Connecticut Unscathed

C&C
CAMPAIGNS & COMMANDERS
GREGORY J. W. URWIN, SERIES EDITOR

CAMPAIGNS AND COMMANDERS

GENERAL EDITOR

Gregory J. W. Urwin, *Temple University, Philadelphia, Pennsylvania*

ADVISORY BOARD

Lawrence E. Babits, *East Carolina University, Greenville*
James C. Bradford, *Texas A&M University, College Station*
Robert M. Epstein, *U.S. Army School of Advanced Military Studies, Fort Leavenworth, Kansas*
David M. Glantz, *Carlisle, Pennsylvania*
Jerome A. Greene, *Denver, Colorado*
Victor Davis Hanson, *California State University, Fresno*
Herman Hattaway, *University of Missouri, Kansas City*
J. A. Houlding, *Rückersdorf, Germany*
Eugenia C. Kiesling, *U.S. Military Academy, West Point, New York*
Timothy K. Nenninger, *National Archives, Washington, D.C.*
Bruce Vandervort, *Virginia Military Institute, Lexington*

Connecticut Unscathed

Victory in the Great Narragansett War, 1675–1676

Jason W. Warren

University of Oklahoma Press | Norman

Library of Congress Cataloging-in-Publication Data

Warren, Jason W., 1977–
  Connecticut unscathed : victory in the Great Narragansett War, 1675–1676 / Jason W. Warren.
      pages cm. — (Campaigns and commanders ; volume 45)
  Includes bibliographical references and index.
  ISBN 978-0-8061-4475-7 (hardcover) ISBN 978-0-8061-7562-1 (paper) 1. King Philip's War, 1675–1676. 2. Connecticut—History—Colonial period, ca. 1600–1775. 3. Mohegan Indians—Connecticut—Government relations—History—17th century. 4. Pequot Indians—Connecticut—Government relations—History—17th century. 5. Connecticut—History, Military—17th century. I. Title.
  E83.67.W37 2014
  974.6′02—dc23
                           2014007137

Connecticut Unscathed: Victory in the Great Narragansett War, 1675–1676 is Volume 45 in the Campaigns and Commanders series.

The paper in this book meets the guidelines for permanence and durability of the Committee on Production Guidelines for Book Longevity of the Council on Library Resources, Inc. ∞

Copyright © 2014 by the University of Oklahoma Press, Norman, Publishing Division of the University. Paperback published 2021. Manufactured in the U.S.A.

All rights reserved. No part of this publication may be reproduced, stored in a retrieval system, or transmitted, in any form or by any means, electronic, mechanical, photocopying, recording, or otherwise—except as permitted under Section 107 or 108 of the United States Copyright Act—without the prior written permission of the University of Oklahoma Press. To request permission to reproduce selections from this book, write to Permissions, University of Oklahoma Press, 2800 Venture Drive, Norman OK 73069, or email rights.oupress@ou.edu.

Interior layout and composition: Alcorn Publication Design

*To the memory of
Lieutenant Colonel Sean Judge, Ph.D., USAF—
no better officer or friend*

Contents

List of Illustrations	ix
Acknowledgments	xi
Introduction	3
1. Forging an Alliance: The Pequot War, Mohegan-Narragansett Competition, and the Coming of the Great Narragansett War	15
2. "Endangering Also the Neighbor Colony of Connecticut": Connecticut during the Great Narragansett War	43
3. Puritan Outlier: Connecticut Colonists and Local Indigenous Groups	78
4. Influences of the European Military Revolution on the New England Frontier	96
5. The Defense of Connecticut	122
6. "To Prosecute the Enemie Wth All Vigor": Connecticut's Offensive Operations	139
Conclusion	173
Notes	183
Bibliography	225
Index	237

Illustrations

Figures

Hill House	68
Beckley Homestead	70
Stiles's drawing of Windsor fortification plan	115
Archaeological dig at Denison Fort site	117
Reverend Street Garrison House	120
Model of Mohantic Fort	168

Maps

Overview of New England	34–35
Topography and avenues of approach	48–49
Connecticut hostile incidents	58–59
Connecticut garrison defense	108–109
Evolution of fortifications on Saybrook Point	111
Connecticut transition to fortifications from garrison defense	118–119
Narragansett country and Indian forts	137

Acknowledgments

This is the most important section of this book, as the project would never have come to fruition without the support, advice, and guidance from family, teachers, and friends. I want to convey special thanks to my children, William and Alice, as well as to Lisa Warren for bearing the brunt of my research and writing absences. I would like to thank my mother, LouAnn, who cultivated my interest in Native American history, as well as my father, James; cousins William and Cheryl Bacon, Jason Lineen, and Jackson Huang; and my entire family for their tireless support. My brother, Adam, has especially supported all of my efforts. A heartfelt thank you to Sara Jones, who edited various portions of this book and supported me. I fondly remember the late James Burke, who gave me Ellis and Morris's *King Philip's War*, sparking my early interest in the conflict. I am fortunate to have experienced caring and skilled teachers, especially the late Pat Duplin, Patricia Panetta, the late Lawrence Nyhan, John Montemerlo, the late Robert Fitzsimmons, John Darrow, and Chris Kolenda.

The writing of this project began in graduate school at The Ohio State University under the skillful direction of John Brooke and with additional guidance from Margaret Newell. I am most grateful for my advisor, John Guilmartin, Jr., whose breadth of historical knowledge and cultivation of camaraderie have no peer, as he oversaw the transformation of this topic into my master's thesis. He led my expert masters committee, which included Geoffrey Parker and Allan Gallay, and all three scholars have continued to assist in the development of this project. I would like especially to thank Geoffrey Parker, not only for his unmatched scholarly example but also for his generous commitment to complete this project for me in the event of my impairment as a result of my tour in Afghanistan. Wayne Lee, University of North Carolina at Chapel Hill, and Daniel Mandell, Truman State University, selflessly provided critical insight, without which this project would have been impossible. Lee spent hours advising me on the phone about early colonial American warfare and introduced me to other scholars of the topic. I would like to thank my fellow graduate students, who from 2007 to 2009 as members the department's unofficial military-history reading group provided a sounding board for my ideas, particularly the late Sean Judge, Robyn Rodriguez, William Waddell, Sarah Douglas, Leif Torkelson, and Robert Clem. Group member Ed McCall commented on an early version of my thesis. Having transformed my thesis into a dissertation, I was fortunate to maintain my original master's committee and was honored to add Peter Mansoor and Kristen Gremillion, both of whom provided essential direction. A special thanks to Graduate Assistant Joby Abernathy (ret.), who guided me through the administrative hurdles of the Ph.D. program, as well as Sean Judge, who represented me in the department after I departed for West Point.

Continuing this project while teaching in the Department of History at the U.S. Military Academy, West Point, I received further recommendations from Sam Watson, Pilar Ryan (ret.), Gian Gentile (ret.), Greg Daddis, Tom Rider, Gail Yoshitani, Casey Doss, Jackie Whitt, Jonathan Gumz, Josh Bradley, and Josiah Grover. Clifford Rogers commented on a critical chapter of my dissertation. Matthew Muehlbauer advised me on the Pequot War. I am grateful to John Stapleton for translating Dutch for me and for our discussions of early modern European tactics. I am indebted to USMA's Dean's Office and the General Omar N. Bradley Research Fellowship in Military History for subsidizing many of my research trips. I appreciate the efforts of the History Department's Lance Betros (now at the Army War College), Ty Seidule, and Deborah Monks, who approved my research endeavors and procured funding, and especially the indefatigable Melissa Mills for her administrative support of my research endeavors. I would like to thank all of my students, from whom I learned more than I could ever hope to impart. I especially want to acknowledge my incredibly talented cadet-senior-thesis advisees Ryan Waldorf, Blaz Marolt, Nick Lemza, Mike White, and Judd Noel.

I possess the deepest gratitude for my supervisor in the department and professional mentor, Kevin Farrell (ret.), who encouraged and challenged me to complete this project. The epitome of the officer corps' professional ethic, his example guided my efforts and best decisions. I am grateful for my academic mentor and good friend Larry Tritle, Loyola Marymount University (Los Angeles), who gave me a chance with my first academic publication and has been an incredible source of strength and guidance ever since. I thank Nate Rosenstein, OSU, for his friendship and wisdom. John Hall, University of Wisconsin, has provided invaluable feedback and advice for both ethnohistory and military history. I am most appreciative of my cousin Vince Pitts, Quinnipiac University, for his advice and encouragement.

The crafting of this book would have been impossible without the extraordinary backing of Kevin McBride and his Mashantucket Foxwoods Museum research team. Kevin is not only an incredible friend but also the most generous scholar I have met. I am indebted for the unfettered access he gave me to the museum's records and artifacts, which he and his team have diligently collected. I am grateful for the assistance of Ashley Bissonnette, Foxwoods's researcher par excellence, who over the last five years has provided me with invaluable resources. I also value the help of Foxwoods's Laurie Pasteryak and David Naumec. Thank you to the staff of the Denison Homestead Museum, Mystic, Connecticut, for the informative tour.

I greatly appreciated the support of Assistant Connecticut State Library Archivist Bruce Stark (ret.) and his entire staff during my many research visits. Faith Davidson also provided me with a critical resource from the Mohegan archives. Charles Gerhing of the New Netherlands Project recommended New York sources. Paul Grant-Costa, Yale University, and Walter Woodward, University of Connecticut, commented on papers used as a basis for this book. Kyle Zelner, Southern Mississippi University, advised me to consider New England's town histories. I acknowledge cartographer William Keegan for his precision and attention to detail in constructing my maps. I have a profound appreciation for my most loyal friend, Edward A. Gutiérrez, whose counsel proved invaluable, as did his timely formatting assistance and photography. Fellow assistant professor Sean McCafferty formatted the first edition of this manuscript. Army planner Iven Sugei advised me on the latest army field manuals.

It has been a pleasure to work with Chuck Rankin's team at the University of Oklahoma Press. I would like especially to thank project manager Emily Jerman and copyeditor Kevin Brock. I appreciate the crucial feedback, as well as friendship, of Campaigns and Commanders series editor Gregory Urwin, Temple University. I am indebted to Greg Daddis of West Point for alerting me to the publishing opportunity with the series.

Even with the incredible support and guidance I have received for this project, it remains imperfect. As such, the mistakes, omissions, and oversights of this manuscript remain my own as do the arguments herein, which do not reflect the views of the U.S. Army War College, the U.S. Army, or the Department of Defense. All dates have been converted to New Style.

Connecticut Unscathed

Introduction

In the early morning hours of 12 August 1676, a pair of soldiers—one allied Indian and one Englishman under the command of Captain Benjamin Church—peered into a shadowy swamp in western Plymouth Colony. Stalking their prey as if hunting, they had located the trail of a hardened band of hostile Indians refusing to submit to English authority, even as many of their comrades surrendered and awaited their fates: death, slavery, or servitude. Suddenly, they viewed an Indian sprinting toward their concealed position. The colonist squeezed the trigger of his flintlock musket, but the early morning humidity had dampened the ignition powder in the pan, and the weapon failed to touch off. His Indian companion, however, managed to discharge his musket, striking their adversary in the vicinity of his heart. When the two men approached their victim, they discovered that they had killed King Philip. This infamous Indian leader would lend his name to the conflict, which his group of Wampanoags had initiated a little over a year before, in the early summer of 1675.[1] This recounting of King Philip's death has often been told in history books. Yet there is an alternate narrative to the event.

An Indian sachem huddled in his makeshift hut. His fatigued body throbbed from the constant campaigning and the long distances he had covered on foot since the beginning of the war. The sachem's heart also ached—his cause appeared to have been defeated by the colonial military colossus and its Indian allies. The latter he considered traitors to native-group sovereignty. Further inflaming the chief's anger and grief, the hated colonists had recently captured his wife and son. A volley of musket fire suddenly ripped the early morning silence, and shot tore through the sachem's sleeping quarters. With the quickness of the panthers he had encountered while hunting, he leapt up, grabbed his musket, and sprinted into the cover of the surrounding swamp. His heart rate accelerated as he made his way through the tangled mass of watery undergrowth, outpacing his noisy English pursuers, who fumbled through the morass behind him. Unexpectedly, he heard the report of a nearby

3

musket to his front. The shock of an incredible pain lifted him off of his feet; the world instantly turned black. He—Metacomet, a freedom fighter for many American Indians inhabiting southern New England—had failed.[2]

Two very different accounts emerge of this much-chronicled event in the early history of colonial America. The first is the standard colonial retelling of the 1676 skirmish from the time of the war itself, based on the diary of the famous Indian fighter Benjamin Church and his son Thomas's later refashioning of it. These and other contemporary sources established a colonial-focused narrative of the war on which historians have relied. The other version of the events of 12 August 1676 attempts to add Indian perspective to this episode, and consequently a different narrative of the war emerges. Daniel Mandell's *King Philip's War* (2010) adds a much-needed American Indian point of view to the narrative that early colonial chroniclers have dominated.[3] Just as historians can mold different accounts together in order to describe Philip's death, so can they to create a new description of the entire war. In this volume I consider the conflict through the point of view of an overlooked colony—Connecticut—and the perspectives of its Indian allies. This methodology revises and alters not only the explanation of colonial-Indian relations in southern New England but also of eventual English and allied Indian victory over the hostile coalition. Further, it places the conflict, often referred to as "King Philip's War," into a coherent frame of reference, relating how this was but one episode —albeit extremely bloody—in an epoch of violence between Native peoples since the arrival of Europeans in the New World. As a result of considering the Native and Connecticut frames of reference for the events in 1675 and 1676, a more effective description of the conflict emerges. In this work, it is referred to as the "Great Narragansett War." Within this framework, the saga of Philip's resistance assumes its proper place.

The conflict that historians have called King Philip's War still ranks as one of the bloodiest, per capita, in American history.[4] An Indian coalition ravaged much of Massachusetts Bay, Plymouth, and Rhode Island Colonies—which along with Connecticut was considered New England—killing six hundred colonial fighting men (not including casualties among their Indian allies). The coalition obliterated seventeen white towns and damaged more than fifty settlements. To fend off annihilation, Plymouth Colony alone expended the then astronomical sum of £100,000 on military expenses during hostilities that lasted little more than a year.⁵ Edward Randolph's report to England's Council of Trade claimed losses in New England of £150,000 "in their habitations and stocks," 1,200 houses burnt, 8,000 head of cattle lost, and "many thousand bushels of wheat, pease, and other grain burnt."⁶ Despite the extensive damage that the Indian coalition inflicted, it suffered a devastating defeat. Colonial and allied Indian forces destroyed forever the power of the belligerent Native groups.

Chronicling the destruction, the Reverend William Hubbard wrote: "The Matter of Fact therein related (being rather Massacres, barbarous inhumane Outrages, than Acts of Hostility, or valiant Atchievements) no more deserve the Name of War than the Report of them that Title of an History."⁷ In contrast to its sister colonies, one colony remained relatively unscathed from the savage conflict Hubbard described. Aside from intermittent raiding, Connecticut suffered the loss of only one major settlement—the town of Simsbury, which had been abandoned. While neighboring colonies such as Plymouth spent exorbitant amounts to defend themselves, Connecticut's direct military expenses for the war amounted to no more than £30,000.⁸ The colony's military forces also achieved a better combat record than those of its neighbors. In contrast to the succession of bloody defeats that dogged troops from the other New England colonies, Connecticut's joint English-Indian forces enjoyed uninterrupted success and suffered much fewer combat losses. Connecticut's achievement and that of its allied Indians in one of America's most terrible wars has not attracted the attention that it deserves.

Historian Hew Strachan argues that "the legacy of literature, and its effects on the shaping of memory, have proved far more influential than economic or political realities."⁹ King Philip's War serves as a testament to this idea. Sachem King Philip of the Wampanoags was an architect of the conflict, but other Indian leaders overshadowed him during the war as Douglas Leach describes: "It has long been recognized that Philip was not the great leader he was once assumed to be. The struggle of 1675–1676 bears his name because he started it, and during those fateful months of war he was accepted as the symbol of Indian resistance to the white men, but once the conflict had spread beyond the bounds of Plymouth Colony Philip lost control of the situation."¹⁰ Yet Philip's early role not only gave name to the conflagration but also became the centerpiece of a war narrative focused primarily on the experiences of Plymouth and Massachusetts Bay.

Jill Lepore, in her acclaimed *The Name of War*, also demonstrates the power of narrative on the issues of war and memory concerning the sachem's centrality in the storyline of King Philip's War.[11] But what if "the name of war" lends itself to an incomplete narrative? Whereas Connecticut lacked a chronicler of the conflict, William Hubbard, Increase Mather, and Benjamin Church developed a narrative focused on Massachusetts Bay and Plymouth Colonies.[12] Historians of early American warfare have concentrated largely on Church's exaggerated account, furthering his trumped-up role in the war because his diary is a rare surviving document from the conflict.[13] The traditional narrative overstates the influence of Philip, whom Church hunted that morning in August 1676, while downplaying Connecticut's role in the fighting. Jenny Pulsipher relates that contemporaries, in fact, did not refer to the war as "King Philip's War" until Church's son Thomas coined the term in the early eighteenth century. Some early New Englanders even referred to the conflict as the "Narragansett War."[14] Only by integrating Connecticut fully into the narrative can historians seat the conflict within the larger context of complicated Indian competition in the region since European arrival.

A recent colonial history claims that King Philip's War "has been covered by every conceivable angle."[15] In truth, historians have replicated the "angle" established by chroniclers from Massachusetts Bay and Plymouth. The twentieth-century accounts of Leach and Eric Schultz and Michael Tougias of the Battle of Bloody Brook is a typical example. Both quote Hubbard to describe the hostile Indians' defeat of Captain Thomas Lathrop's command as "that most fatal day, the saddest that ever befell New England."[16] This phrasing has appeared in almost every description of the battle; as Daniel Mandell's latest history of the war paraphrases, "Bloody Brook . . . became known as the worst day to befall the colonists during the war."[17] Descriptions of events in Connecticut have avoided redundancy because historians largely have overlooked the colony.

By furthering a Philip-centric perspective of the war, historians have marginalized the central role of the Narragansetts and their primary adversaries—Connecticut's English and allied Indians. The Narragansetts, the largest Native group in southern New England, fought Connecticut Indians prior to the arrival of Europeans. As a result of the primary role the Narragansetts played during the sporadic Indian warfare of 1638–74 (recounted here in chapter 1), and given the centrality of Narragansett leadership during the conflict (described in chapter 2), the historically accurate name for the war is the *Great Narragansett War*. For the native groups of New England, this Great Narragansett War continued intertribal strife, which for the first time since the Pequot War of 1637, included the English colonists. While the naming convention of "King Philip's War" accounted for the rising tensions between colonists and Indians, it failed to reflect the relatively minor role the Wampanoags played from 1638 to 1670 and thus downplayed the Indian rivalries that weighed heavily on events in 1675. This was especially the case with the Narragansett-Pequot rivalry and, after the Pequot defeat in 1637, the Narragansett-Mohegan conflict. Connecticut's tacit support for the Mohegans aggrieved native groups in southern New England and motivated some to join the hostile coalition in 1675.[18] The connection of the Mohegan-Narragansett feud to events in 1675 caused the colonists and Indians of Connecticut and Rhode Island to enter the fray, intensifying the conflict in Massachusetts and Plymouth while engulfing all of New England. Yet unlike the other colonies, Connecticut managed to emerge unscathed from the war and was the most effective contributor to its successful conclusion.

In *War and Society in Colonial Connecticut*, a rare piece dedicating a chapter to the colony's war effort, Harold Selesky rightly concludes that "Connecticut survived the war in better physical, economic, and emotional shape than its neighbors because the Indians who lived among its towns were satisfied with the status quo and chose not to join Philip's cause, and because the hostile Indians did not attack simultaneously along the eastern frontier and down the Connecticut valley."[19] My study continues this line of argument by examining in detail why the Indians of Connecticut sought to maintain the status quo, yet it differs from Selesky's social-history methodology by concentrating on the colony's political and military decision making and campaign performance.[20] Focusing on Connecticut's experience permits a detailed examination in chapter 6 of the colony's offensive operations.[21]

Michael Oberg has also identified the importance of Connecticut's Indians in the colony's success, in this case the key role assumed by a Mohegan sachem, Uncas, in sparing Connecticut the "the worst of the slaughter."[22] Uncas formed close personal bonds with the English colonists, entering into an alliance with them during the Pequot War. He and other powerful sachems influenced the course of events throughout the mid-seventeenth century, the English playing a secondary role during the years 1638–74. The current volume expands this theme through the lens of the Great Narragansett War.

In a century of intertribal conflict stretching back to European exploration of southern New England, the Great Narragansett War served as the culminating episode. As a result of disease, shifting alliances, and new military hardware, the arrival of Europeans altered and intensified the already bloody combat between Indian groups.[23] In an effort to settle old scores, Indians allied themselves with Europeans while capitalizing on new economic opportunities. Disease played a critical role in this as well. Native groups along the Atlantic Coast experienced greater contact with overseas traders and suffered the most from epidemics, while those originally without as much European contact, such as the Pequots and Narragansetts, remained relatively unharmed from the ravages of sickness until subsequent decades. Massasoit's band of Wampanoags befriended the original Pilgrim settlers to seek an alliance against the Narragansetts to offset their own losses from illness. Disease, however, does not explain the continuation of the Narragansett blood feud with the Pequots, one of the most important events in early New England; the Pequot War was an interim episode in this struggle. Chapter 1 goes beyond the narration of the Pequot War and the military alliance with Uncas by examining how the Narragansetts and upstart Mohegans—the latter now freed from tributary status and augmented by Pequot refugees—sought to fill the power vacuum that ensued upon the collapse of the Pequot confederacy. The colonies, especially Connecticut, tacitly supported Uncas, angering the Narragansetts and other regional groups. The Great Narragansett War permanently settled the Mohegan-Narragansett-Pequot rivalry.

The Mohegan-Narragansett vendetta continued episodically in the decades after the Pequot War as Narragansett-led coalitions attempted to subdue their rivals. During this period, the colonists prevented a general war through arbitration but backed their principal Native client, Uncas, and to a lesser extent Cassacinamon of the reconstituted Pequots. With this diplomatic and logistical support, Uncas's Mohegans survived these invasions. This assistance, however, set the stage for future violence against Connecticut. Some

Indians sought to undermine the favored status of other groups, such as the Mohegans or "praying" Natick Indians of Massachusetts, within the cultural framework of a multiethnic New England that James Drake discerns as a joint native-colonial society.[24] Obscured cultural fault lines emerged, however, indicating that a significant gulf existed between colonists and many Indians over religion, economic resources, and political sovereignty. The growing power and cultural reach of the English during the seventeenth century magnified these disruptive conditions and threatened the Native way of life. The decades-long power struggle between Mohegan and Narragansett thus anticipated the broadening of Philip's conflict with Plymouth Colony into a New England conflagration.

Philip's perception that the English were interfering with Christian Indians at the expense of his power was at the heart of the initial uprising. With violence previously smoldering between Native peoples, the fresh spark of Philip's resistance to the English turned the slow burn into a full blaze. His hostility to the colonists not only played on traditional intertribal antagonisms but also brought in other formidable regional powers. As many wars trace their proximate causes to events on the periphery of larger power struggles, such as the Serbian-nationalist spark to World War I, Plymouth Colony's local dispute with Philip led to regionwide violence. Indeed, the narrative of "King Philip's War" imposed a "Balkan-centric" view on the years 1675–76. If the Mohegan-Pequots, the Narragansetts, the Mohawks, and Massachusetts Bay and Connecticut Colonies were the seventeenth-century equivalents of the Great Powers in 1914—with Plymouth Colony and the Wampanoags assuming the role of Austria-Hungary and Serbia as powers in decline—then the historiography of King Philip's War has downplayed the roles of Germany and France, relating the story instead through the lens of the minor, diminishing powers.

The Great Narragansett War enmeshed all of New England and surrounding areas, including the fractious Puritan-Pilgrim colonies, apostate Rhode Island Colony, regional native groups, and the Royal Colony of New York. Once Philip's Wampanoags fled to central Massachusetts a month after the war's outbreak, the Nipmucks and upper Connecticut River Indians became the main combatants. With the Narragansetts passively supporting Philip, a number of their warriors also secretly joined his coalition. Narragansett involvement remained furtive until the Great Swamp Fight of 19 December

1675, when colonial forces attacked a main village of the Native group in a now-infamous preemptive strike. Total Narragansett participation drastically altered the nature of the war in terms of its destructiveness and reach, representing far more than a phase in a "King Philip's" war.

Connecticut's leadership formulated the policies that drove the colony's positive local relationships with Indians, which were the foundation for eventual military success. Historians have debated extensively the larger story of New England's relationship with Indians, but the categories historians Alden Vaughan and Francis Jennings have proposed do not reflect Connecticut's policy.[25] Connecticut charted a middle course between those of the other English colonies. Rhode Island's program was as lenient, but it did not boast equivalent military power, and as a result that colony lost many lives and much property during the war. The policy of Massachusetts Bay and Plymouth, meanwhile, led to callous treatment and internment of Indians, alienating the very people that their forces required on the battlefield. This also contributed to high casualties and loss of property for both colonies. By contrast, Connecticut largely avoided violence toward local Natives through negotiation and tribute offerings while maintaining the deterrent of lethal military capability.

Pulsipher comments similarly on Connecticut but attributes its forward-looking policy to its relative security.[26] Connecticut was the most vulnerable of the New England colonies, however, lacking a stable frontier with the Dutch (and then Royalists of New York) and numerous Native groups while remaining exposed to possible French excursions from Canada. Thus its self-interest influenced the colony's sensible treatment toward local Indians, which events during the Pequot War reinforced. This moderate policy served as the bedrock for Connecticut's security: during 1675–76, the continued allegiance of Native groups denied critical intelligence and support to hostile raiding parties. Enlightened leadership in the colony from men such as Governor John Winthrop, Jr., balanced defensive requirements with ethical treatment of Natives, realizing that both related intimately to the other. These attitudes proved influential, generally holding sway over Connecticut's inhabitants. While Pulsipher views Indian-white relations through the prism of sovereignty, Drake perceives such associations as a product of an interwoven society, and Jean O'Brien believes interactions reflected the

Indians' creative resistance to English culture, I consider native-colonial interactions from a perspective of leadership and the mutual quest for survival on an untamed, dangerous frontier.[27]

The Indians of Connecticut chose to accept this moderate policy rather than take hostile action against the colonists. Shrewd political actors, like Uncas, Cassacinamon, and Ninigret of Rhode Island's Eastern Niantics, understood that their best chance of survival depended on cooperation with the English. A greater number of Native groups in New England, however, elected to fight, chancing their survival on military effectiveness. Given this, it is difficult to argue, as some historians do, that the hostile coalition's motivation was suicidal.[28] Another possible option was neutrality, as the Eastern Niantics, the Indians of Nantucket, Martha's Vineyard, and some of Connecticut's native groups attempted, though the latter probably faced some coercion from the Mohegans and Pequots. In addition, some Eastern Niantics and the Narragansetts (until Great Swamp) feigned support or neutrality as a strategy of survival.[29] In terms of their immediate survival, though, Connecticut's Indians made the safest choice.

Spurred on by Royal New York governor Edmund Andros, the Iroquois confederation intervened on New England's northwestern frontier for its own strategic objectives. According to many historians, it was this participation that ultimately carried the day for the English.[30] But as examined in chapter 2, Iroquois influence was not the cause of colonial victory, rather it was a contributing factor. New York's participation in the war—largely overlooked in the traditional narrative—serves as a valuable counterpoint in evaluating the years 1675–76.

A surprising number of Pequot War veterans survived the forty years between conflicts to influence policy during the Great Narragansett War. The memory of 1637 informed decision making in 1675. Connecticut leaders directly imparted the lessons of 1637 to their progeny or through correspondence and military texts, while the second generation of colonists cultivated its own military experience during the English Civil Wars (1638–52) and the Anglo-Dutch Wars (First, 1652–54; Second, 1665–67; Third, 1672–74). Geared toward European enemies, New England's defenses derived from continental fortress design. Before the Great Narragansett War, Connecticut developed fortifications to combat the threat of a hostile Dutch neighbor as well as to account for the potential hostility of

Native groups in the region. These defenses copied on a lesser scale (due to limited resources) the artillery fortresses of the European military revolution, and veteran European military engineers sometimes constructed them.

Foreshadowing future American military policy, colonists allowed their defenses to decay during peaceful periods only to rebuild them during times of increased threat. Indians also utilized elements of artillery fortresses. Connecticut complemented these works by maintaining an active militia force, sending patrols on its pathways and into outlying areas.[31] Faced with such measures, hostile war parties were unable to stage a large-scale attack on the colony. Connecticut gained time to reconstitute its defenses as a result of the early neutrality of the Narragansetts. Without the overt participation of the Narragansetts in hostilities until December, the Indian coalition deemed the colony a secondary objective during 1675.

Directing the colony's war effort, Connecticut's War Council—a group of colonial political and military men—managed the conflict more efficiently than the other New England colonies. This was due, in part, to Connecticut's contiguous settlement pattern and resulting population density, easing military operations through the transmission of orders and intelligence. The microculture of the council and the body's relationship with senior field commanders ensured that the latter's lack of combat experience was not detrimental to the war effort. The council more willingly managed military affairs than its Plymouth and Rhode Island counterparts; at times Connecticut's political leaders even dictated tactics to its officers. Massachusetts Bay's council, of similar size and experience, often issued detailed orders as well, but its noncontiguous settlement pattern and much larger population proved more difficult to manage. Chapters 4 and 5 discuss European influences on Connecticut's war effort, including its fortifications, and colony leaders' experience in managing the conflict.

I analyze Connecticut's tactics and operations in chapter 6, addressing a shortcoming in the historiography of early colonial America while proposing an alternate theory for the colonists' change in battlefield fortunes by the spring of 1676.[32] Leach summarizes the standard argument for the eventual colonial victory: "The real answer to the problem of how to deal with the skulking tactics of the enemy, as time was to show, lay in the intelligent adaptation of standard English tactics to forest conditions, and especially the systematic use of friendly Indians as scouts with every English force that moved through the woods. These natives were experts in the art of detecting the presence of other Indians, and whenever they were used ambushes became much less of a danger."[33]

Historians maintain that the colonists eventually adapted to New England battlefield conditions by mimicking the Indians and only then were able to conduct effective warfare in conjunction with Native allies.[34] Patrick Malone argues that these sought-after tactics resulted from a "tactical and technological" revolution in the wilderness prior to the conflict, rendering European practices obsolete in the New World.[35] Yet few colonists, with the exceptions of Connecticut's George Denison and James Avery and Plymouth's Church, actually adopted a semblance of "the skulking way of war." Instead, Connecticut's successes occurred from the utilization of competent Native allies in large numbers from the beginning of the conflict, generating a military division of labor in which colonists and Indians performed duties associated with their respective strengths. This symbiotic relationship served as a basis for effective operations, with Indian battlefield assistance realizing the potential of European tactics.[36] With this support, Connecticut deployed a competent dragoon force, representing a cross-section of its population, including volunteers to boost effectiveness. Without allied Indian assistance, the troopers' skills would have been diminished greatly against the Native tactics that Malone lauds.

The climactic massacre at Mystic Fort in the earlier Pequot War shattered the Pequot confederacy's political power, but the remnant peoples retained their tactical skills, on which Connecticut's English capitalized during the Great Narragansett War. The martial reputation of the Pequots before their defeat in 1637 was, and afterward remained, formidable. Their fighting ability resulted from the confederacy's unenviable geographic position, encircled by enemies as the Mohawk sphere of influence dipped down into southern New England from the northwest, the Nipmuck groups bordered their territory to the north, and the numerous Narragansett groups inhabited Rhode Island to the east. This forced the Pequots, whose dominion at the time included the Western Niantics and Mohegans, to develop a potent military capability to ensure survival. As a result, Connecticut's Indian forces were militarily superior to those of the other New England colonies.

From Pequot tactical wherewithal to the influences of the Military Revolution on warfare in the New World, the following chapters analyze events from the marginalized Connecticut Colony's perspective, challenging long-held assumptions about "King Philip's War." The revised view point of a Great Narragansett War not only brings into focus Connecticut's native and colonial populations but also places the war itself within the context of the New England Indians' struggle to adjust to European arrival. This great conflict was the final chapter of the saga. Connecticut's story in the Great Narragansett War anticipates a paradigm for analyzing military operations from the perspective of relations between colonists and local Native groups in the colonial Atlantic world.[37]

CHAPTER 1

FORGING AN ALLIANCE

THE PEQUOT WAR, MOHEGAN-NARRAGANSETT COMPETITION, AND THE COMING OF THE GREAT NARRAGANSETT WAR

"The Narragansetts will all leave you, but as for myself, I will never leave you," promised Uncas, "chief sachem of the Moheags," to Connecticut's commander, John Mason.[1] As Uncas predicted, many of the Narragansetts abandoned the march once the Indian and colonial force entered Pequot territory, while the Mohegan sachem remained loyal to the English. The Pequot War of 1636–37 forged the Connecticut Colony–Mohegan alliance, which solidified over the following decades. This relationship was mutually beneficial, allowing Uncas to achieve greater power while the Connecticut colonists gained critical intelligence and military aid from their native allies. With similar effect, and under the patronage of future governor John Winthrop, Jr., Connecticut later reconstituted Pequot native groups that had survived the war.

Although the interaction of English and Indians during this period of intertribal conflict in southern New England remains murky and nonlinear, Connecticut ultimately supported Uncas over other groups, especially the Narragansetts. Critically, the colony developed an appreciation for maintaining peaceful relations with local Indians, setting it apart from the other New England governments. While the decades after the Pequot War brought peace for the English, the southernmost Native groups of the region experienced intermittent warfare, particularly between the Mohegans and Narragansetts. This animosity culminated with the broadening of the Great Narragansett War. While violently settling the Mohegan-Narragansett vendetta, that war also vented the acrimony that had grown between many Indian communities and the English. Although the weaker players within a multicultural New England,

Plymouth and King Philip's Wampanoag band, started the war in 1675, it was the more powerful Narragansetts, Mohegan-Pequots, and Connecticut Colony that finished it the following year.

The population pressures of the Great Migration of Puritans to New England, which brought relatively large numbers of Europeans to the region, contributed to increased violence between Indian communities during the Pequot War and the Mohegan-Narragansett rivalry. American Indians, however, were by no means nonviolent in the precontact epoch. Excavations indicate that their warfare featured more than minimal violence, challenging characterizations of it as ritualistic and limited in nature. Blunt-force trauma and arrow penetrations accounted for the fatalities of 15 percent of remains in 119 excavated burial sites dating to 1000–1600 A.D. in southern New England. Women and children, who were often noncombatants in postcontact intertribal warfare, accounted for 25 percent of that number. While 15 percent is a conservative estimate based on only well-preserved remains with clearly identifiable battle scars, the actual number of combat deaths was probably much higher.[2] The years 1636–76 witnessed a continuation of warlike conditions in the region, with European cultural and military power increasing volatility.

The newcomers also introduced diseases. Unfamiliar pathogens reduced Indian communities, nearly eradicating some along the coast. The historiography concerning the toll of European disease on Indian communities remains controversial, and the lack of precise population data further complicates the issue.

Historians estimate that the southern New England indigenous population ranged between 72,000 and 144,000 people.[3] It is generally agreed that these northeastern communities were small compared to other world population centers, subsisting on sustenance agriculture supplemented by local hunting, fishing, and gathering.

The importance of Indian corn as a central facet of life cannot be underestimated, and not only as a source of calories. The Agawams, for instance, developed a lunar calendar in the mid-seventeenth century with five of twelve "months" based on different stages of maize growth.[4] The Agawams were an inland group centered on present-day Springfield, Massachusetts, along the Connecticut River valley, which happened to be the prime maize-growing territory of New England. The entire region, however, did not benefit from the fertile soil and other conditions that made the inland Connecticut River valley prime territory for agriculture. The effects of significant climate cooling, frost, and seaboard conditions combined to challenge the indigenous population's ability to grow maize. Even the Indians' use of Northern Flint corn, which was suited to a short growing season and cool conditions, and the employment of other local techniques, such as cultivation near lakes to combat frost, did not allow for large crop surpluses.[5] Without surplus food, New England Indians of the prehistoric era were unable to generate large populations of the kind found in more temperate river valleys like the mid-Mississippi region.

Where southern New England Indians did cultivate maize, they relied on polycropping or intercropping, a technique that grew it alongside other edible produce such as squash. Based on nineteenth-century Indians' per-acre agricultural output when it employed farming techniques of the seventeenth century, anthropologist Sissel Schroeder estimates that early Indian communities produced ten bushels of maize per acre. Their bushel consumption per acre was reduced by as much as 42 percent, though, when accounting for storage, wasting, ceremonial offerings, tribute collecting, and seed accumulation. Indian villages thus produced between 5–6 bushels of maize per acre during an average harvest on which to subsist. Schroeder bases these calculations on a 2,500-calorie diet for adults and 1,910 for children, assuming that the ten-bushel yield would supply less than 30 percent of a family's caloric requirements when accounting for supplemental dieting such as game, fish, and other plants.[6]

Warriors in combat needed a minimum of 3,500 calories, however, to sustain themselves in the field, and hunters also required a similar intake.[7] Since these men practiced hunting, fishing, and warfare as their primary occupations, Sissel's estimated acreage output sustained even less of a family's caloric requirement than his study indicates.[8] Allowing for a moderate increase in the supplemental foods to offset agricultural output—Indians could only increase fishing, hunting, and gathering activities so much based on natural limitations such as game availability, hunting and fishing success, and weather conditions—the net caloric output of sustenance activities indicates that New England Indians who relied on corn as a major portion of their diet lacked a nutritive surplus necessary to sustain a large population. Thus, another way to conceive of this 30-percent calculation is that maize accounted for a higher percentage of individual caloric intake for a smaller population. Schroeder estimates that there were two parents and three children in a typical family unit, but based on New England–specific anthropology, there was likely an elderly adult in an Indian household and perhaps only two children.[9] While the elderly adult consumed something like an adult's calorie load, family composition also meant that there were fewer children available to someday till their own acreage and increase the population. These factors together point to all Indian sustenance activities as generating a population not just smaller than the historic numbers that Sissel criticizes, but one significantly smaller.

Although Neal Salisbury argues for a factor of 7–1 or 8–1 when calculating an adult-male-to-family ratio, other scholars more generally accept a 5–1 ratio.[10] Francis Jennings argues that the Narragansetts fielded five thousand warriors in the period before European diseases spread, which would have placed their total population at around twenty-five thousand people using this standard formula.[11] In 1675 the Narragansetts fielded around one thousand warriors and hence maintained a population of around five thousand persons, a large decrease from Jennings's pre-epidemic numbers.[12] Although this number of warriors was still considerably more than other native groups could field, the Narragansetts would have suffered a population decline in excess of 80 percent after 1620, according to Jennings's calculations. In addition to natural population growth, however, the Narragansetts from 1637 to 1675 attempted to offset deaths to intertribal warfare and new epidemics by absorbing conquered Pequots and other Indian refugees of colonial expansion. Further, the diseases that devastated the Massachusetts coastal Indians did not strike the Narragansetts (and Pequots) until the early 1630s.[13] At a time of the booming fur and wampum trade, as well as the introduction of European goods, it is likely that these two large groups actually increased their populations before suffering grievous losses from disease in the years before the Pequot War.[14]

These considerations allow for a numerical reevaluation of the Indian population in southern New England in the precontact period. Using the Narragansett population of 1675–76 as a starting point from which to work backward, it is likely that this largest of regional Native peoples fielded around 3,500 warriors prior to 1620, giving the group a population of 17,500.[15] The Narragansetts slightly increased in size until the early 1630s, when the first epidemic to strike them coupled with increased warfare against the rival Pequots to cause its population to decline substantially. The Narragansetts then received a slight salve with the integration of Pequot captives. By the outbreak of the Great Narragansett War, continued disease and warfare had reduced the Native group to 5,000 persons.

As the Narragansetts outnumbered the rival Pequots, the latter probably fielded around 2,500 warriors at the time of the first English settlement.[16] The estimated Pequot population of 12,500 then dramatically declined in the 1630s as a result of a first encounter with an epidemic as well as brutal warfare against other Indian groups, the Dutch, and finally the English in 1636–37. In line with these figures, Pequot population probably was 4,000–5,000 people at the beginning of the Pequot War.[17] The reconstituted western Pequot group mustered no more than 200 warriors by 1675, a dramatic reduction in numbers since 1637.[18] Unlike the Narragansetts and other New England Indian peoples, the English targeted the Pequots in a war of extirpation. The remaining Indians of Connecticut, likely reduced at first by the Delaware invasion and then both by Pequot and Mohawk incursions in later centuries, counted perhaps 1,500 warriors total prior to the first European epidemic. Connecticut's Native population of the early 1600s thus numbered about 20,000 persons.

The Nipmucks and Nashaways of central Massachusetts, and the Pocumtucks and other Indian groups of the upper stretches of the Connecticut River, although less documented than those on New England's coasts, probably each mustered 2,000 warriors.[19] The Mohawks and Mahicans, the latter inhabiting northwestern Massachusetts and northeastern New York, also reduced the population sizes of these groups through intermittent warfare. Prior to decimation from European diseases, Indians on the Massachusetts coast probably included 2,500 warriors, as did the nearby Wampanoags, including those on the islands of Nantucket and Martha's Vineyard.[20] Thus, a high-end estimate based on the generally accepted warrior-to-family ratio indicates a population in *southern* New England of 82,500 persons prior to the first inroads of European disease.[21] This approximation appears within the range of Jennings's estimate but covers more territory and thus argues for a lower population density. All modern historians agree that by the time of the Pequot War, the Indian population of southern New England had experienced a dramatic decline from its pre-epidemic numbers. Indeed, the reductions among the Pequots and their tributaries limited their military response to the English incursions of that conflict.

The causes and conduct of the Pequot War account for a vibrant historiography of its own.[22] Recent archaeology and historical analysis contribute fresh ideas to the existing body of literature, including new evidence concerning the attack on Mystic Fort, the fate of Pequot groups, and exclusively intertribal battles.[23] The war was noteworthy for the lack of battlefield restraint that the English showed to their opponents, leading to atrocities.[24] The Indians also committed horrific acts of violence. The conduct of both sides reflected differing cultural frameworks for waging war.[25] Connecticut's appreciation of good relations with local Native groups and the importance of Indian allies were the critical influences from the Pequot War in determining the colony's future policy. These crucial lessons became a means of survival for Connecticut during the Great Narragansett War.

Although Alfred Cave claims that their reputation for fierceness was overblown, the Pequots were the most militarily competent Native group in southern New England from the founding of the first English settlement at Plymouth in 1620 through the confederacy's defeat in 1637.[26] The group's hegemony over the Mohegans, Western Niantics, and lower Connecticut River valley peoples indicated military superiority as well as the ability to fend off and intimidate the more numerous Narragansetts. In addition to this potent military capability, the earlier conflict with the Dutch (1633) taught the Pequots to avoid fighting a European opponent in the open field.[27] Indeed, the better-known conflict of 1636–37 was far from a lopsided military contest between proficient Westerners and hapless Indians as often portrayed. During the years 1638–76, the Mohegans, Western Niantics, and remaining Pequots retained this military advantage over other Native groups.

In late August 1636 Massachusetts Bay Colony initiated military action against the Pequots, with raids against groups on Block Island and a principal Pequot fort in southeastern Connecticut. Massachusetts launched these attacks because of perceived Pequot provocations. Far from intimidating the confederacy, these failed attempts stirred it to military action. Trouble began with a treaty between Massachusetts and the Pequots in 1634, when the Bay Colony, seeking to weaken the confederacy, demanded wampum and hostages as well as the surrender of the "murderers" of English traders. The Pequots refused to meet all of these stipulations, ignoring a final ultimatum from the colony in July 1636. After the ineffectual Massachusetts raids, the Pequots deployed their closely related Western Niantic tributaries and aided them in besieging Connecticut's fort at Saybrook Point, located at the mouth of the Connecticut River. This force bested the garrison's foraging parties in a number of ambushes. But the fort's commander, Lion Gardiner, a veteran of the Thirty Years' War, directed a successful effort to stave off defeat and annihilation. Gardiner avoided serious casualties and, though besieged, managed to feed his men.[28]

As the siege of Saybrook continued, Sequassen, a Pequot tributary sachem of the central Connecticut region, requested that his patrons raid the colonial settlement at Wethersfield. He desired revenge because the settlers there had swindled him out of a portion of land. On 23 April 1637 the Pequots honored their obligation to their tributaries with a surprise raid on Wethersfield, killing a handful of settlers and carrying off two prisoners. Though a tactical success, the raid was a strategic blunder. The attack escalated the conflict by enraging nearby English inhabitants who previously had been suspicious of the Bay Colony's intentions toward the confederacy, objecting to Massachusetts's punitive expeditions. It also demonstrated to the Connecticut colonists the importance of good relations with local Indians, for Sequassen's supplication to the Pequots precipitated the raid. Revealing that it had learned from its previous mistakes, Connecticut later pardoned Sequassen, admitting wrongdoing in his provocation over the land dispute.[29] Nevertheless, after the Wethersfield raid, the tide turned against the Pequots.

The leader of Connecticut's militia forces and another Thirty Years' War veteran, Captain John Mason, conceived of an operation to take the fighting to Pequot territory. Although initially suspicious of Mohegan intentions, Mason accepted the support of Uncas's band to fight the confederacy.[30] Uncas, who had asserted a claim of hereditary right to the Pequot leadership prior to the war, offered his people's military assistance to the fledgling Connecticut Colony in a search for new allies to further his own political agenda.[31] As was often the case in southern New England, intermarriage dynamics between closely related Indian groups led to political friction and eventual violence. In this case, Uncas claimed the sachemship through his father, who was a son of the principal Pequot sachem. The Pequot council rejected his claim, and his cousin Sassacus assumed the chieftainship of the confederacy. Uncas never forgave this decision, embarking upon years of subterfuge to overthrow his cousin and dominate both the Mohegans and Pequots. The latter even banished Uncas to the enemy Narragansetts on several occasions, only to grant him amnesty after he pledged allegiance to Sassacus.[32] When the Pequots ran afoul of the English in the following years, Uncas recognized an opportunity to finally overthrow Sassacus and to establish the Mohegans, then a tributary group to the Pequots, as the hegemonic Native power between the Pawcatuck and Housatonic Rivers, or much of what is now Connecticut.

Fortunately for the English, Captain Mason capitalized on the opportunity to enlist Uncas in the war.[33] The sachem initiated an alliance with Connecticut early in the conflict by warning the colonists that they had to respond militarily to the raid on Wethersfield or else appear vulnerable to other Indians. A perception of weakness would convince the Mohegans and others to join with the confederacy.[34] Realizing that the Pequots were the local dominant military power—the Mohawks were the only Native group in the greater northeastern region that retained an even greater military reputation—the captain agreed.

Mason's scheme was to utilize the English advantage in sea power by sailing to Narragansett Bay in Rhode Island, then doubling back by land to Connecticut. This maneuver bypassed Pequot territory, allowing the allied force to retain the critical element of surprise. Mason requested that Miantonomi, a chief Narragansett sachem, allow this operation to proceed through his country to the Pequot stronghold at Mystic. Miantonomi agreed. Mason's army consisted of Connecticut and Massachusetts Bay militia along with Mohegans, Narragansetts, and Eastern Niantics, the latter closely related to the Narragansetts. This was the first major operation in New England to include a significant Indian force allied to the English. After joining Mason, the Indians performed scouting and security duties while navigating the expedition through the wilderness.

As the army approached Mystic, most of the Narragansetts and Eastern Niantics fled back to Rhode Island as Uncas had predicted.[35] Mason sheltered his reduced command at a place called Porter's Rock, not far from the Pequot fort, yet in a position that offered excellent cover and concealment: high ground shielded this encampment, while the Mystic River flanked the position on the west.[36] Launching the attack in the early morning twilight, the Mohegans, remaining Narragansetts, and a number of colonists established "blocking positions" around the enemy stronghold as the outer-perimeter guard. This tactical role would become common for Connecticut's Native allies. Mason and another Thirty Years' War veteran, Captain John Underhill, then assaulted the fort from the north and southwest. Mason's force established a position immediately inside the breach of the palisades, while the commander himself took a small detachment down the compound's main thoroughfare, delivering musket salvos into the Pequot lodges. Sustaining many casualties and with the battle very much in doubt, Mason made the controversial (and unethical) decision to burn the fort.[37]

Undoubtedly, the failure of the English and the Pequots to establish ethical reciprocity—the recognition of an adversary as a legitimate military entity and conferred protections for noncombatants as well as surrendered and wounded soldiers—affected Mason's decision. The English viewed the Pequots and their tributaries as brigands and rebels. Categorizing the Indians in this way was not out of the ordinary for English leaders during the early modern era. Wayne Lee has examined the Anglo-American conduct of war in this period, demonstrating how English practices, though also affected by other factors such as the preferences of individual soldiers and the availability of supplies, categorized combatants between "barbarians and brothers." This resulted in the harsher treatment of Irish and Indian "barbarians" compared to ethnically English enemy "brothers."[38] English forces viewed Indians during the Pequot and Great Narragansett Wars as insurrectionists in similar fashion to the Irish and Scots during conflicts in the British Isles.[39] For American Indians, the violent treatment of enemy combatants and prisoners—both Indian and colonist—accorded with a cultural framework of war that was religiously inspired to gain spiritual power from the torture and death of opponents. What the English viewed as horrific acts meant to inflict pain, suffering, and terror, the Indian combatants carried out to increase their manhood and spiritual potency. These practices also respected the spiritual strength of the doomed captive, allowing him to live out his own masculinity.[40] Indians, like Europeans, also fought to revenge violent acts that they deemed repulsive, such as the ferocious Pequot counterattacks against Mason's force after Mystic.[41] A "negative" reciprocity resulted from these differing cultural values, where many colonists and Indians did not observe ethical conduct toward the other group during the Pequot or Great Narragansett Wars.

With Mason's engagement transpiring on the other end of Mystic Fort, Underhill's force did not breach the palisades until the village already was aflame. The Indians then counterattacked this contingent, driving it back outside the compound with fierce hand-to-hand fighting.[42] Many Pequots did not escape the burning fortress, and the colonists even accidentally wounded some of the allied Indians on the outer perimeter in the melee. None of the battle's participants anticipated such a massacre.[43] After Mystic, the Massachusetts Bay forces departed by water, while Mason and the Connecticut soldiers, ably assisted by Uncas, fought their way through the heart of Pequot territory, barely escaping back to Saybrook Fort.[44]

The most important long-term military outcome of Mystic was that the friendly Native forces utilized their military strengths with "skulking way of war" tactics—scouting, security, navigating—while the English demonstrated a willingness to assault fortifications in accordance with more traditional methods of European warfare. The "skulking way of war," however, remains a misleading description of Indian tactics by implying an unwillingness to fight pitched battles. The early colonists who coined the phrase mistook selectivity of military targets and "the ability to exploit particular conditions" as the lack of European courage and tactical wherewithal.[45] This perception downplayed the devastating effects of raids and ambushes during the Pequot War and afterward, usually executed when Indian forces perceived an advantage, as well as the occasional decision to fight a larger battle. The term "skulking" also minimized the role that Connecticut's allied Indians played in the colony's successes during both the Pequot and Great Narragansett Wars.[46] Far from shirking armed confrontation, the Indians sought to maximize their advantages while minimizing the colonists' advantage in firepower. Native tactics utilized both mobility *and* maneuverability. Mobility is the ability to deploy forces around the area of operations, while maneuverability is the positioning of forces on the battlefield (or the larger theater of operations). Indians during the Pequot and Great Narragansett Wars continually positioned themselves in an advantageous way against colonial forces, certainly not a simple task, and no less "tactical" than European methods.[47]

Compared to "skulking," a more accurate description of Indian warfare is the "cutting off way of war." To "cut off" was idiomatic— at times it meant literally to kill as the Indians executed deadly attacks against colonists and other Natives when the opportunity presented itself.[48] Lee further explains: "At war, [the Indians] mobilized through persuasion and consensus, with the significant addition of young men who sought status through success in war. The combination of young men's enthusiasm with the cultural requirement of blood revenge meant that war was common, but for the most part conducted on a small scale."[49] The demand to fulfill the vendetta could lead to escalation or prolong small-scale attacks.[50] In order to achieve increased social status, warriors sought trophies, and thus it was imperative to return alive in order to demonstrate military prowess. This was not always the case with their European counterparts, who often risked life and fortune for religious ideology, loyalty to a sovereign, or individual honor that demanded death before dishonor.[51] For Indians, becoming a casualty brought no increase in martial reputation, and Native groups could not readily replace lost warriors because of lower birth and higher mortality rates.[52] During the Great Narragansett War, the differing cultural understandings of war remained, including the requirement for blood revenge and the occasional torture of captives. For example, the reconstituted Pequots captured two Eastern Niantics, members of a technically neutral group, and tortured them to death at "there forts" to satisfy blood vengeance.[53] Indians also practiced total war aimed at destroying or displacing enemies.[54]

The Mystic operation confirmed Uncas's allegiance and established a basis for Indian-colonial cooperation in Connecticut. The other New England colonies did not capitalize on the lessons from the Pequot War, especially in the cultivation of Native allies, and paid dearly for this oversight in 1675–76. Mystic set the tone for the remainder of the conflict. Afterward, the English and allied Indians pursued Sassacus's band, which desperately attempted to flee the colony. Skirmishing with the Pequot rear guard and tributaries along Long Island Sound, the allied force cornered the main contingent at a swamp in southwestern Connecticut near what is now the town of Southport. Continuing the tactical cooperation established earlier, the Mohegans formed the outer perimeter while the English assaulted the Pequot position. The enemy noncombatants surrendered and became spoils of war, while many of the warriors died in battle. Sassacus penetrated the Mohegan perimeter with some of his closest followers, however, and turned toward New York, attempting to link up with the Mohawks. But he did not know that the Mohawks already had thrown their support behind the English, and a war party ambushed the Pequots at what is now Dover Plains, New York, on the eastern side of the Hudson River. The Mohawks sent Sassacus's scalp to the English as a sign of friendship.[55] The standard account of the Pequot War usually ends with this gruesome incident, but other events transpired that are just beginning to come into historical focus.

Sassacus's defeat did not mark the end of Pequot clans, as a number of groups escaped into the wilderness or simply avoided the conflict all together. Other individuals were held as prisoners or indentured servants, and in later decades Cassacinamon, with English support, even managed to reconstitute Sassacus's tribal band. With the Uncas-Mason forces' attention focused on the sachem, other Pequot bands escaped unmolested. Meanwhile, other Indian groups continued to fight each other such as at the "Battle of the Northeast," where the Narragansetts sought to exploit a weakened Pequot confederacy. Undoubtedly, there were other intertribal battles that have been lost to recorded history. Another significant Pequot band, located on the Pawcatuck River under the sachem Wequash, fought against hostile Indians but not the English. Other fleeing Pequots and Western Niantics integrated into different regional groups, perhaps returning to the reconstituted Pequots in later decades.[56] There are reports of Pequots removing far afield, and in at least one incident (described below), western Long Island Indians brought in Pequot scalps in 1675, suggesting such a migration and perhaps also lingering Pequot animosity toward the English.

The colonists divided a large number of Sassacus's Pequots, Western Niantics, and other captured tributaries between themselves and the Mohegans and Narragansetts. The failure of the English to mediate the Mohegan-Narragansett dispute over war spoils, particularly captives, worsened the relationship between these two peoples.[57] The Mohegans, Narragansetts, and Eastern Niantics scrambled to fill the power vacuum created by the collapse of the Pequot confederacy, and this resulted in a continuation of intertribal warfare, eventually becoming a primary cause of the outbreak of the Great Narragansett War. With combat during 1636–37 transpiring exclusively within the colony or wilderness areas beyond European observation, Connecticut experienced Indian warfare unique from the other New England colonies. Though Massachusetts Bay participated in military operations, its experience differed from Connecticut because it did not directly experience Indian attacks on its settlements or battles on its territory. Massachusetts thus could not fully appreciate the value of noncontentious relations with Indians in preventing attacks or the utility of employing Native allies.

Events in the decades between the Pequot and Great Narragansett Wars proved that the Mohegan-Connecticut alliance was not based exclusively on the Pequot threat. Uncas and Mason understood the importance of what had been accomplished with the shattering of the confederacy, not only at the political level with the extinguishing of Pequot hegemony in southern New England but also of the effectiveness of combined Indian-colonist military operations. Both parties realized the mutual benefits of military cooperation, and even when there were disagreements during the period 1638–74, this realization prevented a severing of ties. Survival in seventeenth-century southern New England was the obvious common interest because of the dangers from both Indians and Europeans. Without the mutual trust forged during the Pequot War, it is doubtful that the Mohegan-Connecticut relationship would have been maintained peaceably given the competing claims over the surviving Pequots, the colonists' encroachment on the Mohegan's lands and religion, and other diverging economic and political objectives. Events in the years after 1637 demonstrated the complexity of this relationship and that, ultimately, this alliance was far from inevitable.

As Uncas built a stronger Mohegan tribe on the remnants of the Pequot confederacy, and as English power continued to expand in Connecticut, colonial ties with the Narragansetts established during the Pequot War began to unravel. This in turn strained Connecticut's relationship (and to a lesser extent that of Massachusetts Bay) with groups on the upper Connecticut River as well as Indians inhabiting eastern Long Island, after 1637, tributaries of the Narragansetts and Eastern Niantics. Connecticut's ties with the upstart Mohegans also strained the colony's association with the Mohawks, who sought to undermine Uncas. As a closely related Native group and tributary, the Mohegans had maintained closer ties to the Pequots than they did to other groups, including the Narragansetts. Uncas's followers (the Mohegans also had factions) inherited not only the Pequots' position of preeminence between the Pawcatuck and Housatonic Rivers but also their feuds with groups outside of Connecticut. In particular, the straining of Mohegan-Narragansett relations occurred from memories of the former's previous support of the Pequots, competition over the Pequot share of the wampum trade, claims over Pequot hunting grounds, and especially competition over Pequot survivors.

The fate of the Pequots was a point of friction between the victorious Indians and colonists alike. All parties looked to exploit the captives for labor and battle.

Uncas took advantage of the colonists' good will at the expense of the now-rival Narragansetts and their grand sachem, Miantonomi. He accused Miantonomi of a conspiracy to ally various Native groups, including the feared Mohawks, against the English. Although he successfully cleared his name at Boston, Miantonomi never forgave Uncas for approaching the English authorities. In 1643 he invaded Mohegan country with a much larger force than Uncas was able to muster. Miantonomi probably thought that he had persuaded the English to remain neutral in the intertribal feud, and thus was confident in his chances of defeating the smaller Mohegans. Traditional accounts claim that Uncas used a ruse by challenging Miantonomi to individual combat, and when the Narragansett sachem accepted the invitation, the Mohegan leader dropped to the ground as his warriors showered the unsuspecting Narragansetts with a barrage of arrows. Surprised, the invaders fled in confusion. The Mohegans captured Miantonomi because he was weighed down by English chainmail that he had worn into battle.[58] Uncas presented him as a prisoner in Hartford, but in a mock show of neutrality, the colonists refused to interfere. Connecticut authorities knew, however, that this was in effect a death sentence, and the United Commissioners at Boston sanctioned his death as long as it occurred in Mohegan territory.[59] The Mohegans subsequently executed Miantonomi. The Narragansetts never forgave Uncas, and through the intervening decades, they invaded Mohegan territory and instigated uprisings against Uncas. Connecticut did not contribute direct military support for the sachem, but it often indirectly supported its ally. The Narragansetts never forgot Connecticut's involvement in the execution of Miantonomi either, targeting that colony during the Great Narragansett War.

Pessicus inherited the Narragansett sachemship after Miantonomi's death and continued the war against the Mohegans. He also achieved more military success than his predecessor. Pessicus raided Mohegan territory over the protests of the New England colonies and even besieged Uncas's main fort at Shantok in 1645. The Connecticut colonists more directly aided the Mohegans by sending relief supplies up the Thames River and over the river's bluffs, where the Narragansetts had failed to place a guard, into the stronghold.[60] Thomas Peters described the action to Governor John Winthrop of Massachusetts Bay Colony in May 1645: "I with your son [John Winthrop, Jr.,] were at Uncus Fort where I dressed 17 men and left plasters to dresse 17 more which were wounded."[61] Not only did the English resupply Uncas, but the colonial gentry also dressed the wounds of their Native allies. Understanding that the mutual relationship was too important for the security of the colony, Connecticut's leaders prevented Uncas's defeat. The other New England colonies also realized the advantages of maintaining Mohegan power, forcing the Narragansetts and Eastern Niantics to accept a humiliating treaty in 1645.[62]

Members of coalitions usually have diverging interests, and divisions within the Connecticut-Mohegan alliance soon emerged. Colonial and Mohegan economic and political interests collided in the conquered Pequot territories. After temporarily blunting the Narragansett–Eastern Niantic threat, both the English and the Mohegans attempted to exploit the resources of southeastern Connecticut. The main source of tension occurred when John Winthrop, Jr., developed economic interests on the lower Pequot (Thames) River. Though he later would figure prominently in Connecticut's moderate policy toward the Indians, at this time he sought to undermine Uncas's power.[63] While Winthrop never resorted to violence to advance his claims, his material interests were at odds with Connecticut's most valuable Indian ally.

As part of his campaign to dominate former Pequot territory, Winthrop also championed the cause of the Pequots in proximity to his settlement, further alienating the Mohegans. The symbolic nature of his Pequot Plantation (also known as Nameag and by 1658 New London) in the vicinity of a former Pequot fortress, along with the location's commercial implications for the wampum trade, was not lost on Uncas.[64] Winthrop, Jr., writing from Boston, detailed to Thomas Peters in 1646 the deterioration of his relationship with the Mohegans from the previous year, when both men were assisting Uncas in person at Fort Shantok: "If the Pequotts be not taken under the English, If these Indians that we must live neere be still under Uncas command, there will be noe living for English there."[65] Uncas had argued that the remnants of the Pequots should act as a tributary people to his victorious Mohegans, while Winthrop advocated for the freedom of those in the vicinity of his new plantation. The underlying tensions centered on the potential use of Pequot survivors as laborers, the disposition of territory for hunting and agricultural development, and the aforementioned wampum trade. In addition to economic pressures, Uncas had the additional concern of cementing his legitimacy as a consequential sachem. He effectively had to wield power in order to maintain it over the lesser Indians in his sphere of influence, especially those he had conquered. Winthrop's interests posed a serious threat to this mandate.

The commissioners of the New England–wide (except Rhode Island) political body known as the United Colonies (the supracolonial political administration consisting of the Puritan–Pilgrim colonies) attempted to strike a middle course so as neither to abandon their loyal ally nor the son of the governor of Massachusetts Bay Colony. Indicating Massachusetts's position, Samuel Symonds wrote to Winthrop, Jr., advising, "Uncas may be kept a friend still to the English; but yet soe that he be not suffered . . . to insult, or wronge other Indians."[66] For their part, the Mohegans did in fact warn colonial authorities of an alleged plot to kidnap Winthrop, Jr., perhaps in an attempt to gain leverage and ingratiate the group with one of their political adversaries.[67]

Tensions boiled over again in 1647, when Uncas used force to back up his demands. He led a party of Mohegans on a raid of the Pequot village adjacent to Winthrop's settlement, roughing up some of the Indians and looting and destroying their property. Although the Mohegans did not kill anyone, this event accelerated Winthrop's lobbying campaign against Uncas, protesting the raid to Boston authorities.[68] Mason, now a major and the patron of Uncas and the Mohegans, composed the resulting treaty, establishing a formal tributary relationship between the Mohegans and Pequots. The agreement dated 24 February 1647 between Uncas and the Nameag Pequot sachem Cassacinamon ordered that the Pequots accept Uncas's status as overlord, pay him tribute, and "attend him in such services of peace or warre as they shall be directed to by the Governor of Connecticott until the meeting of the Comissioners."[69] Uncas's claims had temporarily triumphed over the protests of the colonists at Pequot Plantation.

The relationship between the Mason family and Uncas continued to develop over the intervening decades, and the Masons remained the most vigorous supporters of Mohegan land rights after the Great Narragansett War.[70] The relationship between the major and the sachem often placed Mason at odds with Winthrop, Jr., as the latter continued to remonstrate for the freedom of the Nameag

Pequots from Mohegan authority.[71] Winthrop may have written to the officer from Pequot Plantation on 19 September 1648—the letter appears unfinished, and it remains uncertain if it was actually sent. In it, Winthrop raises his concerns over the hunting disputes of various Native groups and criticizes Mohegan "Surmises and Jelousies."[72] Even if Winthrop never sent the letter, it is a good indication of his continued rivalry with Uncas.

In July 1649 Winthrop wrote to the commissioners of the United Colonies at Boston, again making the case that the Pequots at Nameag should be free from the Mohegans and the Narragansetts, arguing for their autonomy because "Uncas hath sole militia of all the other Pequotts."[73] He sent another letter the next month to Connecticut Colony governor John Haynes, imploring him to prevent Uncas from provoking the Narragansetts. A Mohegan war party had raided a Narragansett village, killing "an old woman," and pursuers had killed one Mohegan warrior in the subsequent skirmish. Winthrop also mentioned Narragansett wampum as a central factor in his desire for keeping the general peace since it was a stipulation of the treaty of 1645: "so they (the Narangasets) may the more securely goe on in the providing the wampam that is yet behind."[74] Although this letter was also unfinished, Winthrop followed it with another on the same day to Governor Haynes, which was sent to Hartford.[75] In 1650 Winthrop advised Captain Humphrey Atherton, leader of an expedition into Narragansett territory sent to collect the overdue wampum, not to provoke the powerful Natives into fighting the English. His penchant for moderate Indian policy intertwined with his economic interests in making this case.[76]

These exchanges exhibit the complicated intersection of colonial and Indian politics, economic factors, and struggles for power, which although present since the arrival of Europeans, accelerated in the former Pequot territory less than a decade after that people's defeat.[77] The complexity of events demonstrated that there was no clear line of demarcation between the interests of the Native groups of southern New England and the English, as Mason supported Uncas and Winthrop supported Cassacinamon. The Narragansetts and Eastern Niantics lacked powerful English patronage, a fact that plagued both groups through the war of 1675–76.[78]

Uncas did not always enjoy the full support of the English, though, especially those colonists whose interests were at odds with his own objectives. The younger Winthrop's ascension as

Connecticut governor later in the 1650s magnified the earlier tensions, and Uncas's prerogatives began to lose support, especially concerning his power over the Nameag Pequots. Winthrop eventually ensured the independence of Cassacinamon's band, which became a critical element in the success of Connecticut during the Great Narragansett War.[79]

The English authorities invariably supported Uncas even when Winthrop, Jr., and others were at odds with the Mohegan sachem. When violence intermittently erupted with the Narragansetts, Eastern Niantics, Pocumtucks, Mohawks, and other Native groups attempting to conquer Uncas, the colonists backed the Mohegans. In 1648, for instance, a confederacy of hostile Indians determined to attack the sachem. By threatening war, the colonists dissuaded these groups at Pocumtuck (later Deerfield, Massachusetts) from molesting Uncas. Soon afterward, the colonists resolved a dispute between the sachem and his brother Wawequa that included the English sending forces to protect Uncas at Fort Shantok.[80]

Uncas also persuaded colonial leaders that Ninigret, sachem of the Eastern Niantics and at that time also leader of various Narragansett groups, was plotting to ally with the Dutch during the First Anglo-Dutch War of 1652–54.[81] The two European powers both claimed Connecticut territory, and the Anglo-Dutch Wars brought these tensions to the surface.[82] A Ninigret alliance would have given the Dutch a powerful partner to reinforce their claims and potentially open another front in their global war against England. Thomas Stanton, who had been the colonial emissary at Pocumtuck, warned Ninigret not to plot against the English. Whether there was an actual conspiracy was beside the point, Uncas had again succeeded in convincing the colonists to protect his interests. The English also came to his assistance in the late-1650s, when the Narragansetts finally succeeding in ejecting the sachem from Shantok, and again when a hostile confederacy besieged him in the Western Niantic fort at Niantic, Connecticut.[83]

There was yet another Dutch-Indian conspiracy in 1669 that even witnessed the disarming of a group of Mohegans by their patron, Major Mason, although the colonists and southern New England Indians again avoided conflict.[84] This event also confirmed the increased power of Cassacinamon and the revival of the main Pequot group less than a decade before the Great Narragansett War, in which it would play a critical role.[85] Even during this period when

Connecticut did not always support Uncas's economic and political objectives, it was unwilling to allow the sachem's power to diminish at the hands of the external Native groups.

The years after the Pequot defeat in 1637 marked an overall strengthening of the Connecticut-Mohegan alliance. New England's English leaders understood that Uncas's continued friendship benefited colonial security, and they supported him, sometimes even over the interests of well-connected leaders like John Winthrop, Jr. Winthrop in turn urged the recognition of Cassacinamon's group, at first to allay the threat of Uncas to his economic interests, but then to the benefit of general New England security. This prescient policy paid off during the Great Narragansett War, as Cassacinamon's Pequots proved critical in the fight against the Indian coalition. But even with Indian assistance, English military methods proved decisive during the Pequot War and as a deterrent afterward, demonstrating that the "Indian way of war" was not the only effective method of fighting in New England. The Pequots, Mohegans, and their tributaries would prove their military effectiveness during the Great Narragansett War, however, after Indians of the region had adapted to English tactics, and allied Indians proved themselves the margin of victory.

The complexity of events during the interwar years marked a tide of shifting alliances and new centers of power in the greater New England region. Connecticut was but one colony within this postcontact mosaic of economic, political, and cultural turmoil. The surprising aspect was that the English colonists were not involved in an earlier widespread conflict resulting from the upheaval after 1620. Tensions occurred over land disputes; the encroachment of Puritanism on Indian religious beliefs; different views of private property regarding trespassing, grazing, hunting, and fishing access; and the jurisdiction of Indians in colonized areas. While the English experienced a tenuous peace during these decades, even exchanging agricultural and military technology with some tribes, Indians of Northeastern America often turned to intertribal violence as a means to adjust to these challenges. Within this framework, the Mohegans and Narragansetts battled each other throughout the 1640s and 1650s. These were no small-scale skirmishes that resulted in the death of Miantonomi and the driving—albeit temporary—of Uncas from his territory. The English, particularly in Connecticut, angered the Narragansetts when they inserted themselves into this

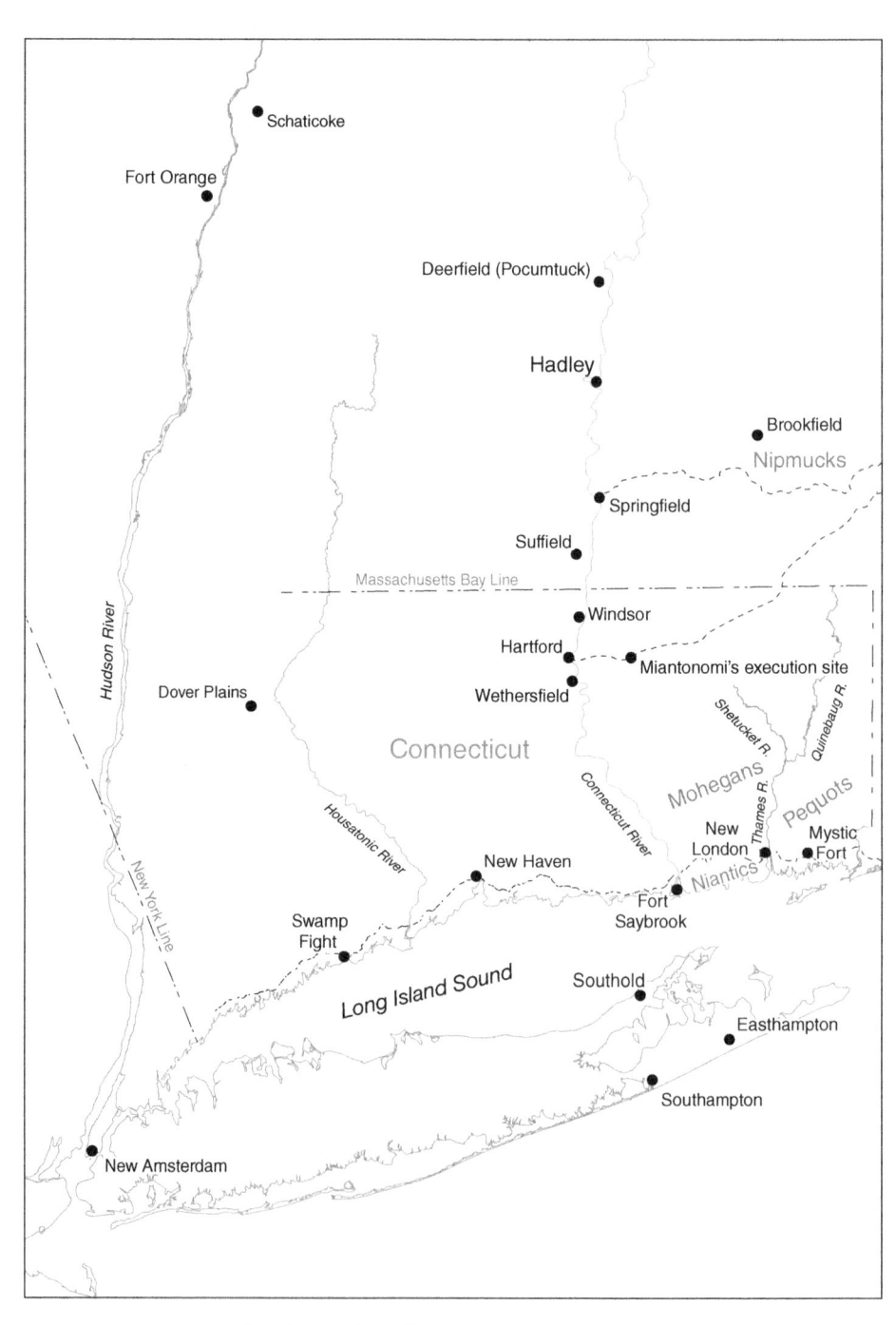

Overview of New England. Map by Bill Keegan.
© 2014, University of Oklahoma Press.

35

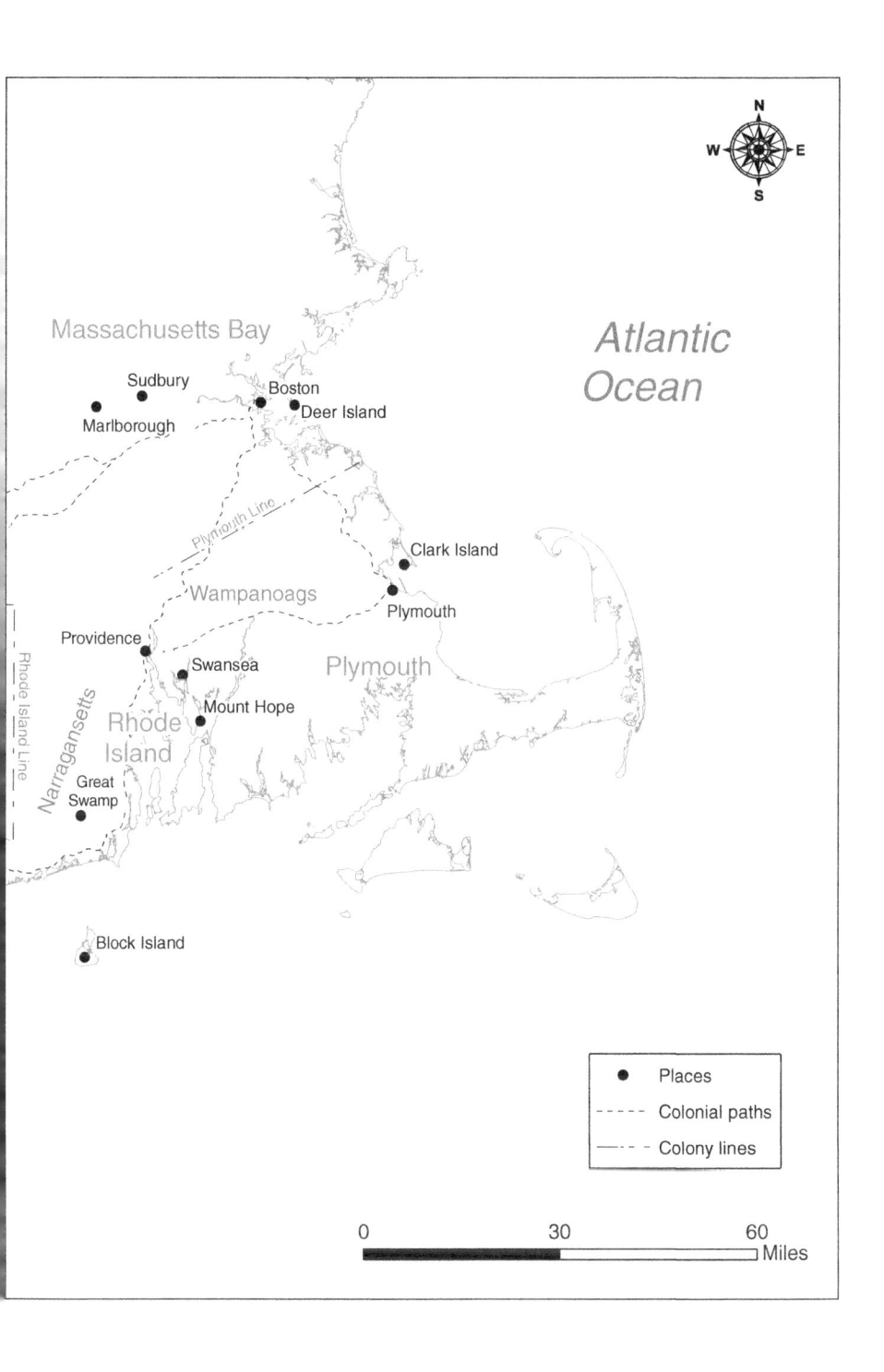

rivalry by supporting Uncas with nonmilitary assistance. The Great Narragansett War was the final chapter in the battle for hegemony after the collapse of the Pequot confederacy, representing also the continuation of violence after 1620. The intermittent warfare of indigenous New Englanders during the years 1638–74 simmered until a skirmish between declining colonial and Indian powers in the region precipitated a general war. This occurred when King Philip's band of Wampanoags retaliated against Plymouth Colony for the execution of a few of its warriors in the spring of 1675, though any similar incident could have engulfed all of New England in flames.

The crisis that ignited the region's underlying tensions involved two smaller entities increasingly relegated to the periphery—Plymouth Colony and the Wampanoags. Since ancient times, declining powers have attempted to regain lost status or maintain even a semblance of relevance in political affairs.[86] These moribund entities sometimes resort to violence or lobby their more robust political patrons to resort to armed intervention or intimidation for them. During the Serbian crisis before World War I, for example, the Serbs counted on Russia for international support. In 1675 Plymouth relied on Massachusetts Bay, and King Philip depended on kinship ties with the Nipmucks.

Disease carried by European traders nearly destroyed the Massachusetts and weakened the Wampanoags in the late sixteenth and early seventeenth century, altering the Native balance of power in southern New England. Losses from epidemics caused the Wampanoag leader, Massasoit, Philip's father, to seek an alliance with the newly arrived Pilgrims of Plymouth.[87] The traditional narrative for "King Philip's War" begins with Massasoit's death, when his son Wamsutta, Alexander to the English, succeeded his father as sachem. In the early 1660s Alexander died soon after visiting the English, and his brother Metacomet, or Philip, succeeded him. Philip suspected that the colonists had poisoned Alexander.[88] This was not the first time that relations were tense between the colonists and Indians since the Pequot War, but it was the first that led to outright violence between them.

Friction between the English and Indians resulted from an intertwined economy, judicial system, and shared religious practices, and thus the Great Narragansett War was to a degree a civil war because the variant cultures had merged to a degree over the preceding fifty-five years.[89] Many colonists considered the Great Narragansett War a rebellion, indicating that they viewed the Indians as the King of England's subjects. Sometimes the Indians viewed themselves in the same way, for instance, using their status as royal subjects to petition the king directly concerning land disputes.[90] Even Philip believed that the English were sovereign in certain matters, including legal jurisdiction over English-Indian disputes.[91]

The demonetization of wampum by 1663 and the related collapse of the fur trade further generated discord.[92] Wampum and the fur trade together formed the basis of the early New England economy. Coastal Indians strung together seashells into belts, creating wampum, which served as currency and was also a symbol of power. In return for wampum, the inland Indians provided furs to the coastal Indians. The Europeans inserted themselves into this economic relationship, and ultimately the demand for furs and beads outstripped supply. When the English demonetized wampum, rendering it useless for financial transactions in this system, land became the Indians' remaining commodity to deal financially with the colonists. Their conception of land ownership, semimigratory lifestyle, and dealings within the English legal system distinctly disadvantaged indigenous New Englanders' property transactions. This became increasingly a point of tension with the expanding colonial population during the Great Migration.[93]

The English cultural colossus relative to the shrinking Indian population induced fears of absorption or worse, the extinction of the Indian way of life. This menacing yet long-term threat—given the decades of tense but peaceful biracial relations since the Pequot War—caused Philip, Uncas, Ninigret, and other sachems to reject Puritan Christianity. It also perhaps explains the apparent rise of women sachems, or "sunksquaws." Women sachems seemed to be rare in the earliest years of colonial arrival.[94] By the outbreak of the Great Narragansett War, however, there were at least four female sachems ruling factions within the Narragansett, Wampanoag, and Quinnipiac groups.[95] Women served important roles within Indian communities, including as the primary providers of food through agriculture and gathering. Thus, many clans recognized this importance "by adopting a system of matrilineal kinship."[96] Women were also arguably the main purveyors of culture to children. With the alternate of a Christian Indian lifestyle available to many Natives in southern New England, and the occurrence of a vastly altered economic and military framework postcontact, perhaps the rise of sunksquaws revealed the growing importance of this transmission of traditional culture to the youth. Mohegan pottery from the seventeenth century even served as a reminder to tribal members about the importance of fertility (and to bring luck in reproducing) and of preserving traditions.[97] Ensuring "Indianness" within clans thus may have provoked a rise in women's political importance within New England groups.[98] The pressure of European arrival and the transformation of indigenous societies existed for some time in the region prior to the outbreak of general war in 1675.

Plymouth Colony's suspicion that the Wampanoags murdered John Sassamon, and the subsequent trial of the alleged perpetrators, was the proximate cause of the war. Sassamon was a "Praying Indian," a Native who accepted Puritan Christianity. He served for a time as a chief advisor to Philip because he was English literate and had experience living and dealing with the colonists. Philip may have believed that Sassamon had cheated him financially in his interaction with the settlers, but in late 1674 Sassamon also reported to Plymouth Colony that the sachem was planning an uprising. He was found dead soon thereafter.

Although a joint Indian-English jury found three of Philip's men guilty of the murder, the circumstances of the trial were less than rigorous. The colonists supposedly witnessed Sassamon's body bleed anew when the suspects approached it, confirming their guilt.[99] The handling of the trial further inflamed the Indians' other grievances, but certainly the trial itself undermined Philip's legitimacy as sachem of the Wampanoags. He stated during a conference with Rhode Island men prior to hostilities that the Sassamon episode angered him because the colonists were meddling in a tribal affair: "The English, they said, took them [Indians] out of the Jurisdiction of their Indian Kings . . . and that the Christian Indians wronged their Kings by lying about them."[100] This indicated that Philip accepted English jurisdiction in colonist-Indian disputes but not in any he perceived as involving only Indians. The colonists, however, considered Sassamon's case as under their jurisdiction because of his religious conversion and English literacy.[101]

This issue of political legitimacy was more important in a practical sense to the Indians than to the colonists. European kings of the period derived the legality of their rule from "divine" authority, thus the Christian God indirectly commanded subjects to action. Indian sachems lacked similar authority over their warriors and did not accept lightly affronts to their more temporal power.[102] The colonists, however, had legitimacy concerns of their own with the Sassamon murder because he had been a Christian Indian, conferring on him an English legal status greater than non-Praying Indians. Had the English authorities left this murder unanswered, it would have had a deleterious effect on their conversion efforts. The controversy over the legitimacy of converted Indians struck at the heart of the colonial-Indian relationship in New England. There was no palatable compromise to diffuse the escalation in tensions over this issue. Only weeks after Plymouth authorized the execution of Philip's men, warfare erupted. The violence from the Indian perspective fulfilled the requirement for blood vengeance, helping solidify Philip's legitimacy with the Wampanoags and potential recruits for the war effort from other groups.

King Philip and other leaders may have decided to fight the English before the Sassamon trial, and it was probably a matter of time before a similar incident triggered a conflict anyway. Most of the Wampanoag clans, the Nipmucks and Nashaways of central Massachusetts, the "River Indians" of the Massachusetts stretches of the Connecticut River, and the Abenaki of northern New England rallied to Philip's cause. The English eventually attacked the powerful Narragansetts for passively supporting Philip, driving them into his camp too. Vaughan estimates that the southern groups by 1675 totaled 6,000–8,000 people, with perhaps 2,000 warriors among them.[103] A more plausible estimate of 10,000–12,500 and 2,000–2,500 warriors, not including the Abenaki of northern New England, better accounts for the Indian coalition since the Narragansetts alone numbered about 5,000 people based on their nearly 1,000 warriors.[104] Individual warriors from neutral groups or those allied to the English also joined Philip, which was unsurprising given the prevalence of intermarriage and clan affiliation as well as the limited political and military control of the sachems.

These Indians faced at a minimum 50,000 English colonists, with around 10,000 men capable of bearing arms.[105] Even with a 5–1 numerical advantage, the English could not win the war without allied Indian support, and at the outset of the conflict, it was not assured that any groups would rally to the colonists. The war certainly did not seem hopeless to the at least 10,000 southern New England Indians who joined Philip, and it was unlikely that the sachem would have won over so many supporters without a specter of success. Philip sent entreaties to the powerful Mohawks of the Iroquois confederacy, as well as to other groups such as the Mahicans and French Indians, likely a combination of St. Lawrence Mohawks and Algonquian groups from as far afield as the Great Lakes region. Some of the Abenaki campaigned on the Massachusetts stretches of the Connecticut River, while others attacked what is now New Hampshire and Maine, drawing off Massachusetts Bay forces from southern New England.[106] The possibility of winning over the Mohawks and other powerful Indian nations was a motivating factor for the groups that joined Philip's alliance and increased the coalition's chance of success.

There was also the reality of indirect Dutch and French support for the coalition. English fear of Dutch and French conspiracies before the war furthered growing tensions in the region. This possibility of support was only logistical, for England had reconquered New Netherlands a year prior to the Great Narragansett War, and there was no central Dutch administration to control support to the hostile coalition. France was allied temporarily with the Catholic-leaning English crown and also could not directly support the coalition. Philip likely aimed at a negotiated peace similar to the one that colonists had granted Virginian groups after a colonial-Indian conflict in the Tidewater. In this scenario he would have retained his honor and restored his legitimacy among his people after satisfying the requirement of blood vengeance for the execution of his warriors after the Sassamon trial.

Philip's motives were not appealing, however, to all New England Indians. The tactically dominant and closely related Mohegans, Pequots, and Western Niantics of Connecticut provided critical military aid to the English colonists as did some of Connecticut's Indians from smaller groups. The Natick Praying Indians rendered military aid to Massachusetts Bay and Plymouth Colonies.[107] Those Natives who determined to remain neutral were also important because they did not add to the fighting strength of either party. The neutrality of Ninigret's Eastern Niantics was critical because this group was powerful and closely related to the Narragansetts. The remaining neutral groups of Connecticut, the Indians of Cape Cod, Martha's Vineyard, Nantucket Island, were smaller and of less military importance.

Maintaining an advantage in numbers, logistics, and the possibility of reinforcement from elsewhere in the English realm did not guarantee the colonists a total victory. Although colonial objectives shifted to correspond with the expansion of Philip's uprising from a local affair to a regional conflict, internal disputes over land and military operations blunted the war effort. The New England colonies, like the Native groups, were not a monolith with identical objectives, though the destruction of southern New England's Indian power became the goal of the United Colonies. This objective proved more difficult to achieve than necessary because of the fractured war effort and the failure of Massachusetts Bay and Plymouth to employ allied Indians in meaningful numbers from the beginning. Particularly, land disputes prevented effective prewar military policy, and this issue surfaced again at the conclusion of major hostilities, when the Puritan colonies sought the occupation of conquered Indian lands, particularly at the expense of Rhode Island Colony.[108] Throughout the war, Massachusetts Bay and Plymouth accused Connecticut of insufficient support and later for failing to participate in the northern Indian war after the defeat of the southern New England coalition.[109] The United Colonies did not survive the political fallout of the Great Narragansett War as England attempted to impose on the region "The Dominion of New England," a more centralized administrative body with the hated Governor Edmund Andros of New York Royal Colony as titular head. This new organization also faced the intransigence of colonial New Englanders, and the Glorious Revolution of 1688 toppled it after Holland's William of Orange invaded England and assumed the throne.

The English faced the possibility of economic ruin and high casualties during the Great Narragansett War, although complete annihilation at the hands of the Indians was by that time impossible given the large colonial population and the lack of artillery support that the coalition needed to reduce their main strongholds. The New England colonists, interestingly, did not believe that the war with Philip would result in a general uprising of the region's Native groups.[110] The historical record makes clear that they genuinely felt betrayed, especially by their local Native groups who joined the rebellion after having been the colonists' peaceful neighbors for decades. The colonists may have been in denial or simply misunderstood their situation vis-à-vis the Indians, remaining ignorant of the animosity that they had engendered since their arrival in the New World. With the exception of Connecticut, a lack of clear policy outlining the Indian's legal status and this sense of betrayal with an accompanying desire for revenge increased colonial violence toward indigenous New Englanders. Brutality on both sides accelerated once the colonists categorized the hostile Indians as rebels in a fashion reminiscent of the Pequot War. Those not killed outright were sold into slavery or indentured servitude, depending on the capturing colony's preference (and the desires of individual colonists), while hostile Indians sold English captives to the French in Canada. The unguarded nature of the frontier and their lack of preparation for war demonstrated that the colonists misunderstood their environment. Most of New England would pay a price in blood for this lack of vigilance. Connecticut was the notable exception.

CHAPTER 2

"Endangering Also the Neighbor Colony of Connecticut"

Connecticut during the Great Narragansett War

All along Connecticut's border, the Indian coalition devastated major settlements, but they did not launch major attacks against the colony itself. War parties destroyed Springfield's abandoned outlying settlements, now Suffield, Connecticut, and Longmeadow, Massachusetts, only six and fifteen miles respectively from Windsor, Connecticut.[1] Reports indicated that Hartford was under imminent threat of attack, and colonists sighted hostile Indians on both sides of the Connecticut River in the heart of the colony near Windsor, Wethersfield, Wallingford, and what is now Glastonbury.[2] Connecticut Colony's eastern frontier was also within easy striking distance of Narragansett territory, once this Native group joined the Indian coalition.

Although the colony suffered far less than the rest of New England, war parties entered Connecticut during the conflict and managed to carry out a number of violent acts, including the burning of abandoned Simsbury. These hostile bands even caused the colony to temporarily withdraw from the upper Connecticut River valley in Massachusetts. Large war parties invaded Connecticut and sought targets of opportunity, temporarily occupying a central position within the colony, as well as striving to destroy Norwich, a critical meeting point for colonists and Mohegans. If they had succeeded, it would have served to weaken allied Indian support for the colonists and diminished Connecticut's ability to raid coalition territory.

The lack of a large-scale attack was not due to the absence of the Indian coalition; rather, it proved to be the product of sound military operations begot of solid relations with local Native groups. War parties operated within the colony, but the historiography does not address their activities, while the primary records scarcely mention their operations in Connecticut. An assessment of the coalition's threat to the colony is necessary for the understanding of the effectiveness of Connecticut's local Indian policy. Without considering the objectives, activities, and capabilities of hostile groups, it is impossible to evaluate the defenses, which were critical elements of the colony's success during the war.

In late June 1675, when the Wampanoags initiated the bloodshed with a revenge attack on Plymouth, Connecticut was not a priority target for King Philip. The area posed no immediate threat to the Wampanoags, with the exception of the early battle of Nipsachuck, in which a band of Mohegans supported colonist forces.[3] When Philip's band successfully evaded capture and joined the Nipmucks and the upper Connecticut River Indians, it transformed the nature of the conflict from a local uprising to a regional war, "endangering also the neighbor Colony of Connecticut, which hath also suffered somewhat by the fury of this Flame, though not considerable to what the other colonyes have undergone."[4] Though he never took command of other groups after fleeing Plymouth territory, Philip's expanded coalition now threatened Connecticut because the Nipmucks of central Massachusetts, who occupied areas that expanded into northeastern Connecticut, were ancient enemies of the Mohegans and Pequots.[5] The upper Connecticut River Indians felt a similar animosity toward Connecticut's natives, acting to curb Uncas's rise since the defeat of the Pequots, which thus imperiled the colony further with the potential of raids across its northern frontier. Connecticut's English leaders were well aware of the threat posed by the groups of central and western Massachusetts, and for his own purposes, Uncas stoked their fear of violence from the Indian coalition.

Beginning in the late summer of 1675, Connecticut provoked the latent animosity of Massachusetts Native groups by sending a joint colonial-allied Indian force to aid the hard-pressed Massachusetts Bay towns along the Connecticut River. Although these forces met with neither defeat nor decisive victory, their actions altered the military objectives of the coalition. With Connecticut forces disrupting their operations and logistics, the coalition had little choice but to attack that colony in an attempt to induce it to abandon operations upriver, thus isolating the Massachusetts Bay towns on the river. Without assistance from Connecticut, these towns stood little chance of success against the coalition. If effective, these operations would have forced the weaker western Massachusetts forces to fight alone or to abandon altogether the western New England frontier. Connecticut's status as an important yet secondary target during the late summer and throughout the fall of 1675 resulted in enemy activity within the colony as early as August.

The coalition sometimes achieved its objective, forcing Connecticut repeatedly to withdraw its forces from the upper Connecticut valley to respond to threats within its own borders. This was short-lived success, however, as the colony's forces returned to conduct offensive operations throughout the war. Massachusetts Bay urged Connecticut to play an even greater offensive role and to supply it and Plymouth with more material aid. Disagreement between the Puritan colonies also included a crisis in the colonial chain of command concerning the theater of operations along the upper Connecticut. This resentment reflected differences in military strategy as well as overlapping territorial claims. The situation in the western theater of operations was a microcosm of the division within the United Colonies. Governor Andros further complicated the English war effort by pursuing his own royalist agenda, although he convinced the Iroquois confederacy to aid New England. The Iroquois in turn entered the conflict against their traditional Algonquian enemies for their own strategic purposes, and they were successful in preventing a widening of the war by upending Philip's diplomatic entreaties and raiding the Indian coalition.

Another objective of the Indian coalition was to weaken Massachusetts and Plymouth forces and then to invade Connecticut with enough warriors to force it to come to terms by threatening vulnerable areas of the colony. Towns geographically isolated from the rest of the colony and relying only on garrison defenses were most vulnerable to this strategy. Warriors would have had to reduce the frontiers of Massachusetts Bay and Plymouth first because of the logistical concern of protecting rear areas against colonial raids in order to concentrate exclusively on Connecticut. This nearly occurred in the spring of 1676 after the Narragansetts joined the hostile Indians, with the rise of Canonchet as the coalition's primary war leader. When the colonists drove the Narragansetts into the hostile camp with the Great Swamp attack in December, Connecticut became a primary target, though one that proved difficult to strike given its (by then) advanced defenses and the coalition's weakened logistical base. Canonchet and many of the Narragansetts despised Connecticut, given events since the Pequot War, and it was only a matter of distance, logistics, and Canonchet's death that prevented a successful *major* incursion into the colony. Even with these favorable circumstances during the winter-spring offensive, primary documents show that war parties raided the colony despite the best efforts of Connecticut forces. The colony did not completely prevent raiding not only because of the size of enemy war parties but also because of their ability to avoid detection, not to mention the unfavorable ratio of friendly forces to the territory involved. In addition to the handful of Connecticut Indians who joined the rebellion, others entered from surrounding areas. Intelligence records and enemy activity in the colony demonstrate that it was not a matter of coalition inattention that led to the colony's success, but rather the positive actions of both its English and Indian inhabitants. Sound military operations predicated on good relations with local Indians prevented the violence witnessed in the rest of New England.

Though rugged in many areas, Connecticut's highest point in the area of hostilities was only approximately eighteen hundred feet. The difficult terrain and rivers served as obstacles, though not impenetrable barriers. There were four main "avenues of approach" for enemy forces into the colony.[6] The northern approaches were from west-central Massachusetts, where hostile forces operated with impunity, into north-central Connecticut. The first and primary avenue of approach was the Connecticut River valley, a band of flat terrain, five to ten miles in width, running on either side of the river.[7] This terrain is suitable for even the movement of a mechanized division with large vehicles, let alone small groups of lightly armed American Indians. The second avenue was a north–south corridor on the western side of the river divided from the Connecticut valley by a trap-rock ridgeline running from north of Holyoke, Massachusetts, south to the outskirts of New Haven, Connecticut. This valley is five miles at its greatest width and also would have been accessible to war parties.[8] Simsbury is in this valley, and hostile warriors obviously had gained access to this area when they burned the abandoned town to the ground.

The third approach, more rugged than the river valley, led from Narragansett country into southeastern Connecticut. There is a near continuous ridge running in a north–south direction along the entire Rhode Island–Connecticut border until flattening in the area of North Stonington near the Atlantic Ocean. (Where the ridgeline ends is in fact where route I-95 now runs from Connecticut into Rhode Island.) From this location, the Narragansetts would have had the same freedom of movement as Philip's other allies in western Massachusetts.

The final avenue of approach into Connecticut was from Nipmuck country in the northeastern corner of the colony, moving southwest toward the Thames River and ultimately the Connecticut River. This was a narrow corridor of approach, and Connecticut's Mohegan allies likely observed it as it led toward their territory. The Wabbaquasett Nipmuck group inhabited the northern portion of this area and traversed south through it when submitting to Uncas. These were the main entry points into the colony, though other, smaller approaches existed, which also were passable given the small size of many war parties.

There were other obstacles that disrupted any invaders besides the natural terrain features of Connecticut's hills. Hostile war parties traveling along the Connecticut River would have had to negotiate water barriers. These included flooded lands, tributary rivers, and numerous bends along the river, all of which would have increased the physical danger and infiltration time from Massachusetts. Such terrain increased straight-line distances. From a defensive perspective, these barriers were beneficial by channeling enemy forces into passable, more easily challenged areas, especially fords on rivers and larger streams.

Hostile warriors gained access into Connecticut even with the defenses and terrain because of the nature of their war parties. Even with natural impediments increasing direct distances by a few miles from Springfield's southernmost plantations—initially a mere six to eight miles from Windsor, Connecticut—an Indian war party would have rapidly covered that distance. A modern combat infantryman carrying full combat gear is expected to march twelve miles in three hours.[9] An Indian patrol, carrying relatively little in comparison and inured to traveling long expanses from hunting, could certainly match that pace.[10] As historian Patrick Malone explains, "Stealth, surprise, and high mobility were major assets in the irregular warfare

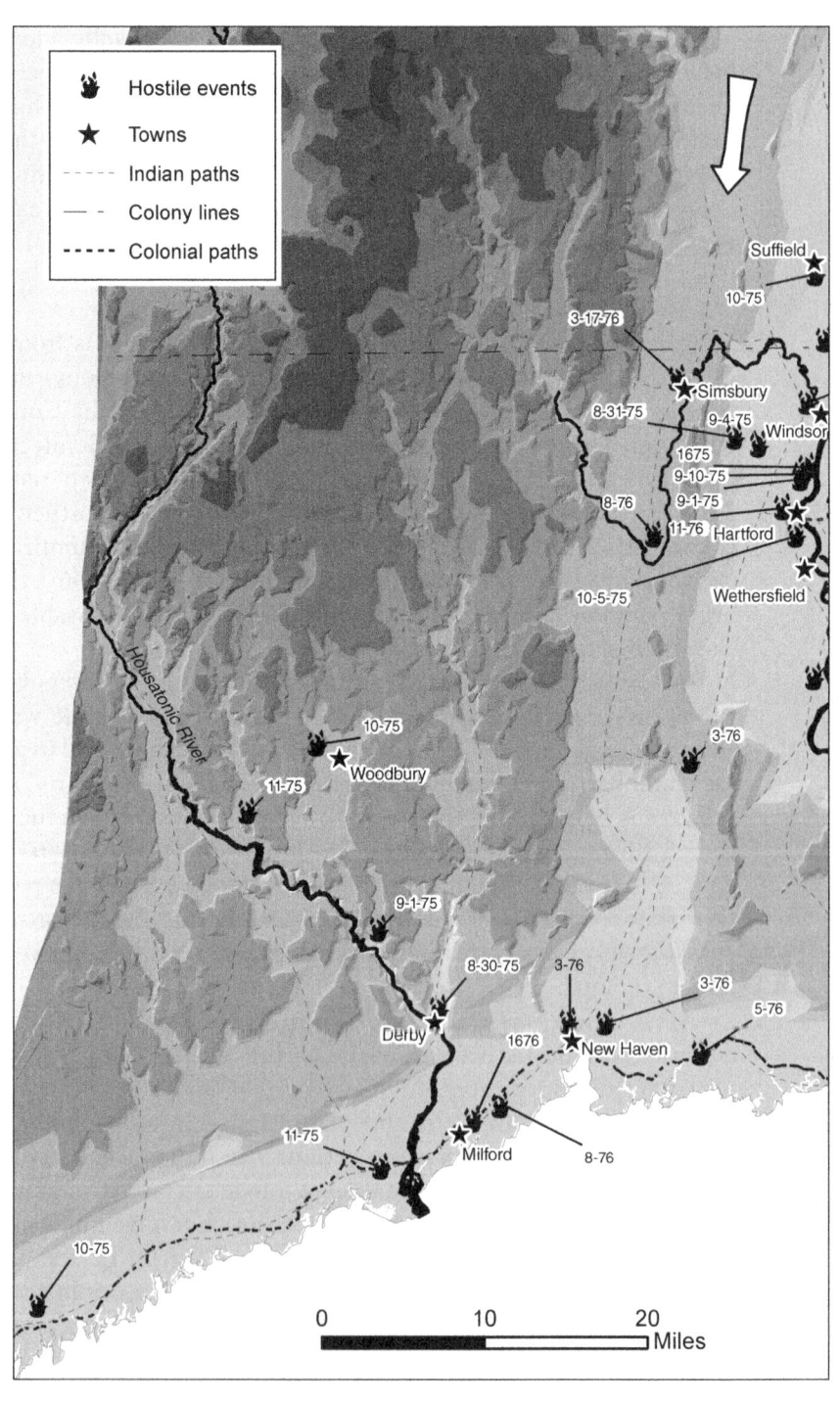

Topography and avenues of approach. Map by Bill Keegan.
© 2014, University of Oklahoma Press.

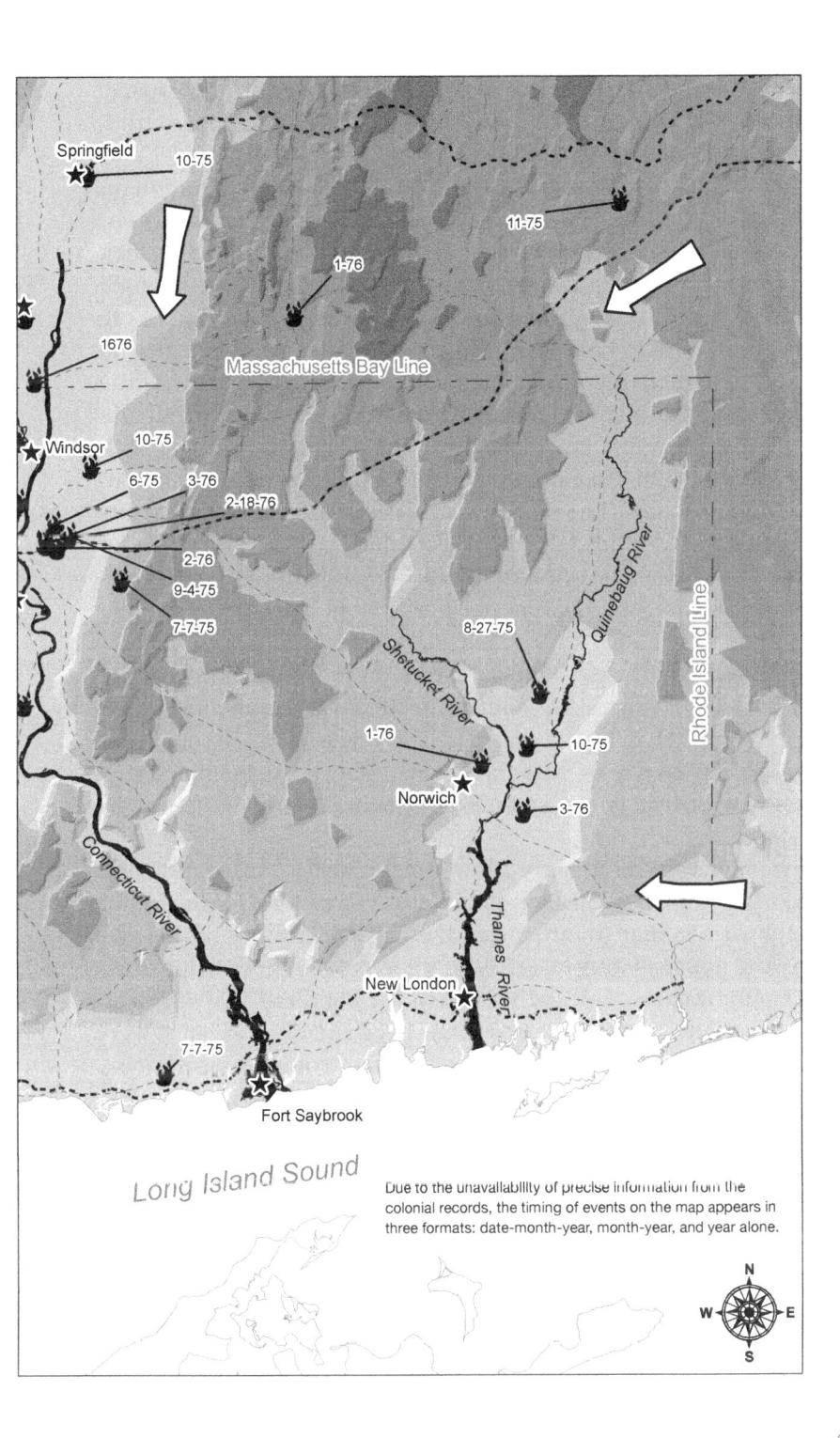

Due to the unavailability of precise information from the colonial records, the timing of events on the map appears in three formats: date-month-year, month-year, and year alone.

at which the Indians excelled."[11] This high degree of unobtrusive mobility in the wilderness allowed hostile warriors to bypass frontier obstacles and defenders alike to enter Connecticut.[12]

The Indians eschewed the burden of excessive equipment, which not only made noise while traveling through the woods but also required more energy to carry. Besides the ubiquitous flintlock musket or a bow and quiver of arrows, a hatchet or knife, a pouch for bullets, a horn for powder, and a purse for ground maize, the Indians carried little else. They simply added water to the ground maize for a high-energy ration and occasionally hunted game while on the warpath to supplement this crude mixture.[13] L. Foxhall and H. A. Forbes demonstrate that "exceptionally active" men, such as military personnel conducting field operations, need 3,382 calories daily.[14] Donald Engels estimates that Macedonian warriors consumed 3,600 calories a day during combat operations in arid conditions.[15] The Indians' ground-maize ration, with around 4,000 calories per kilogram, contained more calories than both the wheat and whole grain considered by Foxhall and Forbes and Engels respectively.[16] Averaging the two studies' estimates for the required caloric intake to 3,500 calories for soldiers in field operations, an Indian warrior would have had to carry slightly less than 2 pounds of rations per day to satisfy this threshold.[17] They also supplemented the maize with fish, game, and berries, further reducing the weight of rations.

A warrior's ability to carry a low-weight, high-calorie ration and supplement it on the route of march eliminated a logistical tail of resupply wagons that so influenced European operations of this era. During the Great Narragansett War, some colonial formations utilized supply wagons, especially early in the conflict.[18] As such, the Indians had an operational advantage over their European adversaries and were inherently more mobile than colonial formations. Wayne Lee argues, however, that this was only a short-term benefit because warriors, a critical link in the Indian food chain as hunters, could not remain away from their villages indefinitely, especially in winter when hunting was critical to the Indian diet. Allied Indians, though, could and did capitalize on this short-term operational advantage because the colonists became their groups' long-term ration supplier.[19]

The absence of supply trains allowed Indians to negotiate difficult terrain since the only physical constraint on their mobility was the natural limitations of the human body, not the restrictions of machines or beasts of burden that often determined the course of European operations. Even with the ability to move across difficult terrain, the natural human tendency is to take the path of least resistance, which requires less energy and thus reduced caloric expenditure. This accounts for many trails traversing flat terrain and passing near waterways, which tend to be of lower elevation. War parties preferred to move along the flat valley bottoms and only traversed more difficult terrain if obstacles or enemy forces blocked their primary route of march.

Whereas the Indians wore very little during combat operations for most of the year, their English contemporaries clothed themselves heavily with sturdy leather or quilted jackets for protection.[20] This was an improvement over the equipment worn when the colonists first arrived in New England, which in addition to helmets consisted of "a back and breast-plate (corselet), tasses for the thighs, thules for the groin, and a gorget for the neck."[21] The vests or quilted jackets also reduced mobility and required more calories to wear when on foot. Hirsch claims that the colonists stopped wearing steel armor once the Indians adopted muskets, but this would not explain why some still wore heavy leather or quilt during the Great Narragansett War.[22] Quilted or leather vests could stop arrows, which were the primary weapons of American Indians through midcentury, with many still so armed in 1675. Most Indians used some version of flintlock muskets by then, however, and the colonists' vests would have been of little protection. The change in English equipment likely resulted from the loss of mobility when wearing armor, not because of the Indians' adoption of firearms. That the colonists still wore vests also suggests that they had not completely transitioned their equipment to meet the new threat. Lacking combat experience—the ultimate agent of change for military technology—against Indians since the conclusion of the Pequot War as well as intelligence concerning their military developments, the English continued using equipment of an earlier era.

Contrary to historian Harold Peterson's account of colonial weaponry during this era, many Connecticut soldiers still carried swords.[23] Colonists utilized these weapons to close with the enemy, for there is little evidence that New World soldiers used plug bayonets, the precursor to the socket bayonet. Soldiers in the early modern era did not rely on killing their opponents from a distance but instead sought to close the distance across the battlefield to dispatch them with edged weapons. Swords and plug bayonets were the tools used in Europe, with the latter weapon not in use in America.[24] Before the Great Swamp expedition, the Connecticut War Council ordered that each county equip ten soldiers with hatchets as opposed to the standard-issue swords, the former beginning to be recognized as a more effective all-purpose tool for fighting and hewing through the wilderness.[25] But Massachusetts Bay militia still used swords to close with the enemy at the battle of Turner's Falls in 1676.[26]

Most Connecticut troops were mounted, which restricted their mobility to trails and open land generally free of debris, except when dismounting to fight.[27] At the outbreak of hostilities, the colony's field forces consisted of both cavalry and dragoons.[28] Dragoons mostly armed themselves with long muskets because they fought on foot and thus did not need the shorter-barreled carbines that the cavalry carried in order to fire while on horseback. The uneven and wooded terrain of New England limited the opportunities for mounted troops to maneuver, even in the rare occasion that enemy Indians could be caught in the open. Based on such considerations, the Connecticut General Court ordered its cavalry to arm themselves with long muskets, which had longer ranges and fired a heavier round than carbines, essentially turning this force into dragoons.[29] Lighter flint-lock carbines, or "fusils," were also in service since there was a lack of firearm uniformity throughout New England.[30] The industry was unavailable in North America to produce firearms, causing delays while awaiting shipments from overseas.[31]

Historian Harold Selesky argues that Connecticut soldiers were mounted all of the time, but the standard militia companies assigned to garrison defense operated dismounted unless scouting. The General Court ordered town officials to distinguish between the dismounted traditional trainband militia and the ad-hoc mounted field forces that conducted operations outside of their local communities.[32] An exception was the march to Great Swamp in late December 1675, when Connecticut assigned a horse only to every third soldier, perhaps lacking the mounts and the fodder necessary (during the winter) for such an unusually large force.[33]

Horses were more tactically effective and logistically efficient when operating over shorter distances, while dismounted soldiers retained the locomotive and logistical advantage over longer distances.[34] This explains how Connecticut's dismounted Indian allies maintained a rate of march on par with their mounted colonial comrades, a factor aided by the less encumbered nature of Indian tactics, which the use of horses did not complement. A small number of prominent Indians might have been mounted at times during the conflict, as the General Court in 1674 granted Uncas's son Joshua, sachem of the Western Niantics, "liberty to purchase two horses, the one for himselfe and the other for his Interpreter, that they may be the better capacited to attend their meetings with Mr. Fitch; the markes of the horses to be entered at Norwhich with the recorder there."[35] An English prisoner observed three hundred horses at Philip's great powwow east of Albany in the winter of 1675–76 before the Mohawks drove his party back into New England.[36] After their aborted assault on Hatfield in October 1675, the hostile Indians withdrew from the area carrying their dead and wounded on horseback.[37] Lacking a sufficient number of mounts and the means to supply them, the Indians only employed horses occasionally for transport and not as a means of maneuver.

When war did come at the end of June 1675, it did not immediately encompass all of New England, occurring initially only in a narrow portion of Plymouth Colony around the Wampanoag stronghold of Mount Hope (now in eastern Rhode Island). Philip's warriors first struck at Swansea, then elements of his Wampanoags raided the English settlements on Plymouth's border with Massachusetts Bay and Rhode Island Colonies.[38] Although colonists sought a knockout blow before Philip could escape and widen the war, their forces were unable to corner him. At this point, Connecticut was the farthest colony from the conflict.

Abandoning his headquarters, Philip and his band repeatedly escaped the colonists. Following standard "cutting off" tactics when pursued by a larger force, the Indians fled to the nearby Pocasset Swamp. The colonists believed that they had surrounded them and even built a fort that dominated a main access point into the morass. Taking advantage of local flooding, however, Philip's band crossed the Taunton River on rafts and doubled-backed past Mount Hope into northern Rhode Island.[39] A colonial force soon picked up his trail.

With the assistance of local Rhode Islanders and joined by Uncas's son Owaneco's Mohegans, this motley crew surprised the Wampanoag camp at Nipsachuck.[40] Forced to stand and fight while his noncombatants fled, Philip lost a significant number of warriors and a few key leaders, but he escaped once again. Connecticut's only participation during this early phase of the conflict had been Owaneco's chance presence in the area, returning from a mission to Boston to swear fealty to Massachusetts Bay.[41] Connecticut also sent a force in July under Wait Winthrop, the governor's son, along with soldiers from the other New England colonies, to force a treaty upon the Narragansetts.[42]

As early as two weeks after the outbreak of violence, Hartford received warnings about the questionable intentions of some local Native groups. On 7 July 1675 the colonists suspected that Indians from the coastal area around Saybrook had joined with Philip, while Uncas warned them not to trust the Narragansetts near Hoccanum and Podunk east of Hartford.[43] These fears surfaced amid the news from late June that the war had spread beyond the area of Philip's traditional territory. In early August after Nipsachuck, Philip led his band north from Rhode Island into Nipmuck country in central Massachusetts. The union of the Nipmucks and the closely related Nashaways with the Wampanoag bands represented the very expansion of the conflict that the colonists had sought to avoid.

Prior to Philip's arrival, the Nipmucks ambushed an expedition from Massachusetts Bay led by Captain Thomas Wheeler, which confirmed the group's "disloyalty" to the colonists. With most of his force slain in the ambush, Wheeler, wounded and hotly pursued, barely limped into Brookfield, the lone English settlement in the heart of Nipmuck territory, and sounded the alarm. Before a relief force saved it, the town's garrison house scarcely withstood a multiday siege that witnessed the Indians employ a number of ingenious techniques to break through its defenses.[44]

On 24 August, reacting to the new threat on its northern border after the Brookfield raid and other hostile activity to the north, Connecticut leadership commissioned Uncas's son Joshua to interdict Philip's forces, which reportedly were moving toward Norwich.[45] No additional intelligence followed that would have indicated hostile forces in the area. On 30 August colonists of New Haven, Milford, and Derby were "alarmed with the hostile conduct of Indians in these parts, who it was apprehended were marching in a Body towards Paugasset [Derby] to make an attack upon it."[46] Though again no attack materialized, the alarm demonstrated a high level of insecurity on the part of some Connecticut colonists. The misperceptions of some in New Haven County resulted in repeated alarms during the war.

The groups of the upper Connecticut River next went over to Philip's hostile coalition, exposing the Massachusetts towns there to attack. The colonists had failed to court good relations with these Indians, and in some cases they even exacerbated tensions during this period of mutual suspicion. The Pocumtucks of Deerfield, the Norwottocks of Northampton, the Woronocos of Westfield, and groups of Western Abenaki in what is now Vermont all joined Philip's coalition. War parties raided Massachusetts's Connecticut valley settlements on 1 September at Deerfield and on 2 September at nearby Northfield (Squakeag). On 4 September hostile Indians annihilated Captain Richard Beers's command as it attempted to relieve isolated Northfield. Those colonists not immediately killed or incapacitated rallied on a small knoll not far from the site of the ambush, but they eventually succumbed to the Indians. The victors mutilated the dead and tortured the survivors. Soon after Beers's defeat, Captain Thomas Lathrop led a contingent from Deerfield on 18 September south to harvest sorely needed crops. Hostile Indians ambushed his men while they were crossing a creek thereafter known as Bloody Brook, killing nearly the entire party.[47] These defeats filled the colonists with terror, demonstrating that they had underestimated the development of Indian military capabilities since 1637, this fact epitomized by Beers and Lathrop, who were veterans of the Pequot War. Connecticut forces drew off the Northfield garrison, and the colonists subsequently abandoned Deerfield. The hostile groups had wrested the initiative from the English during this phase of the war.

In late summer 1675 Connecticut experienced scattered violent acts, though nothing near the magnitude of the carnage that the colonists experienced in Plymouth and Massachusetts Bay. On 31 August, in one of the first acts of violence in Connecticut, four out of an estimated party of eight Indians shot at Christover Crow while he was traveling from Simsbury to Hartford.[48] A hostile war party thus was operating in the corridor between Simsbury, Windsor, and Hartford, for it also fired upon John Coalt the next day in the north meadows of Hartford. That same day colonists claimed to have observed hostile warriors in arms on the lower Housatonic River.[49] Raiding parties continued to harass the colonists in the area of Hartford, where four Indians surprised Major Talcott's oldest son in the north meadow, though he appears to have survived the incident. On the same day as Beers's defeat, war parties shot at lone colonists between Simsbury and Hartford and in the woods across the Connecticut River at Podunk.[50] On 10 September a friendly fire incident occurred north of Hartford during an operation to clear this area of these raiders: "Some [soldiers] were sent out after Stray Indians in our Meadows in the night & my Man was amongst them & being forward in seeking After them was shott by one of ye Company in Sted of an Indian, one bullet stroke his arm & broke it but I hope it may be recovered it is set & the wound Mr. Bulkly hopes is Mending."[51] War parties were probing Connecticut's defenses as Philip's coalition sought to develop intelligence while simultaneously launching attacks upriver on the Massachusetts Bay towns. These raids also gathered evidence concerning the loyalty of local groups toward the English. If the coalition had convinced Connecticut's unaligned Native groups to join their efforts in the early fall of 1675, a combined force might have exploited the colony's unprepared defenses.

The anti-English confederacy's successes on the upper Connecticut River focused actions outside of Connecticut as it sought to reinforce its successes.[52] Philip's confederates would have next turned their attention south had they forced most of the Massachusetts settlers to abandon their towns along the upper Connecticut, but even with tactical victories, this strategic success never occurred. Throughout the fall, Connecticut's forces assisted in preventing colonial evacuation as they reinforced Massachusetts's forces.

While colonial forces failed to locate its enemy in the wilderness, one of the most shocking attacks from the colonial perspective occurred on 5 October at nearby Springfield. The local Agawam group shielded members of the Indian coalition before joining with them in an attack on the town. Although Springfield's English leadership had received intelligence of an imminent assault, they doubted the veracity of the report, relying instead on the settlers' perception of good relations with the Agawams. Lieutenant Thomas Cooper, ignoring the warnings of the town's few naysayers, opted to confirm the Agawams' loyalty for himself. While en route to the Agawams' nearby fort, hostile Indians ambushed and mortally wounded him, but the lieutenant managed to return to Springfield to sound the alarm before expiring. Crowded into garrison houses, the inhabitants watched helplessly as the Indians destroyed most of the town.[53]

Soon after this devastating attack, only miles from Windsor, the Connecticut War Council received reports of enemy activity on the east side of the Connecticut River and near Hartford.[54] This caused the council, the decision-making apparatus during the war, to recall its commander, Major Robert Treat, and many of the Connecticut forces from upriver, much to the chagrin of Massachusetts Bay.[55] This retreat also validated, at least temporarily, the coalition's strategy of isolating the Massachusetts towns by demonstrating against the Bay's southern Puritan neighbor. Intelligence gathered from the field in western Massachusetts pointed exactly to this operational design. On 15 October Connecticut's War Council, in an exchange of letters with beleaguered western Massachusetts's commander Captain Samuel Appleton, explained that Philip's targeting of Norwich and the nearby villages of the Mohegans and Pequots would delay further military support. This intelligence came from two separate sources, the Reverend James Fitch of Norwich and John Stanton of New London.[56] Western Connecticut also experienced alarms during the fall of 1675. In early October Stamford alerted nearby New York of potential violence from local Indians.[57] Prior to the abandonment of Woodbury, hostile forces shot at guards who had been sent from Milford to protect the fledgling settlement.[58] It was not until 19 October that the Indian coalition faced its first significant setback in this region. Major Treat's Connecticut troopers, having returned upriver, and Massachusetts Bay soldiers garrisoned at Hatfield defeated an attack on the town, claiming to have inflicted numerous casualties.[59] This victory preempted the continuation of the coalition's raiding into Connecticut during the late fall and early winter, as the colonists observed its forces moving northward from Hatfield and away from the colony line, abandoning their previously successful offensive.[60] It is unclear if Connecticut's leaders understood that offensive operations upriver had bought critical time for its towns to establish an effective defense, but this was the effect of forcing the coalition to concentrate on the colony's field forces operating in Massachusetts Bay.

Nearly a month later, after hostile activity had ceased in the vicinity of the Massachusetts Bay river towns, Appleton speculated that some of the coalition Indians had withdrawn to the Stratford River region in Connecticut due to reports of increased Native corn planting the previous spring. From that locale, the colonists assumed that hostile forces would target towns west of the lower Connecticut River.[61] Two days later on 12 November, Appleton

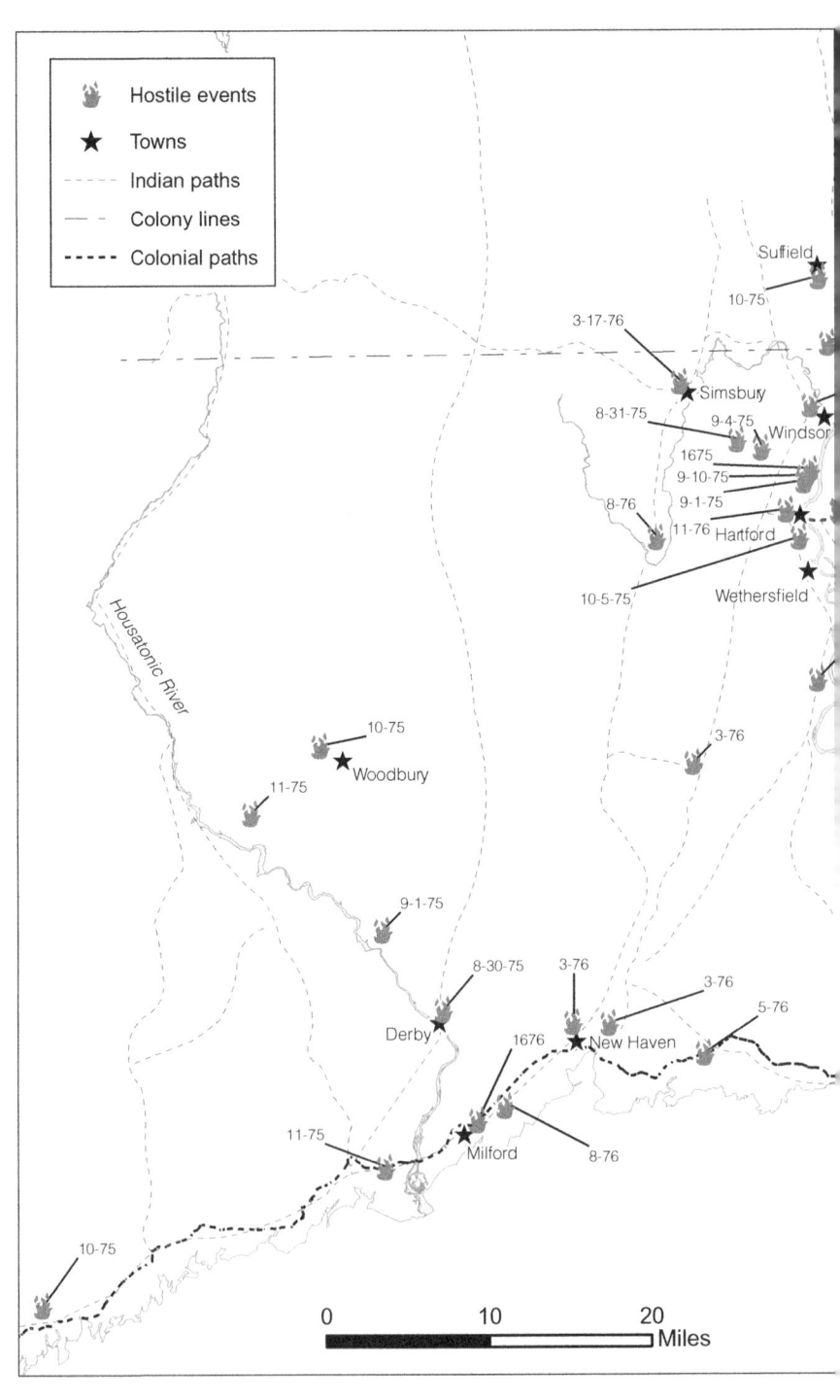

Connecticut hostile incidents. Map by Bill Keegan.
© 2014, University of Oklahoma Press.

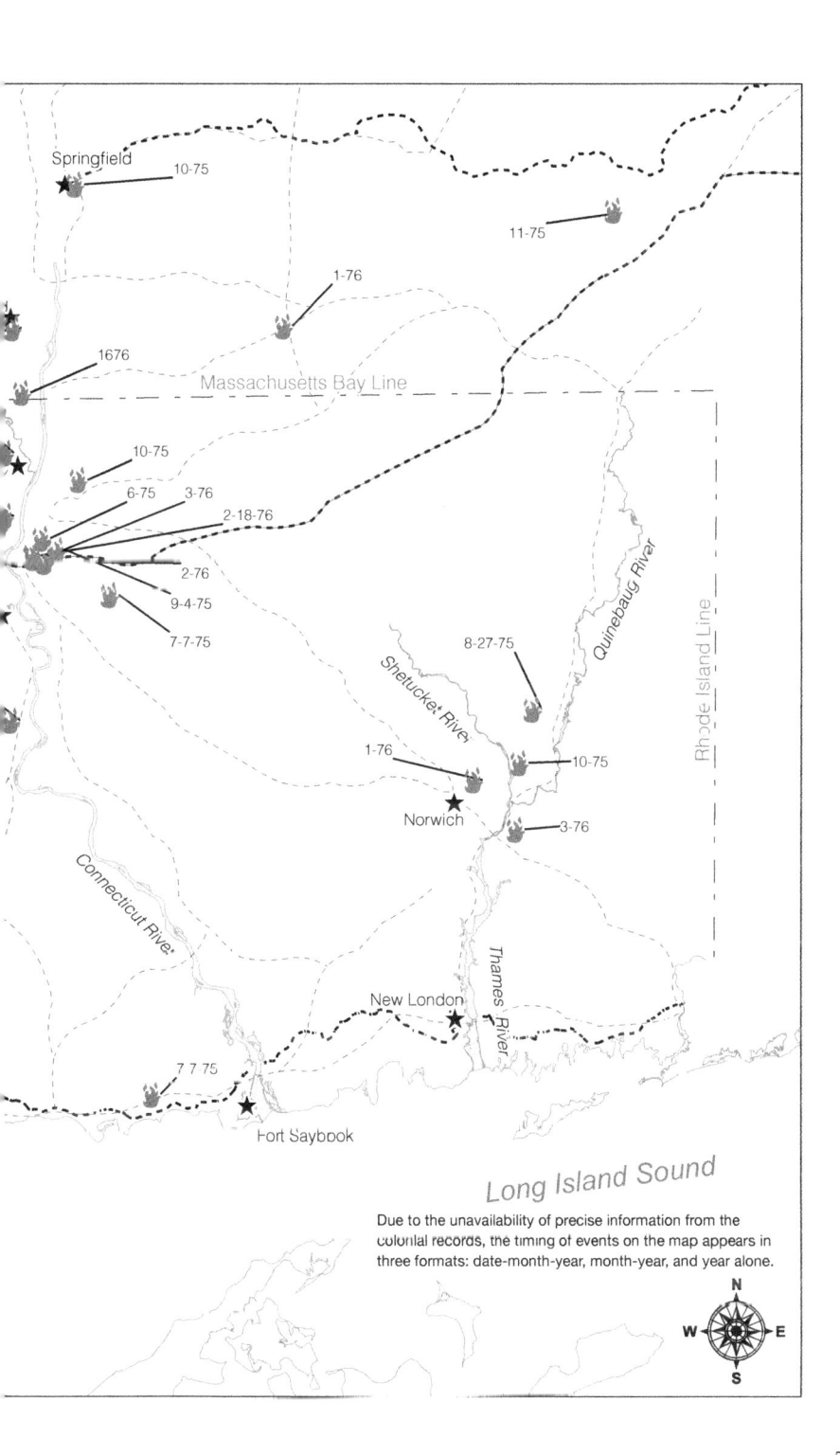

Due to the unavailability of precise information from the colonial records, the timing of events on the map appears in three formats: date-month-year, month-year, and year alone.

learned that Owaneco had informed Connecticut authorities that Philip intended to send 600 warriors to attack Massachusetts and 400 to raid Connecticut. Other reports suggested that a great powwow was about to transpire at Stratford but that the loyalty of the attendees remained unknown.[62] This intelligence, when combined with the hostile and suspicious activity, pointed to Connecticut as an important, though secondary, objective in the fall of 1675.

Early November also witnessed tensions increase between the colonists and Narragansetts in the lead up to the Great Swamp Fight, when Hartford residents blamed Miantanomi's son Masecap for the burning of a barn and warehouse within town limits. The English arbitrarily detained the young man as a hostage, even though it was uncertain if he had committed the arsons.[63] This episode perhaps fulfilled Uncas's augury not to trust the Narragansetts, who were near Hartford, or the sachem's prophecy led to a mistrust that influenced the colonists' decision. It also demonstrated the fluid nature of Native culture, as the Narragansetts traditional territory centered on central and southern Rhode Island, but Masecap resided near Hartford; perhaps he was serving in a diplomatic capacity or retained kinship ties to other Indians in the area. For the remainder of November through the Great Swamp expedition of mid-December and into January 1676, either Connecticut's inhabitants did not report hostile activity or the records of such events have been lost. With hostile Indians entering winter quarters to regroup and resupply, the remaining western Massachusetts Bay towns also experienced a weather-induced armistice.

The United Colonies shattered this tranquility by launching a daring, though morally dubious, preemptive strike on the Narragansetts. This resulted in the Great Swamp Fight, one of the best-known episodes of the war and the largest colonial action, with more than a thousand soldiers deployed. In council at Boston, the United Colonies coordinated this action, though not all Connecticut leaders approved of the plan since the Narragansetts technically remained at peace with the English. Governor Winthrop, Jr., a member of the council, insisted that the colonists refrain from launching the attack, which would constitute a violation of accepted diplomatic norms governing neutral parties.[64] The majority of Puritan and Pilgrim leaders, however, vetoed his position, maintaining that the Narragansetts had violated the terms of two recent treaties that forswore aid to Philip when its members sheltered Wampanoag noncombatants and provided other logistical support.

Plymouth's governor Josiah Winslow led the expedition, though the army represented a proportional contribution from the Puritan colonies. Massachusetts and Plymouth forces marched into Rhode Island, while Connecticut troops arrived by water. Rhode Island officials did not sanction the operation but did provide local support to Winslow's army. Minor raiding and skirmishing with the Indians occurred as the combined colonial force entered Narragansett country. A renegade warrior then led the column through the wilderness toward a main fort at Great Swamp.[65]

On 19 December 1675 the guide located the fort (the site of which is in present-day West Kingston, Rhode Island). While the army's Connecticut Indian allies, led by Captain James Avery, formed the outer cordon as joint tactics dictated, the colonials assaulted the well-hidden bastion across a frozen swamp. The Narragansetts initially prevented the English from gaining entrance until part of the colonial army happened upon an unfinished portion of the stockade and stormed through. Heavy fighting occurred within the stronghold and played to the colonists' strength of massed fire at close quarters. They eventually overcame the Indians, driving them out. Aiding this expulsion was, in a scene reminiscent of Mystic, the burning of the wigwams, killing many noncombatants and preventing the reoccupation of the fort. The Narragansett population suffered serious losses, though most of the warriors escaped the melee and inferno. The Indians inflicted heavy casualties on the English force, especially the Connecticut contingent, which stumbled upon a heavily guarded entrance protected by a blockhouse. After the battle and over the protests of Plymouth and Massachusetts Bay, Major Treat withdrew his command from the field in order to replace casualties and reequip his men.[66] This was possible because the colonists maintained the population and logistical base to replace losses whereas the Indians could not. Great Swamp thus marked a major turning point in the war since it resulted in the Narragansetts losing their logistical base. Though the strongest Indian group now joined the hostile coalition, it did so in a weakened state.

After Great Swamp, many Narragansett groups made their way north to join the uprising, evading another colonial army, which failed to follow up the earlier success. The union of the Narragansetts with the coalition combined with Philip's diplomatic failure during the winter to enlist Native groups from outside New England marked the decline of the Wampanoag sachem. His wartime strengths had been diplomacy and eluding enemy forces, not battlefield acumen. Once he escaped to Nipmuck country after the disaster at Nipsachuck, there is no evidence that Philip directed a single battle in the conflict. His diplomatic position began to unravel as winter set in without a sign of abating hostilities. The hostile coalition suffered from a lack of provisions as English and allied Indian patrols drove them from their logistical bases. There was at least one inside plot to kill Philip, and other tribal groups indicated a willingness to surrender to the colonists.[67] Coalition prerogatives changed, however, when the Narragansetts joined the conflict en masse after Great Swamp. Narragansett leaders maintained more clout than Philip, controlling a greater number of warriors than any other group in New England, and probably dictated new objectives for the coalition. There were soon at least seven hundred Narragansett warriors bolstering the ranks, dwarfing Philip's tiny remnant band of Wampanoags.[68] Seven hundred, though probably more since not all Narragansetts went directly to Nipmuck country, was the largest number of warriors for that period in southern New England. This contingent doubled, for example, the total number of Connecticut's allied Indian warriors.

Sachem Canonchet, son of Miantonomi, who inherited the Narragansetts' animosity toward the Mohegans and Pequots, emerged as the leading military leader within the Indian coalition. Canonchet was a more respected warrior than Philip and determined some of the coalition's operations during the winter and spring of 1676. The leading historians of King Philip's War all agree that Canonchet occupied the central leadership role in the conflict after the Great Swamp Fight. Daniel Mandell argues that "with Metacom[et] away seeking Mohawk help, Canonchet became the most influential war leader among the swelling force of Natives fighting the Puritans."[69] Jenny Pulsipher calls Canonchet's later death "a critical turning point in the war" after comparing his military leadership in the late winter and early spring with the absence of any from Philip.[70] Pulsipher's "turning point" reasoning is accurate, for having enjoyed a string of successes leading up to Canonchet's death, Philip's forces afterward managed to score only the notable triumph at Sudbury.

There is evidence that the Indian coalition, which originally included more Native groups than actually ended up fighting the English, even selected Canonchet as its primary war leader in a great powwow in 1674. The Narragansetts even may have led the coalition from the start if Philip's warriors had not precipitated the conflict after the Sassamon affair before the other Indian groups were prepared to fight.[71] William Hubbard also notes that the English and their Indian allies greatly benefitted from the early precipitation of the war: "However the good hand of God was seen in so ordering things, that the Narragansetts were for the present restrained from breaking out into open hostility against the English, at that time when Philip began; which if they had then done according to the eye of reason, it would have been difficult, if [even] possible for the English to have saved any of their inland plantations."[72] The colonists received intelligence that Canonchet secretly fought around Hadley, at a time when the upper Connecticut River Indians joined the coalition months before the Narragansetts.[73] Connecticut colonists also reported observing wounded Narragansetts streaming back to Rhode Island from the upper valley.[74] In addition to Canonchet, the elderly Pessicus was another leading Narragansett sachem within the coalition, though too old for field service. Pessicus's group of Narragansetts and assorted allied Native peoples established a presence upriver from the Massachusetts settlements on the Connecticut and participated in attacks on these towns in 1676.[75]

The Narragansetts were more disposed to attack Connecticut than Philip given their longstanding intermittent warring with the Mohegans and Pequots stretching back to the precontact epoch. After the defeat of the Pequot confederacy, the Narragansetts repeatedly attempted to annihilate the Mohegans and had grown to distrust and dislike the United Colonies, especially Connecticut, because of its support for Uncas. They never forgave Connecticut for tacitly approving the Mohegans' execution of Miantonomi, and Canonchet continued this blood vendetta into the Great Narragansett War.[76] Soon after that execution, the peoples hostile to the Mohegans "conclude[ed] then that the only way to succeed against the English was to begin with Uncas."[77] When the Indians exchanged peace feelers with the English in the spring of 1676, their leadership explained that their true enemy were the allied Indians and not the colonists.[78] Even the Mohawks, when flirting with Philip's entreaties prior to turning on him, promised to attack the Mohegans but not the English.[79]

After the colonists drove them from their traditional territory in the winter of 1676, the Narragansetts decided to risk the outcome of a total war rather than pursuing Philip's more modest goals. The Narragansetts were behind the rejection of two Connecticut peace proposals, and although groups of Nipmucks and Wampanoags eventually defected from the coalition, no significant Narragansett group attempted to submit to the English.[80] The one possible exception was the female sachem Quaiapen (also called Sunk Squaw by the colonists), who had been negotiating with Rhode Island authorities when Connecticut forces attacked her band.[81] Given their enmity for the colony, the Narragansetts included Connecticut's destruction high on their list of objectives, a fact confirmed by intelligence that both New York and Connecticut received from various sources.

Connecticut always feared that the Narragansetts would join with Philip, acting in the beginning of the war to secure its eastern border and sending a force to ensure the people's neutrality.[82] At Boston, Connecticut's Governor Winthrop argued against the Great Swamp expedition in part to avoid Narragansett retaliation against his colony's eastern frontier. Afterward, faced with the Indian coalition's threat to the north during the late summer of 1675, Connecticut now faced a two-front war. The determining factor for the future operations of the hostile Indians, now led by the Narragansetts, was that that tribe had lost its food stores, having abandoned their traditional territory after Great Swamp. As starvation threatened the people's noncombatant population during the winter, the Narragansetts fled north, the only direction in which they could find shelter with their coalition allies, placing them even farther from the increasingly militarized Connecticut frontier. When Connecticut forces captured and executed Canonchet, the coalition lost one of its only leaders capable of directing a concerted effort against that colony's now-hardened defenses.

Though it probed Connecticut's defenses many times in early 1676, the Indian coalition continued to press its best military option given a lack of supplies (having abandoned hidden stores of food): attacking the nearby and less fortified Massachusetts Bay, Plymouth, and Rhode Island settlements. These colonies, having interned friendly Native groups out of poor policy borne of distrust, lacked large numbers of competent Indian scouts to provide intelligence on and early warning of enemy activities. This not only negated their best asset against an Indian foe, but it even drove some friendly Indians into the enemy camp.[83] The coalition's turn to the weaker colonial targets after Great Swamp spared Connecticut the worst of the war's fury, its winter–spring offensive inflicting some of the worst losses upon Europeans in America's Indian wars. This was ultimately a losing strategy for the hostile Indians, however, as Connecticut remained unharmed, launched the expeditions that played a vital role in defeating the coalition, and continued to supply the other Puritan colonies with food and material. Although war parties prior to Canonchet's death entered Connecticut, as did some afterward, without the support of the local Native groups, facing more-advanced defenses, and lacking Canonchet's leadership, these groups were unable to deliver a decisive blow. The winter of 1675–76 also witnessed Philip's failed attempt to strengthen the coalition.

With the approach of winter, Governor Andros enlisted the Iroquois confederacy to support the New England colonists. The Iroquois disrupted Philip's diplomatic entreaties by driving his winter camp away from the upper Hudson River valley. This site had been about twenty miles northeast of Albany on the eastern side of the Hudson along the Hoosic River at an Indian meeting place named Schaghticoke. It was a critical location for Indian diplomacy, for the area represented a Native cultural fulcrum: Mahican territory surrounded Schaghticoke; the Iroquois confederation bordered it to the west; the southern New England Algonquians bounded it to the east and southeast; French Indians and northern New England Algonquians encompassed it to the north and northeast; and Delaware groups delimited it to the southwest. At this meeting place of Indian nations, Philip attempted to enlist the support of other groups for his cause. A report from escaped English prisoners through Governor Andros indicated that Connecticut was a priority target the coalition's winter–spring offensive.[84] Bringing clarity to events of the previous winter, on 29 April 1676 an interrogation of "Wuttawawangkcssnek Sucqunch Messenger of Pessicus" revealed that Mohawks had killed five, three, and three more of Philip's men respectively in three winter raids, one at Schaghticoke, and the latter two at "Squackheag" (Northfield).[85] Philip was attempting to recruit five hundred French Indians (identified by straw in their noses) and the neighboring Mahicans to his cause. Before the Mohawks arrived, Philip had been entertaining 2,100 young warriors at his camp.[86] Despite the low number of casualties that the Iroquois inflicted, they did succeed in ending

Philip's diplomacy with approximately 2,000 warriors from outside of southern New England.

Spurred on by Andros, the Mohawks and other warriors of the Iroquois confederacy chose to intervene directly on New England's northwestern frontier. John Grenier summarizes the argument for the Iroquois's supposed defeat of the hostile Indians: "Indeed, without Iroquois participation on the side of the colonists, it is difficult to imagine an English victory over King Philip."[87] Although acknowledging Mohawk raids, Connecticut remained skeptical of the overall effect of their involvement in the war.[88] The colony was suspicious of Andros's intentions, which led its leaders to view the Iroquois as an arm of the Royal Colony's military apparatus and thus, warily. Fearing also a revival of the Mohegan-Mohawk feud, Connecticut denied entrance within its borders to Iroquois warriors.

A colonist seeking aid from the royalists in England and thus lacking motivation to downplay the role of the Mohawks (supported by the *Royal* Colony of New York) asserted that the Mohegans and Pequots were more effective partners in defeating the hostile Indians.[89] In recognition of the traditional "Mohawk argument," though, the Iroquois did significantly aid the colonists by containing the war to New England and raiding the remnants of the coalition in the late spring. But if the confederacy had been so effective in degrading coalition forces that winter in northern New England, this does not explain how in the spring of 1676, hostile war parties launched the most devastating offensive of the Great Narragansett War.

Regardless of Iroquois involvement, reports from various sources consistently described Connecticut as a major target beginning in the winter of 1676. Major Edward Palmes, headquartered at New London as military leader of southeastern Connecticut, received intelligence that hostile bands would operate southward from Nipmuck country into the colony.[90] Governor Andros also warned of imminent attack on numerous occasions.[91] During the winter–spring offensive, Connecticut issued orders to clear the Wabbaquasset country in the northeastern section of the colony of enemy bands based on another of the New York governor's letters, corroborated by Palmes's intelligence.[92] Although Andros desired to acquire all of Connecticut west of the Connecticut River for the Duke of York's royal colony, New York records confirm that he did not inflate or otherwise alter the raw intelligence concerning Connecticut that came into Albany or his headquarters at Manhattan.

Governor Andros's suspicious role in the war began in July 1675, when he attempted to enact the Duke of York's charter by using Philip's rising as an excuse to invade Connecticut.[93] Throughout, he was playing a double game. The governor at once claimed to his Hartford counterpart that the presence of his forces at the mouth of the Connecticut River was to assist the New England colonists against the Indians, while on the same day as his invasion he wrote to Massachusetts Bay that he was making good the duke's charter claims.[94] This royal claim was dubious, though, as the duke himself admitted in private correspondence with his governor.[95] Andros also offered refuge to hostile groups, to the chagrin of New Englanders, if these bands agreed to live peaceably and under satellite control of the Mohawks.[96]

After Great Swamp there was a hiatus in the coalition's operations until launching a counteroffensive in late winter that lasted through mid-June 1676. By the middle of January 1676, Deputy Governor William Leete reported to the United Colonies that Connecticut's enemies had infiltrated its defenses—the eventuality Connecticut leaders feared after the preemptive strike against the Narragansetts.[97] The colony came under attack on 28 January from a raiding party that killed two men and captured a teenager near the Shetucket River in the vicinity of Norwich.[98] The fourteen- or fifteen-year-old boy was "carried away and kept a fortnight" before a "Martha's Vineyard Indian rescued him."[99] The colonists attributed this incident to Narragansetts as an act of revenge for Great Swamp. Intelligence that never made it to Connecticut from John Stanton, who was with colonial forces harassing hostile groups in Massachusetts during the winter, however, indicated that "Sagamore" Sam led a party of Nipmucks or Nashaways in the attack.[100] If this were indeed the infamous Sachem Sam, a senior war leader of the coalition, then this raid was intended against Norwich itself, a more important target than a few farmers sowing flax. It also indicated the improvement of Connecticut defenses, which prevented a more serious assault. The aborted attack confirmed the intelligence that in the spring hostile bands would begin raiding Connecticut from Nipmuck country as a primary target in their war effort.

The other New England colonies were not as fortunate. Hostile war parties destroyed or badly damaged the towns of Lancaster, Medfield, and Northampton in Massachusetts from 10 to 21

Hill House, 2013. Courtesy Edward A. Gutiérrez.

February.[101] During this onslaught, on 18 February, warriors wounded William Hill near Hoccanum, Connecticut. Hill survived the attack through a ruse: "Fryday Night Will Hill att hockanum was shott by two Indians who . . . [made] his Escape to the house & Caled out as though there was more at wch the Indians forsook the ho[u]se but Drove away 10 or 12 Cattle. Its thought ye man will not live."[102] He also defied his prognosis, surviving to petition Connecticut's General Court in 1684 to compensate him for his wounds sustained in this raid, which had prevented him from properly providing for his family.[103] The scars of battle marred the Hill House some three centuries after this attack, as a local teacher brought his students to view the arrow marks remaining in the structure.[104] After this attack, the War Council ordered inhabitants on the east side of the Connecticut River into garrison houses because of the "evident" threat of hostile war parties.[105]

As events would confirm, March was the climatic month of the spring offensive. The bloodshed and devastation escalated when the hostile Indians destroyed the settlements of Groton, Marlborough, Sudbury, Rehoboth, and Providence, as well as other towns in

Plymouth, Massachusetts Bay, and Rhode Island Colonies. The English military response during February and March proved ineffective. Coalition forces had regained the initiative and even caused Massachusetts Bay to debate abandoning its frontier by withdrawing its population behind a large wall the colony would erect in the vicinity of Boston itself.[106] Connecticut also witnessed a corresponding increase in enemy activity, facing a substantial series of threats, including the worst attack within the colony during the war—the burning of an abandoned Simsbury toward the end of March, the greatest loss of property the colony suffered. A hostile party nearly burned Milford as well, but the fire petered out in a swamp adjacent to that settlement. Local residents claimed that Indians had started the conflagration to eliminate Milford's partially constructed palisades.[107]

Considering the near disaster at Milford, the threat of violence was not concentrated only on the colony's northern border. Further demonstrating the hostile menace to all of Connecticut, in early March a letter to Governor Andros described the incarceration at Saybrook along the coast of an Indian prisoner named George, who was later transferred to Hartford. Authorities detained him for "thefts and deceits," though the letter did not specify if George was a source of information or even if he was operating as part of a larger band.[108] On 26 March, the same day as the Simsbury burning, a war party abducted a man at Windsor, demonstrating that hostile Indians were operating between the two towns.[109] This group also killed Henry Denslow near Pine Meadow (now the Suffield–Windsor Locks area).[110]

The most salient evidence of the existence of hostile war parties, however, was a 30 March letter detailing a group of approximately one hundred warriors operating in the area between the Blue or Hanging Hills (in what is now Meriden and the south Kensington portion of the town of Berlin) and the Mattabassett-Lamentation Hills of Wallingford, Middletown, and Berlin. This rare piece of specific intelligence came to the English from a party of friendly Indians possessing a movement pass from Major Treat. The Indians claimed to have spent the night at Sergeant Beckley's house of Wethersfield (later referred to as the Beckley Quarter of Berlin), which stood adjacent the important colony highway running through the wilderness from Hartford through Wallingford and New Haven to New York or to Haddam and the coast beyond.

Beckley Homestead, 2013. Courtesy Tom Trask and James Warren.

This letter from John Moss, Sr., and Nathaniel Merriman, the town leaders of Wallingford, alerted the council that a Goodman Cole's house burned in the town's outer limits early that morning. They originally suspected that "Rum" Tom's friendly band of Quinnipiacs had attacked the homestead.[111] Moss and Merriman reconsidered their original inclination, however, because Cole's house had burned "quickly after sun sett, which made us think they were not soe much to be suspected."[112] Henry Cole was the unfortunate buyer of the farmstead only two years prior to this attack, in what is now Meriden.[113] Cole perished probably along with his wife, as Nathaniel Merriman filed his remaining inventory in New Haven Probate Court on 12 May 1676, a month and a half after the incident.[114] Various histories place the Cole's estate in north-central Meriden, not far from present-day Berlin, astride the Old Colony Path between Hartford and New Haven. This was the same path that the Quinnipiacs in question would have traveled to Wallingford from Sergeant Beckley's farmstead.[115]

There was a tavern and inn to the north of the Cole farm, extending from present-day Meriden into Berlin, known as the Gilbert farm and later the Belcher farm, located on the same colony route as the Cole residence.[116] The tavern-inn served as a waypoint for those journeying from New York and the coast to Hartford and Boston. It is possible that this structure existed before the Great Narragansett War, and if so, it interestingly survived the attack on the nearby homestead. Nothing else existed at the time but the colony path and wilderness between the Gilbert farm and Beckley homestead, and Wallingford proper was then miles south from these two northerly residences. Moss and Merriman did not see the flames from Cole's burning farmstead because of the distance involved, relying instead on the friendly Indians' report. If it existed at the time of the incident, then the Gilbert dwelling had been converted from a tavern-inn into a garrison house as was later reported, and the hostile war party opted instead to destroy the "softer" target of Cole's farmstead.

The Quinnipiacs also provided a troubling estimate of the enemy's numbers within the colony, as the Wallingford men reported to Hartford in the same letter: "And these indeans say that they saw a great many traks, and some of them went to ward Matabesut mountaines, and others toward the hanging hills as they did judge near a 100 These things being considered wee doe judge the enemie is near us and therefore doe desire that you would speedyly consider our condition, and send us some help." Considering the usual number of men for a raiding party, one hundred warriors was a significant force, larger than many bodies of Indians reported throughout the conflict. The intelligence reinforces that Connecticut was a major target of the coalition, now influenced by Narragansett leaders, who viewed the colony and its Indian allies as inveterate enemies. That Connecticut did not succumb to a large-scale attack from this force sheds light on the overall quality of its defenses and the underlying loyalty of the local Indians. March ended with another report of Indians "skulking" in the proximity of the colony's towns.[117]

Canonchet's annihilation of Captain Michael Pierce's force outside of Providence, Rhode Island, in March 1676 was one of the greatest Indian victories of the war and further contributed to the colonists' siege mentality.[118] Canonchet outmaneuvered Pierce, waiting until the English and allied Indian force had crossed a river, and then ambushed him with the water to his rear. Canonchet's warriors outnumbered the colonial force, which could not maneuver from its position. Few in Pierce's command survived the battle.[119] Connecticut forces avenged this defeat by killing Canonchet early the following month.[120] English and allied Indian search-and-destroy operations and smaller raids, especially those launched by Connecticut patrols led by George Denison and James Avery and Plymouth's Benjamin Church, increasingly disrupted the logistics base of the hostile coalition and caused the decline of its war effort. The loss of Canonchet, though, was a crippling blow. His final mission to retrieve seeds for planting indicates the concern of coalition leaders with the critical resupply activity of planting crops. The hostile Indians never managed to plant enough crops for sustenance because of the constant harassment of English-Indian forces.[121] Combined with the loss of leadership, this failure of logistics eventually led to defeat.

In early April a hostile band at Hoccanum, Connecticut, killed Deacon Goodman and carried off his compatriot Thomas Reede. Reede later escaped from Pessicus's encampment near Turner's Falls, on the Massachusetts-Vermont border, and transmitted intelligence used by the English to launch an attack there.[122] Reede's captivity revealed that raiding parties in Connecticut operated in conjunction with coalition members far to the north in the western Massachusetts theater. Shortly thereafter, around 3 April, Connecticut forces overheard a "great shouteing" from Indians at "Thawtuckett," which is a version of Shawtuckett or Shetucket, near where the two Connecticut settlers had been killed in February.[123]

Also in early April, Governor Leete wrote to Connecticut leaders on the coast acknowledging receipt of one of their letters to the council at Hartford, which described a house burned and a colonist shot at in the woods.[124] The original letter appears to have been lost, but Leete's reply was further confirmation of hostile raiders in Connecticut, even though larger attempts by war parties at Wallingford and Norwich had failed to overcome sound defenses. Sepawcutt, a member of one such band, claimed to have killed seven colonists of the "seaside."[125] The "seaside" in Connecticut records referred to the colony's coast, usually New Haven County, indicating that the deaths had occurred there. In early May in fact, a band of Indians ambushed Anthony Howe from a nearby swamp, killing him as he was rounding up cattle near Branford along the New Haven coast.[126] The colonists again suspected local Quinnipiacs, who they handled roughly but eventually released. The next day a sortie of colonists and Quinnipiacs picked up the trail of the assailants and followed it as far as Guilford, where it turned north toward Middletown. Running low on provisions and nearly outside of the county's bounds, the group turned back. Connecticut never identified Howe's killers.[127] Raiding parties between Wethersfield and Middletown also accounted for the killings of G. Elmore of Podunk and a man named Kirby.[128] While coalition groups were harassing Connecticut without a significant breakthrough of its defenses, in late April at Sudbury, Massachusetts, hostile Indians scored one of their last tactical successes with the destruction of Captain Samuel Wadsworth's command and much of the town. Wadsworth had responded to an earlier attack on Sudbury, and an enemy group lured him into an ambush. He managed to lead his force to a strong defensive position on a hilltop with clear fields of fire. His assailants set fire to the fields, however, causing the colonists to break ranks. The Indians, maintaining a decisive edge in individual combat, then killed most of Wadsworth's men.[129]

As English field forces—particularly those of Connecticut under Major Talcott and Captains Denison and Avery—enjoyed more success in the late spring and throughout the summer 1676, the hostile coalition's ability to carry out offensive operations dramatically declined. On 19 May the colonists stunned the Indians at Turner's Falls (bearing the name of the colonial leader) in the upper Connecticut River valley with a surprise attack on a major encampment there. Although inflicting heavy losses, the English force failed to regroup, and the camp's warriors nearly destroyed most of Turner's command. The Indians then counterattacked against Hatfield, where the raid had originated. In this running battle, the English sustained losses that they could replace, but the Indian noncombatants at the falls suffered heavy losses, lowering coalition morale and damaging its already weakened logistical base. Many of the noncombatants were swept over the falls and drowned when they jumped into the river after rumors spread that the Mohawks were present among the attackers, adding to the terror of the assault.[130]

Connecticut forces assisted in defeating another assault on Hadley on 12 June, which was one of the last major coalition attacks of the war.[131] Colonial operations followed up this victory with raids that destroyed most of the remaining hostile forces, fracturing the coalition in southern New England by the late summer of 1676. Connecticut forces, led by Major Talcott and Captain Denison, played a key role in this effort, inflicting massive defeats on the hostile groups, particularly the Narragansetts. In July Talcott massacred Quaiapen's band not far from the first Nipsachuck battle site.[132]

Accelerating the decline of the hostile coalition in the late spring and throughout the summer, Indians began to desert and join with the colonists to hunt down their former comrades. By this stage of the war, the other New England colonies had copied Connecticut's use of large numbers of allied Indians, as well as volunteer colonial troops, and also began to score successes that a few months before were all but unimaginable. Benjamin Church, one of the few non-Connecticut leaders who utilized allied Indians throughout the conflict, led the party that eventually killed Philip near Mount Hope.[133] In the late summer of 1676, in the last major engagement of the war, Talcott again destroyed a fleeing coalition group, this time on the upper Housatonic in the wilderness between New York and western Massachusetts.[134] Over the next year, parties of colonists and Indian allies continued to pursue hostile remnants, and many of which surrendered. The war in southern New England was over. Native groups in northern New England continued fighting with more success, however, and violence between English and Indians in this region continued throughout the French and Indian Wars.

In August, with general military operations winding down throughout southern New England, a hostile Indian named Menowalett was captured in the wilderness near Farmington, Connecticut.[135] He had been hiding in the woods with a very small band, which the combined forces of colonists and allied Indians captured when scouring the woods for remnants of the hostile coalition. Upon his interrogation by colonial leaders, Menowalett confessed to belonging to the party that had burned Simsbury and killed Kirby between Middletown and Wethersfield as well as Elmore of Podunk. He had also participated in battles against the English on the Massachusetts stretches of the Connecticut River, indicating again the coalition's operational connection between the upper Connecticut and the colony.

In an incredibly detailed account, Menowalett claimed that his war party had consisted of seven to nine warriors from a number of different Indian groups, including Narragansetts, the Norwottocks of Northampton, the Agawams of Springfield, the Quabogs of the Nipmuck confederation, renegade Mohegans, and a Native group the English abbreviated as "Wer," likely the Woronocos of Westfield. He himself was half-Mohegan and half-Narragansett.[136]

This evidence, if uncorroborated, would have been difficult to rely on alone. Prisoners have not always been known to reveal critical intelligence, and Menowalett undoubtedly knew that other captives who had killed Englishmen already had been handed over to the allied Indians for torture and execution. He could have related events without incriminating himself, only confessed to one event instead of three, or not have said anything about these attacks at all, but he seems to have revealed everything.

In early September 1676 another renegade named Cohas, whom allied Indians captured between New Haven and Milford, confessed to two murders and the burning of a farmstead, all of which Menowalett had earlier accused him of committing. The council turned Cohas over to an allied Indian, who promptly executed him.[137] Before his death, though, he corroborated three of Menowalett's allegations against him, confirming the validity of most, if not all, of his comrade's testimony. If Menowalett had refrained from giving specific names and only generally described his activities, and then Cohas had admitted to the attacks, there would have been lingering doubt about the veracity of the latter's confession. Menowalett, however, had named Cohas in his testimony.

The examples of Menowalett and Cohas not only reveal the nature of war parties in Connecticut but also illustrate the complex nature of identity and tribal loyalty during the Great Narragansett War. As Uncas had warned early in the conflict, at least a number of Narragansetts who inhabited Connecticut supported Philip; what he failed to mention was that a number of Mohegans did too. The case of Menowalett and Cohas demonstrate that the colonial method of identifying Indians—based largely on the political entities established by the colonists themselves, and mostly used by historians today—is insufficient in discerning identity and loyalty during the war. The high degree of intermarriage between southern New England Indians and the fluid political nature of their warrior societies clouded the colonists' cultural understanding of allies and enemies alike.

As half-Mohegan and half-Narragansett, Menowalett either identified with Philip's cause or fought for personal gain, though more likely a combination of both. He might have switched sides, a not uncommon occurrence during the war, nor one uncommon for Europeans to do in the early modern era. Rhode Islander William Harris, writing to the king's Privy Council in the summer of 1676, revealed just that: "It is Indian custom not to distinguish their men by place of residence but by voluntary obligation, that is, they are or are not this or that sachem's men."[138] Unfortunately, Menowalett's English interrogators did not ask the critical question of why he joined Philip's confederation.

Based on his testimony, Menowalett clearly did not support Uncas's faction of Mohegans, which was the majority of that Native group. Perhaps he resented the sachem's domineering leadership or his continuing conflict with the other side of his family, the Narragansetts. The Mohegan "tribe," like other Algonquian groups, was hierarchical and leadership was inherited, with Uncas's sons Owaneco and Joshua dominating the Mohegan war effort in support of the colonists. Menowalett might have resented this lineage or perhaps belonged to a rival family. Kinship-based identity was common in American Indian culture, and it trumped band affiliation. As bands and tribes intermarried, this could weaken band cohesion in favor of kinship.[139] This might have influenced Menowalett's preference, even more so if he were married. Finally, he possibly identified with the anti-English cause of the coalition.

The effect of violence on Native communities further loosened traditionally transitory band membership. Military operations forced migrations upon the groups, altering in turn the fabric of Indian communities. As discussed, the bands of Narragansetts and Wampanoags hostile to the English fled to central and western Massachusetts, joining Nipmucks and upper Connecticut River Indian communities there. This changed the already loose groupings of tribal peoples based on intermarriage and shifting political loyalties. These new communities represented the mixed-warrior parties that threatened Connecticut during the conflict. The sometimes pan-tribal nature of the Great Narragansett War indicates that Indians identified with anti-English sentiment to some degree. Once these warriors joined in battle with the colonists, perhaps they derived an identity of fighting against the English, and violence in turn reinforced anti-English feelings from before the war.[140]

The Indians who chose the colonial faction or no side at all reveal as much about identity and loyalty as those who joined Philip. The Indians of Connecticut, excepting a scattered population among the Mohegans, the Narragansetts, and perhaps other groups, remained loyal to their English neighbors. Connecticut's colonial leaders cultivated this relationship through moderate policy. In the end, the local Indians were agents of their own destiny, although the colonists' military capability and fear of the Mohegans and Pequots influenced this decision.

The Menawolett and Cohas interrogations, rare Native voices from a sparse colonial record, demonstrate that small war parties still survived in Connecticut after the conclusion of major hostilities. A number of these with members of diverse lineages had been operating within the colony's borders during hostilities, revealing that the participants in the Great Narragansett War were more difficult to define than through traditional "tribal" delineations. These bands, which identified and exhibited loyalty to Philip's cause for a host of reasons, ranged in size from small groups to large bodies of one hundred or more, and they had been able to infiltrate Connecticut undetected. As Governor Andros and Major Palmes had predicted in the early winter of 1675-76, the coalition had intensified its operations within the colony. A few weeks later, Cohas's band wounded William Hill at Hoccanum, and Sagamore Sam's party killed the men on the Shetucket. In light of these events and the subsequent testimony of Menowalett and Cohas, Connecticut had remained a coalition target throughout the war.

When Philip fled his traditional tribal area and enlisted the support of the Nipmucks and the upper Connecticut groups, he began to lose control over the coalition's war aims. Connecticut came under eventual attack because of its reinforcement of the colonial settlements upriver and the traditional hostility of Native groups there toward the colony's Indian allies. Connecticut became a primary target once the powerful Narragansetts joined the coalition. Their traditional antipathy toward the Mohegans and Connecticut's support of Uncas resulted in the regionwide conflagration. With a view of the Great Narragansett War that incorporates Connecticut's perspective, these events become more understandable within the framework of episodic Mohegan-Narragansett conflict since the defeat of the Pequot confederacy and the violence exacerbated by the issues underlying English colonization. Although targeted to varying degrees throughout the war, Connecticut generally avoided the violence and devastation that similar marauders had caused in the other New England colonies through cooperative local relations with Native groups.

CHAPTER 3

PURITAN OUTLIER

*CONNECTICUT COLONISTS AND
LOCAL INDIGENOUS GROUPS*

> As for your Postcript Respecting a house burnt, and a man shott at in the woods, nott known by whom, we Can but ad vise that it will be well lookt into and finding matters cleard against any that justice be done yet must likewise desire that injustice may pass instead of justice, and we wish due Consideration be had that as yett [no] Indian hath appeared Convict[ed] of breaking out into hostility that belongs to this Colony in any part of it since the warre began wh we acct a favour therefore we would have one Care taken that ye grounds be very cleare, ore we drive them to hostility as is by some doubted to have been don in other Collonies too hostile but we Can well trust your Good discretion in these matters and must have it to God and you that right may be don for both and against all Indians & Remain
> Yours to affectionately to seek peace & well fare off the whole.
>
> WILLIAM LEETE BY REQUEST OF THE COUNCIL

Acting Governor Leete's prescient guidance to the "Assistants sea side" at New Haven, Connecticut, reveals how the colony's leadership sought to maintain an environment of understanding and cooperation between the Native groups and English settlers.[1] Although he did not know at the time that a handful of local Indians did join hostile forces, Leete understood that the vast majority remained allied or neutral. Good policy—mostly obeyed by Connecticut's colonists and accepted by local Natives—created mutual security for both communities. This prevented the hostile coalition from gathering intelligence to launch attacks. Connecticut's colonists experienced firsthand the importance of maintaining Indian allies during the Pequot War, learning that their security rested in part on good relations with their indigenous neighbors. During an October 1675 meeting of the General Court as the threat to Connecticut was increasing, the court proclaimed, "But its advised that all due care be taken to treat the Indians amicably in all parts, and not to put them upon any unrighteous or intollerable tearmes to be obserued."[2] This proclamation and others like it indicated a critical difference between Connecticut and the other Puritan colonies. Leaders like Leete and Governor John Winthrop, Jr., enacted moderate and practical policy toward Native groups that combined security concerns with a sense of justice, unlike their counterparts elsewhere in the rest of the region.

There was a trend in the other New England colonies of local Indian-settler disputes turning violent and thus paving the way for the entry of hostile forces. Philip and his confederates adeptly took advantage of these local disputes. When Captain Wheeler's expedition aimed at determining the Nipmucks' position toward the Wampanoags, it turned into a disaster. Local Brookfield men insisted on the Native group's loyalty to the English and led the force into an ambush. The Indians then besieged the town itself.[3] Brookfield residents misunderstood the close relationship between the Nipmucks and the Wampanoags while overestimating their own ties with the Native community. Underlying tensions over land served to exacerbate the situation as this irritant had with Philip's own band vis à vis the local colonial community at Swansea, Plymouth Colony.[4] At Northampton, along the Massachusetts stretch of the Connecticut River, "the Improvident demands of Captn Lathrop made upon the Narwartteck Indians" drove the tribe into the coalition by attempting to disarm them as a preventative measure, an action Connecticut leadership considered a blunder.[5]

On 2 September 1675 at Northfield, the northernmost settlement along the Massachusetts Bay's stretches of the Connecticut, a band of River Indians surprised the English even though hostilities had been ongoing in the region for almost two months.[6] The colonists' lack of military preparation signified that they also trusted the local Indians, misunderstanding the loyalties of their indigenous neighbors.

The situation replayed itself at Springfield, where inhabitants refused to believe that the local Agawams would turn against them. Rejecting town leader Major John Pynchon's developing suspicion of the Indians, constable Lieutenant Thomas Cooper was ambushed on his way to the Agawam village.[7] Members of the hostile coalition, now joined by the Agawams, who had clandestinely sheltered them in their nearby fort, then struck the town, destroying most of it.[8] Governor Winthrop, Jr., had recorded only weeks earlier that the Indians "up the river (as those have to us) have assured Maior Pynchen of their fidelity to the English."[9] The colonists' trust of the local Natives was manifest in such communications and apparent in the general lack of English military mobilization in Nipmuck country and along the upper Connecticut.

This trusting posture helps explain the colonists' sense of outrage at the perceived disloyalty of the Indians once those groups joined with Philip. From the coalition perspective, there were legitimate grievances that the English failed to comprehend. Indian outrage over the colonists' confiscation of firearms and disillusionment over their encroachment on agricultural and hunting-fishing grounds aggravated Native apprehension of burgeoning English economic power and cultural influence in much of New England.

The situation was markedly different in Connecticut. Not only did the colonists there allow the Indians to maintain their firearms, they did little to incite the ill will of their indigenous neighbors. By 1675 the Indians of southern New England had fully adopted the flintlock musket as their primary tool for fighting as well as hunting, and disarmament would have meant disaster for their families: "They had become quite dependent on those Arms to procure the Means of living, and hence it is not strange that they should consider the Seizure of them an Act of great Injustice."[10] Most warriors also had adopted the flintlock by the outbreak of the Great Narragansett War as well, "not making Allowance for the Difference of Times, when they before engaged us, only with Bows and Arrows; but now came to fight us with our own Weapons."[11]

Connecticut previously had disarmed a handful of Mohegans during the scare of a New England–wide Indian conspiracy of 1669–70.[12] The patron of the Mohegans, Major John Mason, Sr., was so convinced of the threat that he "pursuade[d]" Owaneco and a number of other warriors to hand over some of their weapons.[13] Reconsidering the disarmament policy it had employed only a few years earlier, the Connecticut War Council during the Great Narragansett War not only disapproved of the "improvident" disarming of the Norwottocks of Northampton in Massachusetts Bay Colony but also refused the request of the town of Stratford to disarm its local Indians in mid-August 1675.[14]

Connecticut's colonists also arranged local peace agreements with neighboring Indians after the outbreak of hostilities in exchange for English clothing.[15] This was more than a practical offering of garments for protection from the elements. The Indians' acceptance of these gifts indicated that a friendly relationship existed between the parties, and the wearing of English clothing identified them as allied or neutral in regard to the neighboring colonists. Nathaniel Gold, a town leader of Fairfield, wrote to the council urging it to provide the local Indians with a young female Indian captive to replace a captive warrior who had been executed.[16] Prisoners replaced material goods in this case, but Connecticut's leadership sought to look after the local Natives' interests. Apparently, the colony did so more than judiciously, for a senior war leader complained to the War Council in Hartford during the summer of 1676 that the allied Indians took all of the prisoners and war booty, even though the English volunteers had signed on to share in the trophies.[17] That Captain George Denison referred the matter to arbitration as opposed to handling the issue through force himself demonstrated the desire of many colonists to treat Indians respectfully and within the limits of established policy. In the same letter Denison eschewed bitterness toward his Indian allies over the war trophies, asking the council to resupply them with corn.

There were several occasions when the War Council requested that the allied Mohegans cooperate with local neutral Indians. The body sanctioned Owaneco to establish a fort with local Indians near Hoccanum for their joint safety and undoubtedly to watch over these groups.[18] Allowing Indians to deal with Indians ensured that the colonists would not violate indigenous taboos and demonstrated that groups in good standing would be empowered to act as leaders within their regional communities. Any policy entails risk, and there was some danger inherent in establishing a fort at Hoccanum if the Mohegans mistreated other Native groups. Connecticut's leadership, in fact, often had fielded complaints from local Indians about mistreatment at the hands of Uncas prior to the conflict.

Reminding the colonists of Milford to treat the local Native groups fairly, the War Council instructed: "we must desire that you would cause all your people to carry so tenderly towards the Indians that they may not receive any just provocation to stir them up against us. We have enemies eno, and let us not by any harsh dealing stir up more yet."[19] This was a similar warning to the colonists as Governor Leete had made, and the council remarkably issued the latter after Connecticut came under attack in the spring of 1676, with a house burned and a colonist shot at in the woods along Long Island Sound.[20] Colonial leaders also sought to provide security for the allied Pequots' noncombatants while the warriors were away supporting English forces.[21] The protection of these families was an incentive for the warriors to take the field against the hostile coalition. Connecticut also provided sustenance for Uncas's Mohegans during the war, and likely the other allied Indians as well.[22]

The General Court ordered that the towns establish methods for identifying local Indians to keep them from becoming confused with Philip's confederates, preventing friendly fire incidents.[23] When Connecticut's allied Indians joined colonial troops in western Massachusetts Bay at Brookfield, the council instructed Marshal Gilbert to ensure their safety through proper identification as well as to ascertain why more friendly Indians did not join the expedition.[24] It later ordered Major Treat on 19 January 1676 to see to the identification and general good treatment of the allied Indian contingent remaining in Narragansett country after the Great Swamp Fight.[25] The council issued this directive after reports that other colonists accidently targeted Connecticut's Indian allies during the battle.

The most significant and notable element of this policy occurred when the War Council "desired" Wethersfield, Middletown, and Hartford to allow the local groups *into* their towns, along with their corn, for mutual protection from hostile Indians.[26] That the council would even consider such a step during a time of tension indicated that peaceful relations existed at least along the stretches of the lower Connecticut River valley in the colony. The leaders also encouraged Norwich to do the same, and some Mohegans, noncombatants, lived within that settlement for some time, the town leaders later requested reimbursement for feeding them.[27]

This was remarkable policy relative to the other New England colonies and New York. Massachusetts Bay Colony, for example, forcibly drove off peaceful local Native groups or imprisoned them on Deer Island in the bay.[28] Captain Samuel Moseley, a privateer for the colony and commander of a volunteer company made up of pirates and other ruffians, raided a loyal Indian village near what is now Concord, New Hampshire. As a result, Massachusetts Bay sent a delegation to attempt reconciliation. On another occasion Moseley sent eleven friendly Indians to Boston for execution, though authorities there eventually released them.[29] The captain's worst act of anti-Indian violence occurred at Springfield, where he had a captured Indian woman "torn in peeces by Doggs" even though she had provided intelligence to the colonists.[30] Such violent acts were the prelude for Massachusetts Bay's policy of removing Praying Indians from Natick and other communities to Deer Island. This action caused irreversible damage to the colony's relationship with neutral or friendly Indians, causing some to join with Philip. James Quannapohit, himself a Praying Indian and spy for Massachusetts Bay, reported that Praying Indians previously loyal to the colonists had fled to the hostile Nipmucks after Deer Island. A number of these people "went willingly, others of ym unwillingly as they told him for befor they went away they were in a great straigt, for if they came to the English they knew they shold bee sent to Deere Iland, as others were."[31] Massachusetts' early spring effort to supply the Deer Island internees was too late to prevent the defection of some loyal Indians as well as mass suffering.[32] Perhaps as many as five hundred friendly Indians endured detention on the island, yet many still remained loyal to the colonists.[33]

Massachusetts Bay was not alone in detaining friendly or neutral Indians on inhospitable and unfamiliar islands off the Atlantic coast. Plymouth joined with its neighboring Puritan colony in such a brutal Indian-removal policy: "The councell of war now assembled doe order, that the Namassachessett Indians be speedily removed to Clarkes Iland, and ther to remaine, and not to depart from thence without lycence from authoritie upon paine of death."[34] Historians have focused on the Deer Island episode as the epitome of Puritan mistreatment of New England's indigenous population, but none have connected Plymouth's Clark's Island as part of New England's larger story of Indian mistreatment.

Plymouth authorities ordered the people's removal to this small island in Plymouth Harbor between the end of February and early March 1676 at exactly the worst time for Indians to be able to fend for themselves on barren, windswept islands. Like Deer Island, Clark's was devoid of adequate shelter or food sources. In 1620 a small scouting party from the *Mayflower* had originally landed on the island, naming it after the ship's first mate, when a storm forced them to seek shelter before reaching the mainland.[35] Clark's Island exemplifies a dual narrative sometimes found in early America history, representing on the one hand a "positive" discovery narrative, which locals still celebrate today with a picnic and religious services at the original Plymouth rock, yet on the other is a little-known account of atrocity committed against an indigenous people.[36] The Namassachessetts undoubtedly suffered a fate similar to the Natick groups removed to Deer Island. With little sense of irony or justice, Plymouth instructed that its press masters compel into military service twenty to thirty local Indians at the same time as the Clark's Island removal, as if such actions would not affect the motivation of such men to fight alongside the English against other nearby Indians in Philip's coalition.[37] Later that month Canonchet's force wiped out Captain Michael Pierce's expedition from Plymouth, leaving one to question the loyalty of the pressed Indians who accompanied the doomed column.[38]

Perhaps the Clark's Island episode was a culminating event in Plymouth's anti-Indian policy, for earlier on 6 December 1675, the colony enacted a precautionary measure against its local groups: "Wheras great damage may acrew to the collonie by the southeren Indians theire frequent resort to Plymouth, the councell have ordered that speedy notice be given to those Indians to come noe further towards Plmouth then Sandwich, which shalbe theire confine, on paine of death or imprisonment."[39] Plymouth's policy stood in stark contrast to Connecticut's actions in inviting the local Indians into their communities. Misunderstanding the local situation proved devastating for English settlements outside Connecticut. At the same time, such misguided actions, xenophobic and perhaps racist in nature, lessened the willingness of Indians to cooperate militarily with the colonists.

The colonists of Rhode Island and Providence Plantations, the outcast colony of New England, treated their local Native groups relatively better than Massachusetts Bay and Plymouth. Roger Williams was known for his special relationship with the Narragansetts, yet even he provided intelligence for New England colonists before and during the Great Narragansett War. Members of the colony appear to have maintained a close relationship with Philip, as was the case when the Wampanoag sachem revealed his rationale for war to Rhode Island men soon after the outbreak of hostilities.[40] Governor William Coddington believed that Rhode Island could have ensured Narragansett neutrality at the start of the conflict without resorting to armed intimidation before Puritan forces compelled the Indians to accept a treaty.[41] Even with a relatively better relationship with local groups than Plymouth and Massachusetts Bay, no Rhode Island town appears to have cultivated or sustained the relationship with its local Indians as had been done in Connecticut towns like Wethersfield, Middletown, and Norwich. In fact, an order from Rhode Island's War Council on 13 March 1676 ordered that Indians must be "bound" if out of doors, while its colonists had to escort Indians by day and lock them up by night.[42] This was a harsher policy of control than any Connecticut enacted during these years.

The Indian coalition, unlike in nearby Connecticut, devastated Rhode Island during the war, destroying nearly the entire colony except for the settlements and seat of government on Rhode Island (or Aquidneck Island) itself.[43] The Narragansetts had little capability of launching an amphibious operation to thwart Rhode Island's coastal defense of four patrol boats manned by five or six soldiers each.[44] The colony's reputation of leniency with respect to Native groups appears to have been exaggerated at least during the Great Narragansett War. A special relationship with local groups, which would have spared destruction in Rhode Island, did not exist.

Williams lacked enough influence to persuade the region's most powerful Native people from passively supporting Philip at the outset of the uprising, which provided the pretext for the colonial attack on Great Swamp. If the Puritans had considered Rhode Islanders' religious beliefs as tolerable and hence the colony as deserving of an equal political relationship and territorial integrity, then the colony might have worked within the apparatus of the United Colonies to soften that body's distrustful perception of the Narragansetts. Likewise, the Narragansetts had cultivated the least-influential New England entity as a patron, even though the tribe had the most influence among Native groups in the region. The imbalance between the Narragansetts' real power and their lack of an effective colonial advocate in New England's political circles caused the embers of discord to smolder in the years after the Pequot War.[45] This disadvantageous political position along with the people's kinship ties to the Wampanoags led to the Narragansetts' sympathetic stance for Philip, and ultimately their entry into the war.

Although not directly involved in the conflict, the Royal Colony of New York also enacted policy to deal with its local Indians in the event that the fighting spread beyond New England. New York had a different cultural framework than its eastern English neighbors since it was a more centrally administered and non-Puritan colony. It also had a more complex task of dealing with the three major Indian cultures within its borders—the Iroquoian and the two Algonquian peoples, the Delaware along the Hudson River and western Long Island, and the Native groups on eastern Long Island associated with New England's Algonquians. This affected the colony's policy formulation, which serves as an interesting counterpoint to New England. The groups living within New York did not openly join the hostile coalition, though this was unlikely a result of the colony's Indian policy, which was somewhat severe for neutral Native peoples. Though Governor Andros on at least one occasion reminded his people to treat Indians fairly, he had disarmed local groups at the outbreak of violence in New England.[46] On 15 September 1675 he countermanded this with an "Order to restore to the Indians of Long Island their arms except to those of Easthampton and Shelter Island, who have paid contributions to the Narragansetts."[47] Long Island Indians were related closely to the Narragansetts and Eastern Niantics and had been considered part of the earlier suspected Dutch-Indian conspiracies. The colonial inhabitants of Long Island either ignored this second order or confiscated weapons at another time after 15 September, for the local sachem at Southampton petitioned the New York Council to return his arms a month after Andros's countermand.[48] Colonists might have also associated Southampton's local Indians with Easthampton's and disarmed them as well. On 7 October the New York Council ordered colonists not to sell powder or shot to Indians.[49] This order did not apply to the Iroquois confederacy, which the government equipped to fight the hostile Indians.[50]

New York's restrictions on local Indians did not only concern arms and ammunition. Andros congratulated the constable of Harlem on 21 October 1675 for prohibiting the movement of ten to twelve canoes of friendly Indian women and children with provisions for failing to have a movement pass.[51] Two days later he again ordered the disarmament of Native groups on Long Island. Recent intelligence of suspicious Indians from neighboring Stamford, Connecticut, might have precipitated this decision.[52] Three months later Andros wrote to officials on Long Island detailing that local Indians there also needed a movement certificate to leave their immediate environs.[53] The disarmament of neighboring Native peoples continued, when the governor wrote to a local leader named Huntington on 13 December to disarm the Rockaways and Sequatalkes.[54] The colonists appear to have retained these firearms until the end of May

1676, when they were released back to the Long Islanders and presumably other New York Indians.[55] In late April 1676 Andros did negotiate directly with the Indians of southwestern Connecticut and Westchester, New York, trading "ten deerskins, a beareskin and four small beavers" for English "Duffells Coates" in a cultural exchange signifying friendship.[56] The Indians near Southampton, at the urging of the local minister and with the support of Andros, were invited to join with the colonial settlement, although they were disarmed first.[57] Even with these two examples of positive relations, New York's policy witnessed the same disarmament and restrictions that characterized the policy of Plymouth and Massachusetts Bay, and this without the immediate threat of violence toward the colony. It was harsher during peace than Connecticut's was even at war, and the royal colony was fortunate that it did not lead to open hostilities. New York's Indian policy, however, probably generated sympathy for the cause of New England's hostile coalition.[58]

Personal relationships between Indians and colonists were important in maintaining good local relations. Wayne Lee considers the close association between certain Indians and settlers as characteristic of "resident alien" status; a number of Connecticut colonists' relationships with similarly influential Natives fit his categorization. This association sometimes existed in combined colonial and Indian villages or those indigenous towns adjacent to English settlements. As the case of Connecticut indicates, the influence of the "resident aliens" mattered for local defense and security. Indians desired the symbol of colonial protection, if not actual joint defense, in return for providing intelligence to the colonists. This intermingling of peoples was in accord with Indian cultural norms for diplomacy, with those living with the colonists serving as "diplomatic 'entry points,' go-betweens, and early warning mechanisms."[59] The Indians also at times invited colonists to live with them for many of the same reasons, though especially to demonstrate their loyalty to the English. The Natick Praying Indian community of Massachusetts Bay, after the onset of the Great Narragansett War, convinced two Englishmen to live with them. The positive experience of these men, however, did not influence the attitudes of enough Massachusetts Bay colonists to prevent the internment of the Natick on Deer Island.[60]

In recent times of extreme crisis, people have sometimes resorted to an insular tribal instinct like that of Massachusetts Bay and Plymouth Colonies in 1675–76.[61] Connecticut's policy was at once ethical and security conscience, denying critical local intelligence to enemy forces. Without this information, the hostile Indians were unable to carry out such attacks as they had managed in the other New England colonies in conjunction with local groups. Neighborhood intelligence was of critical importance for the type of warfare that the coalition practiced: "As the Indians had lived promiscuously with the English in all parts of the country, they were generally as well acquainted with their dwellings, fields, and places of worships, as themselves. They were perfectly acquainted with their roads, times, and places of resort. They were at hand to watch all their motions, to attack them at every difficult pass, and in every unguarded moment."[62] But Connecticut colonists were able to obtain critical information from the local groups. For instance, an Indian from the locality of Windsor named Toto exposed the hostile plot against Springfield, though unlike their neighbors to the south, Springfield's inhabitants were unwilling to believe this intelligence and suffered the consequences.[63]

Connecticut extended its moderate policy also to the hostile Indians. The War Council sent a letter by way of a Narragansett messenger named Tiawakesson (alias Watawaikeson) to hostile forces requesting a prisoner exchange and proposing a peace conference two days after the burning of Simsbury.[64] Simsbury, located to the northwest of Hartford and Windsor, was then an outlying settlement, and it became the only town in the colony destroyed by enemy activity. Certainly the council could have been motivated by a sense of weakness after the attack, but this seems unlikely since Simsbury had been abandoned and no inhabited towns had been attacked.[65] Connecticut's field forces, heavily aided and guided by Indian allies, also had been the most effective of the colonial commands. It seems that the colony was offering conciliation out of a position of strength rather than weakness, hence continuing its moderate policy. When there was no definitive reply to this entreaty, another proposal was approved on 18 April 1676, with a force sent to Hadley to affect this meeting on the first of May.[66] The coalition never acted on these overtures. Connecticut forces in Narragansett country later killed Tiawakesson in combat; the "ticket for his free passage" from the English was found folded in his pocket.[67]

Compared to Massachusetts and Plymouth, Connecticut had a relatively forward-looking internment policy: "Connecticut was alone in forbidding the sale of other Indians into foreign slavery. Instead, the colony sentenced captives to ten years of domestic servitude if they were sixteen or over at the end of that term; those under sixteen served until age twenty-six."[68] Rhode Island's internment policy was slightly more lenient, with a term of nine years.[69] Connecticut's nonslavery policy does not appear to have been obeyed universally. A little-known letter from the summer of 1676 names New Londoners Sam Rogers and Ralph Parker as communicating about the slave trade of hostile captives, then running through Boston. The unknown author was complaining that the twenty to twenty-five Indian women captives he intended to sell were only likely to fetch five to six pounds each.[70] Other Connecticut residents probably were involved in contravention of the colony's policy as it was a relatively lucrative business in human trafficking, requiring little investment other than perhaps military service. These were individual cases of malfeasance, however, unreflective of any official sanction.

As throughout New England, Connecticut enacted the death sentence for Indians convicted of killing colonists. This was not breaking with the standard English practice at the time for citizens who had committed murder or treason, which was how the colonists viewed Philip's "rebellion." Many Indians viewed slavery, especially far from their native land, as a fate worse than death, however, and Connecticut's move to outlaw this form of punishment for those hostile Indians who were not known to have killed colonists was therefore moderate in comparison to their regional counterparts. More effectively, Connecticut's policy moved away from the Indians' fear of slavery, creating an incentive to surrender to authorities instead of continuing to fight (of course only if hostile Indians did not know about the clandestine slave trade).

The controversy over the disposition of Philip's captured wife and young son also demonstrated that Massachusetts and Plymouth were in no mood to offer quarter after a number of influential ministers sanctioned the pair's execution. Samuel Arnold, John Cotton, Increase Mather, and James Keith all used Old Testament passages to formulate a legal opinion on the disposition of Philip's family.[71] Only Keith argued against a death sentence. The colonists eventually sentenced the family to slavery in Bermuda.[72] Connecticut's opinion on the matter was not recorded, but it is difficult to imagine the colony supporting a death sentence even for Philip's immediate family given the ethical tilt of its leadership and the colony's relatively lenient views.

The treatment of the Indian coalition in the field by Connecticut forces, however, might not have been as humane as the reintegration or voluntary-surrender policies. The colony's field forces did not always provide quarter if they captured hostile warriors, as opposed to enemy Indians coming in of their own volition: "[T]hese Connecticut men capture very many Indians, and kill all they capture except some boys and girls. This so frightens the Indians that they hasten to surrender themselves to Massachusetts, Plymouth, or Rhode Island, where their lives are spared, excepting known notorious murderers."[73] There was also debate over the severe defeat suffered by Sunk Squaw's band of Narragansetts at the hands of Major Talcott, which appears to constitute a massacre. Nevertheless, colonial forces did take prisoners throughout the conflict.

Connecticut's record was not completely unblemished either when dealing with local Indians. In Hartford, for instance, colonists required Indians to register and did not allow them to leave the vicinity of the town without a special permit. Authorities mandated where the Tunxis tribe of Farmington could establish its village.[74] The New Haven Town Committee prohibited Indians from entering the town for fear that they would observe its defensive capabilities.[75] The motivation for these rules, however, was partly for the Indians' own protection so they would not become victims of circumstance. On 1 September 1675, however, the War Council passed an ordinance that allowed colonists to shoot Indians on sight if the latter did not immediately throw down their arms and profess friendship.[76] Connecticut troopers also witnessed the torture and killing of prisoners at the hands of their Indian allies.[77]

Connecticut forced its local Native groups, including their primary Indian allies, to provide hostages, though Uncas petitioned the court to allow a grandson to remain at Norwich with Reverend James Fitch in Mohegan territory.[78] The court released sachem Turramuggus of the Wangunks or closely related Mattabassett group and two other Indians on 23 June 1676, acquiescing to another Indian petition.[79] The hostage policy deserves special consideration because Governor Winthrop, then at the convocation of the United Colonies commissioners in Boston, disapproved of demanding hostages from the Narragansetts while they were neutral. Perhaps this policy was the action of Deputy Governor Leete and other magistrates acting in the governor's absence. The case of Turramuggus was especially troubling, however relaxed the conditions of internment, because he had led a body of ostensibly friendly River Indians as part of the relief force for Springfield on 6 October 1675.[80]

The colonists' worst example of Indian mistreatment during the war was the murder of two captured Narragansetts in a New London prison. The motivation for this ugly episode was that a Narragansett raiding party allegedly killed two English colonists and captured a teenage boy not far from Norwich. When Major Palmes attempted to bring the perpetrators to justice, local civilian leadership frustrated his plan.[81] A letter from a soldier to Governor Andros that apparently never made it to Connecticut authorities, however, revealed that Nipmucks carried out the attack.[82] But the colonists had already lynched the Narragansetts in a case of mistaken identity.

In late August 1676, when the coalition's capabilities had significantly diminished, the War Council told Uncas that the victory was ultimately the colonists' own and, therefore, so were the prisoners of war. Connecticut apparently waited until the services of the Mohegans were no longer critical to its survival to assert authority over one of the last remaining powerful sachems of southern New England. This incident was not indicative of a complete realignment of policy, however, as the colony only a week later allowed Uncas to maintain jurisdiction over any Wabbaquasset tributaries who had surrendered to him.[83] A year later the council also sent representatives asking Andros to intercede with the Mohawks to release Owaneco, who had been captured by a raiding party.[84]

Although certain actions against local Indians represented the worst of the colonists, Connecticut throughout the war maintained more tolerant relations than its Puritan neighbors. The colony's inhabitants generally adhered to this policy. Connecticut never employed the large-scale concentration camps of Massachusetts and Plymouth, refrained from disarmament, maintained a lenient voluntary-surrender policy, and took positive actions—such as inviting local Indians into their towns for mutual defense and feeding them in the process—to maintain good relations. It avoided unnecessary irritants such as disarmament, which New York even implemented. This pragmatic and ethical approach to local Indians led to sound relationships and ultimately better security.

Why did the Connecticut settlers—members of the same Puritan-English cultural background as those in Massachusetts and

Plymouth—treat their neighboring Indians better? The brutal experience of the Pequot War forty years prior to Philip's rebellion was the vital experience that the other New England colonies did not share. Their settlements were never in danger from the Pequot confederacy, although some Massachusetts Bay troops participated in that war. Connecticut colonists, however, quickly learned that they could only wage successful war in the New World with Indian allies. The alliance with the Mohegans helped generate Connecticut's respect for its indigenous neighbors during the Great Narragansett War. Both parties maintained connections during the intervening years through personal relationships, such as that of Uncas and the Masons and the Pequot sachem Cassacinamon and the Winthrops. When local Indians in 1637 invited the Pequot raid on Wethersfield because of a local disagreement, the colonists experienced firsthand the dangers of poor local relations.[85] A nearby group provided intelligence and assistance to the colonists' enemies, just like neighboring Indians did for the hostile coalition in the other New England colonies during the Great Narragansett War. Connecticut colonists capitalized on the memory of that sometimes brutal experience from forty year earlier. A number of them, who had experienced the Pequot War, survived until 1675 to continue to influence policy, including Governor John Winthrop, Jr.[86]

Connecticut's policy of moderation was, in part, a reflection of its governor's leadership. Winthrop had long experience in matters of governance and war. He began his professional career as an executive officer to a Captain Best on the man of war *Due Repulse* as part of Admiral Lord Buckingham's armada sailing in relief of Huguenot forces at the besieged fortress of La Rochelle in 1627.[87] Winthrop experienced the ugliness of war, particularly at the battle of the Ile de Re, where he witnessed the royal French Catholic army slaughter poorly marshaled English forces.[88] Biographer Robert Black claims that this experience colored young Winthrop's view of war and that he thereafter sought diplomatic solutions to solve disputes: "from war itself he would shrink as from an evil beyond calculation."[89] Although Winthrop preferred diplomacy, there is no evidence that he feared war. Whether or not he disliked his first military experience during the aborted relief effort in France, he was waiting anxiously to sail back to England: "I hope we shall not stay here long after [relief from England arrives] I thinke soone after Michaelmas."[90] Throughout the course of his public service, Winthrop tried to resolve crises through diplomacy. During the events leading up to the Pequot War, Massachusetts Bay appointed him as chief negotiator for that colony's diplomatic mission to the Pequots.[91] His actions in Connecticut during the years between the Pequot War and the Great Narragansett War indicate his preference for negotiation over force. In the events prior to the latter conflict, Winthrop was again an active force in Indian affairs.

By 1675, Winthrop was an old man suffering from chronic illness.[92] He was in a state of semiretirement and had twice attempted to resign the governorship so that he could return to England.[93] But the General Court simply would not accept his resignation, especially after the onset of hostilities. Winthrop returned to work and resumed leadership of the colony, presiding over a number of meetings during the crisis of late June and early July.[94] Connecticut's policy of moderation toward the Indians was undoubtedly a hallmark of Winthrop's predilection for a diplomatic solution to resolve disputes. Even during the early days of Puritan hysteria, fostered by the uncertainty of the scope of the uprising, the governor maintained his composure and on 9 July argued that the Wampanoags, who had fled to Ninigret, should have "hopes of good quarter if delivered to us, &c."[95] Three days later he penned guidance to New England field commanders then in Narragansett country, reminding them of Narragansett assistance during the Pequot War and "to cosider whether it be not far better to take up wth such ingagements of amity as can be attained freely & willingly [from the Narragansetts], than that the potetest [most potent] of all our neighboring heathen should be made open, professed enemies."[96]

Winthrop argued against a "so absolute" position regarding the surrender of Narragansett hostages, pointing out that European nations did not require hostages from "newtralls." Given his veteran experience in these matters, the governor undoubtedly saw more room for negotiation with the Narragansetts, a powerful tribe and a former English ally with an unknown view toward Philip. Underlying his argument for treating the Narragansetts like fellow Europeans was also a realist view of affairs: "I believe there is difficulty ynough wth that one enemy, & why to stir up an other before an issue wth ye first [is settled]."[97]

Connecticut took appropriate measures for its defense, but its leaders did not allow xenophobia to carry the day. Winthrop left his mark on the colony's Indian policy before he was summoned to

Boston on 19 August 1675 as a senior representative to the assembly of the United Colonies.[98] The governor's sons, Majors Fitz-John and Wait Winthrop, not only continued their father's service to the colony but also maintained his policy toward indigenous communities. Fitz-John distributed cloth to loyal Indians, while Wait led a mission to trade coats to the friendly Mohegans, Pequots, and Western Niantics in exchange for those people's handing over hostile Indians.[99] Wait also participated in the expedition to the Narragansetts in July 1675.[100]

Governor Winthrop would see neither Connecticut nor England again. He died in service at Boston, succumbing to an illness apparently exacerbated by other health problems.[101] Before his death, Winthrop enraged the other colonial leaders by not countermanding Deputy Governor Leete's decision to withdraw Connecticut forces from Massachusetts Bay.[102] He was later ignored by the other delegates when he argued against the December 1675 Great Swamp expedition that he believed was "unnecessary," preferring another negotiated settlement with southern New England's largest Native group.[103] His ethical leadership far exceeded that of his fellow governor John Leverett of Massachusetts. Leverett tacitly accepted the unethical and murderous leadership of his cousin Captain Moseley, who wrote to the governor describing his feeding of the cooperative squaw to his dogs. Leverett also failed to prevent the Deer Island removal, as did Plymouth governor Josiah Winslow for the Clarke's Island removal.

Winthrop advised Deputy Governor Leete to allow Uncas and Ninigret to "draw of fro the enemy all yt will come ine & live quietly," implying good treatment of those who surrendered. He considered that such a measure would be "an expedient towards peace" and would open the possibility of a treaty with Philip, perhaps setting the stage for Connecticut's peace offerings later in the spring.[104] Regardless of the other New England commissioners' animosity, Winthrop was given an extravagant (by Puritan standards) state funeral after he died on 5 April 1676 to pay tribute to his long public service.[105] One of his last major acts at the United Colonies was to urge a policy of leniency for captured or surrendered Indians instead of the slavery advocated by some of his peers.[106] This argument was consistent with his earlier positions and provided a moderate point of view to his fellow commissioners. Winthrop's leadership was a critical factor in Connecticut remaining unscathed during the Great Narragansett War.

The majority of Connecticut's Indians, for reasons that were not recorded, elected to accept the colony's policy of moderation and remain allied or neutral. Undoubtedly, the decision not to disarm local Native groups influenced the Indians, who thus still possessed the means to hunt and protect their families. The colonists inviting Indians into their towns and in some cases feeding them also eased tensions. Connecticut's leadership also observed indigenous cultural norms in terms of exchanging gifts and respected Indian leadership of the allied groups by empowering them to lead other Indians within the colony. Uncas, Cassacinamon, and other sachems had long before thrown their lot in with the colonists and derived their influential political positions and economic security by such cooperation. The Indians of Connecticut were largely the ancient enemies of the groups that formed the hostile coalition. This probably led them to distrust the motives of the coalition and to understand that these groups could turn on them too if they first succeeded in weakening or defeating the English. Finally, the Delaware-related groups west of the Housatonic River valley lacked the Algonquian associations of greater New England, perhaps in part dissuading them from joining the Indian coalition.

Connecticut survived the worst of the conflict because it benefited from the experience of an earlier major Indian war on its soil and profited from its leaders' implementation of a practical policy of moderation. While the colony succeeded in maintaining solid relations and effective policy, its Puritan neighbors misunderstood the loyalties of their local Indians and miscalculated their willingness to assist the hostile coalition. Conversely, Connecticut's indigenous communities chose to remain allied or neutral during the conflict, and good relations with their colonial neighbors undoubtedly were a significant contributing factor. This relationship prevented the coalition from obtaining the critical local intelligence and support necessary to carry out large-scale attacks in the colony. The presence of allied or neutral groups in the vicinity of the English settlements there, as with cohabitation, improved security for both communities. Although local relations were the critical aspect in Connecticut emerging generally unscathed from the Great Narragansett War, there were other factors that contributed to the success of the colony's military operations.

CHAPTER 4

INFLUENCES OF THE EUROPEAN MILITARY REVOLUTION ON THE NEW ENGLAND FRONTIER

Connecticut's positive relationship with local Indians established a foundation for successful defensive operations. The colony established a more advanced defensive posture than the rest of New England throughout the course of the Great Narragansett War. Its defenses were similar in style, though on a smaller scale, compared to Europe's fortresses. The Old World's early modern era witnessed the development of fortifications based on geometrical design, termed *trace italienne*.[1] Europeans developed these works in response to the increased firepower of deployable field artillery, which could systematically destroy the vertical stonewalls characteristic of Medieval defenses.[2] Connecticut was on the frontier of New England and retained the traces of some European-style fortifications built to ward off other European forces, reconstructing these works during the Great Narragansett War. The hostile coalition did not immediately target the colony due to its remote location from the heart of the conflict and the initially passive nature of Narragansett support for King Philip's effort. This allowed the colony to reconstruct its fortifications and increase its defensive posture before it became a primary target for the coalition, once the Narragansetts took over, in the winter and spring of 1676. A surprising number of Pequot War veterans also survived to fight again in this later Indian conflict, a relative advantage over other New England colonies, which relied on less-experienced military leadership. Connecticut commanders passed on martial knowledge directly and through military texts bequeathed to subsequent generations. The members of the War Council capitalized on their own experience by adequately managing the conflict. The concentrated nature of the colony's towns and the density of its population in these settlements also aided the council's management of the war. Finally, Connecticut maintained an active defense, utilizing friendly Indians in addition to colonial forces to patrol the countryside.

The inability of attackers to overcome easily developed defenses often led to military stalemate in Europe: "As the English military writer John Cruso observed in 1632: 'The actions of the modern warres consist chiefly in sieges, assaults, sallies, skirmishes etc., and so affoard but few set battels." Another military writer from this era, "Johann Behr stated that, in Germany, 'Field battles are in comparison scarcely a topic of conversation. . . . Indeed at the present time the whole art of war seems to come down to shrewd attacks and artful fortification." The great Sebastien de Vauban, the most famous military engineer of the era, described the importance of fortifications in Europe just prior to the outbreak of the Great Narragansett War: "its importance has increased to the point where one can say that today it alone offers the means of conquest and conservation."[3] New England's, and especially Connecticut's, reliance on elements of modern European fortifications and the general absence of set-piece battles during the Great Narragansett War, signify the similarity in fighting styles between Europe and New England. In Connecticut's case, during the early part of the conflict when it was not a primary target, the colony created hardened defenses that Indians without artillery found difficult to assault. This was compounded by the absence of support from the local groups, who would have tipped off the fortified areas' weak points to the attackers. The coalition stood little chance of offensive success in the colony by late winter 1676.

Considering that during the war, most of New England was under siege, with colonists crowded into garrison houses and other fortifications and very much afraid to harvest their crops, warfare in the New World was not much different from warfare in the Old World. But sometimes there were pitched battles. The combat during Great Swamp and Pierce's Fight resembled a standard European battle, with opposing forces firing close-order musketry.[4] The majority of nonsiege fighting in the region, however, consisted of "shrewd attacks" (ambushes) or the "sallies" that European military writers lamented. The Great Narragansett War provided numerous examples of war parties attacking garrisons in all of the New England colonies, except Connecticut. The Great Swamp Fight, for example, saw the colonists battling Narragansetts behind fortifications until successfully storming a breech in the palisade. This and Pierce's Fight resembled the conditions of warfare in Europe. What can we now make of the assertion that "neither [the English nor the Indians] observed traditional European military conventions" because it was incompatible with American conditions, the Indian way of war having to be adopted for the ultimate success of the colonial effort during the Great Narragansett War?[5]

With the combatants generally waging war using the methods then en vogue among Europeans, they faced similar problems, namely the inability to capture fortified positions. Warriors would normally burn any outlying and abandoned homes and farm buildings but were often unwilling to attack (in accord with the "cutting off way of war") or unable to defeat the garrison houses.[6] Hubbard confirms this: "For [only] at *Lancaster* where they seemed to have had the greatest Cause of boasting for their Success in any Assault (although it were since known, that they had five hundred fighting Men when they assaulted that small Town of about fifty Families) yet were they able to surprise but one Garrison House, which neither was fenced round, nor were the Defendants able to ply their Shot behind it, but so as the Enemy came to the very Walls, and Roof on the back Side with their Fuel, or else they had never been able to have dispossessed the Inhabitants."[7]

The garrisons normally held, though usually at a high cost. Without artillery and military engineers, Indian forces did not normally have the capability to defeat them, and especially those inside full-scale fortifications, in a direct manner. Victory through infiltration and surprise could never have been entirely ruled out except for Connecticut, where the neighboring groups did not provide the hostiles with intelligence. Some of the colony's towns relied on the same strongpoint system of defense that utilized reinforced garrison houses, but large settlements constructed more-advanced fortifications, more so than the other colonies.[8] The garrison houses served as "the first line of defense for frontier communities," and the inhabitants were sometimes required to shelter there at night.[9] A standing guard was required to defend them effectively. A typical garrison house in Connecticut was "palisaded . . . a deep ditch was dug all around the house; logs were then placed perpendicularly in the ditch all around it, leaving space for a gate. Logs sharpened at the top, placed close together, and [standing] about twelve (12) feet above the ground. The ditch filled in and the earth replaced and stamped down, and here part of the ditch open; this with the gate was a good defence against sudden attacks."[10]

Garrison houses were sometimes similar to European fortresses but on a much smaller scale. They typically adopted at least two of the features of early modern European defenses. The "open ditch" was a small-scale moat, and soon the War Council ordered garrison houses in Hartford (and eventually elsewhere) construct flankers, another standard feature of European geometric design.[11] Consisting of wood, these defenses were especially vulnerable to attacks with fire. Malone claims that the Indians adopted incineration as a tactic from the English during the Pequot War, which is highly unlikely given the bloody warfare of the precontact era.[12] Only a limited number of colonists, an "uncomfortable 'heap' of humanity," could squeeze inside the garrison houses, essentially slightly larger than normal dwellings for the time period converted for defense.[13] By the late fall of 1675, Connecticut mandated the fortification of its major towns because of these weaknesses of a garrison defense, the proven effectiveness of the hostile Indians in destroying towns in other colonies, and the entry of the Narragansetts into the conflict.

Whether in Europe or the Americas, fortifications alone made for insufficient security. During the Great Narragansett War, garrisons failed to protect property and sometimes even the lives of the colonists, while almost all fortifications even in Europe at this time succumbed to siege if no relief force was forthcoming and the supplies of the offensive forces held out.[14] This was in fact what happened at Fort Saybrook during the Pequot War, when a lack of provisions forced Gardiner to send parties beyond the walls to bring in corn and hay. The Pequots successfully ambushed these missions.[15] Attackers also frequently bypassed fortifications: "Initially, the colonial governments tried stationing small, immobile garrisons in forts situated on the major avenues of approach into the settled areas. However, the Indians quietly bypassed the forts and ambushed the surprised settlers."[16]

Military engineering capability from Europe crossed the Atlantic with veterans like John Mason and "Lion Gardener, [who] had fought as a youth against the Spaniards with an English volunteer force in the Netherlands.... He stayed on in Holland, winning appointment as a lieutenant of engineers on the staff of the prince of Orange. Having twelve years' experience with the Dutch as a master of fortifications, Gardiner was ideally suited to supervise the building of a refuge for Puritan noblemen in the American wilderness."[17] At Saybrook Point in the 1630s, Gardiner "constructed a very respectable fort. The placement of the two cannons on 'Fort Hill,' a ten-foot-high mound within the palisade, enabled Gardener to command the treacherous, sand-clogged channel at the [Connecticut] river's mouth."[18] Captains Mason and John Underhill also served successful yet controversially political and bloody military careers during the early history of New England after having served together as sergeants in Colonel Vere's English regiment in Dutch service in the Netherlands. The English and Scots maintained five standing regiments with the Dutch during part of the Eighty Years' War in support of their Protestant coreligionists on the Continent.[19] Mason probably served during the siege of S'Hergatobosch, where the Dutch commander implemented a daring and unique plan to capture the fortress.[20] Perhaps Mason employed the same flexibility (though unethically) he observed at the siege by setting fire to the Mystic Fort, when the English were losing that battle.[21] Although Gardiner, Mason, Underhill, and many other military leaders of the Pequot War had died or were too old for field service by the time of the Great Narragansett War, the knowledge that they brought from the Old World survived with the soldiers they had trained, the texts they had bequeathed, and the fortifications they had designed.

With the passing of the first American generation, historian Guy Chet argues, "colonial commanders, as a group, were simply remarkably inexperienced and unprofessional. Unlike Miles Standish, Lion Gardiner, and John Mason, most of the colonial commanders during King Philip's War were not professional soldiers trained and seasoned on the battlefields of Europe."[22] A number of Pequot War veterans survived to fight in both wars, and others *did* gain experience fighting other Europeans in North America. The military experience garnered by survivors from the 1630s proved invaluable for Connecticut forces during the Great Narragansett War. By 1675, many veterans had become senior civic and military leaders of their respective communities. The following men were documented to serve in both wars, but given the longevity of the colonists, it is certain that others served in both conflicts, though their service cannot be confirmed due to lost records. In addition to Governor Winthrop, a veteran diplomat from the Pequot War, there were a number of military men who attained leadership positions by or during 1675–76. Captain Thomas Bull, who led Connecticut forces at Fort Saybrook against Governor Andros, was a Pequot War veteran.[23] He responded not only to the War Council's order to repair Fort Saybrook in July 1675 but also to the request for assistance from fellow Pequot War veteran Captain Robert Chapman of Saybrook. Joining Chapman nearby were Pequot War veterans Lieutenant William Pratt and Thomas Munson. Lieutenant Thomas Tracy served as local quartermaster in the vicinity of Saybrook and disposed of the surrendered weapons of hostile Indians. It is probable that he had served in the 1630s.[24]

Farmington's Burnham brothers, John and Thomas, were veterans of Massachusetts Bay forces during the earlier Indian conflict. The War Council ordered Lieutenant Edward Culver, Pequot War veteran, out on at least one scout for marauding war parties. Hostile Indians killed Edward Elmer, who was a veteran of both wars. Narragansetts killed Captain John Gallop Jr., another Pequot War veteran, "while in the command of a company of Pequot Indians" at Great Swamp.[25] Jacob Waterhouse also survived the Pequot War only to die of wounds on 1 September 1676. Captain Merriman of Wallingford, who wrote to the council about the burning of the Coles' house, was a Pequot War veteran as was John Stanley, who after the war settled in what became Kensington and whose family lent its name to a part of the city of New Britain. Nicolas and Richard of the leading Olmstead family of Hartford both served in the Pequot War.[26]

Connecticut's second generation of leaders, as had their parent's generation, cultivated combat experience in the Old World as well as in the New. Captain George Denison, Connecticut's most effective field commander, not only served in the Pequot War but also was wounded fighting in the English Civil Wars. After the former conflict, Denison had returned to England to fight with the Parliamentarians against the Royalists. Genealogical accounts assert that he was wounded at the Battles of Marston Moor and Naseby.[27] At Marston Moor Oliver Cromwell snatched victory from the jaws of defeat in a daring nighttime cavalry assault, supported by the Earl of Manchester's infantry.[28] Though Denison absorbed some tactics for later use from this experience, he definitely learned how to handle stress, fear, and pain on the battlefield. He also increased his knowledge from his earlier Pequot War experience about how troops respond to combat, perhaps also drawing some conclusions about what leaders should do in battle and how they should do it.

Dension also witnessed the utility of employing dragoons at Naseby. During that battle, General Thomas Fairfax (who also had led troops earlier in the Netherlands during the Eighty Years' War) employed his dragoons as an ambush force in the hedges on the New Model Army's left, perpendicular to the army's main line. The dragoons played a decisive role in the battle, pouring in enfilading fire down the lines of the advancing Royal Army.[29]

Captain Fitz-John Winthrop (son of the Connecticut governor and later governor himself) prepared to fight in 1658 for Charles II's restoration. Though this happened without major combat, and thus not gaining any direct combat experience for the young man, he witnessed training and administration of military forces. Fitz-John would enter combat in 1673-74 while leading Long Island and Connecticut militia against the Dutch in a number of skirmishes, gaining tangible experience.[30] These actions, though not as extensive or intense as those that Denison experienced in England, also prepared him for decision making during the Great Narragansett War.

Although the tactics were sometimes different in Indian warfare (as discussed in chapter 6), general leadership experience and the ability to manage fear and make decisions under fire mattered as much in the seventeenth century as they do today.[31] Celebrated military theorist Carl Von Clausewitz asserted that only an experienced commander can come to terms with friction on the battlefield, whereas pure theoreticians without combat experience risked catastrophic failure: "Is there any lubricant that will reduce this [friction]? Only one, and a commander and his army will not always have it readily available: combat experience."[32] The battlefields of Europe and North America provided Connecticut leaders such experience.

Besides the use of dragoons, there were administrative and organizational similarities between the New Model Army (and earlier Parliamentarian armies) and Connecticut forces during the Great Narragansett War. The trainband flag at Fort Saybrook was even a replica of the "Blew Trayned Bands" of the city of London from the English Civil Wars.[33] The New Model Army, as at Naseby, employed its mounted forces generally in squadrons of three hundred troopers and officers, which corresponded roughly to the number of dragoons who deployed on large field missions for Connecticut during 1675-76.[34]

New England's colonial forces also employed tactics similar to the type that Parliamentary forces utilized in Ireland, focusing on disrupting the enemy's ability to produce food. Although research has not uncovered a direct link to Connecticut colonists' participation in Cromwell's Irish campaign, undoubtedly New Englanders were familiar with the methods used in attempting to deny the Irish sustenance. The New Model Army's extirpative warfare in Ireland sought to break the population's will to resist in a way similar to the New England colonists' targeting of Indian food supplies: "Elsewhere [in Ireland] the inhabitants ate grass and green corn. A year later widespread starvation was reported in Wexford. The effects of starvation were compounded by the plague which swept across the country in 1652. The new settlers were dismayed to discover the drawbacks of occupying a graveyard."[35] Although there were similarities in tactics used to subdue resistance in both cases, the New England link to the English Civil Wars can be taken too far. Ian Gentles argues that Parliamentarian policy was to eradicate the Irish Catholic population and supplant it with English Protestants.[36] This genocidal plan aimed at making way for ethnic English settlers reeks of an early notion of *lebensraum*. Francis Jennings views this colonial policy toward Indians in the New World as derived from Europe in places like Ireland. Unlike in Ireland, however, Native allies played the key role in English success, and neutral groups in Connecticut and Rhode Island generally remained unharmed.

Colonial settlers employed military-engineering techniques that they had learned on the Continent and in European schools. In addition to Gardiner's engineering acumen, Winthrop, Jr., knew of the design of England's Fort Harwich, and its pattern influenced the methods of his fortification building. Before his political career, Winthrop, Jr., was commissioned chief fortifications officer at Boston and later at the mouth of the Connecticut River at Saybrook.[37] He wrote to his father, the governor of Massachusetts Bay, concerning the fortifications at "Langer Point," England, which he visited with a "Kinges workman" and copied: "I have now a perfect plot thereof, wth the dementions of the whole & parts. I will have it read sgt [sergeant] you come downe."[38] The fortress at Langer Point was a "pentagonal structure with angle bastions and a dry ditch" and meant to compliment the Harwich works.[39]

A vibrant discussion of military affairs also was carried out between North America and Europe, such as one between Winthrop, Jr., then in London, and his father in Boston concerning the Thirty Years' War: "The Spaniard hath a mighty fleete prepared to goe agt the Dutch at Parnambuco. . . . The King of Sweden prvaileth in Germany, he hath lately given Tilly an overthrow wth a small army agt his mighty army."[40] Given the great distances concerned and the slow travel between the Americas and Europe, the English colonists surprisingly remained well informed of political and military events around the world. Winthrop, Jr.'s letter was not an anomaly, for the Reverend John Russell at Hadley, even on the besieged New England frontier during the Great Narragansett War, received information from Europe that he subsequently forwarded to Connecticut with a touch of humor intact: "The Emperor demanding all of the ffrench interest in Alsatia the greater and lesse. The Duke of Larraines Territories wth two cities of Concern in fflanders The answer is that is to aske one of his eyes. The Emperors Reply is yt he will have more than that viz all yt he holds in fflanders. This the kg of ffrance saith is to demand both his eyes and therefore if they would have it they shall win it by inches to eeke great prparacons For war on both hands."[41]

Winthrop, Jr., also maintained the largest personal library in the New World by the mid-seventeenth century, possibly consisting of more than one thousand tracts, some of which concerned military affairs, including Robert Ward's *Animadversions of Warre; or a Militarie Magazine of the Truest Rules and Ablest Instructions for the Managing of Warre* (London, 1639).[42] The complete title for Ward's text includes information about the Thirty Years' Wars and, specifically, fortifications:

> Anima'dversions of vvarre; or, A militarie magazine of the truest rules, and ablest instructions, for the managing of warre: composed, of the most refined discipline, and choice experiments that these late Netherlandish, and Swedish warres have produced. With divers new inventions, both of fortifications and stratagems. As also sundry collections taken out of the most approved authors, ancient and moderne, either in Greeke, Latine, Italian, French, Spanish, Dutch, or English. In two bookes / By Robert Ward, gentleman and commander.[43]

Winthrop, Jr., was not the only Connecticut leader with access to military texts, which should not be entirely surprising given the literate state of New England's white-male population. Captain Merriman bequeathed his military texts to his son: "I give to my son Caleb my military books, my cutlash & sash, my best gun &

all other accoutrements belonging to military affairs."[44] He chose to highlight "military books" first in his 1692 will, indicating perhaps that such items were more valued and important than weapon systems, even at a time when New England lacked a weapons-production capability. With an emphasis on texts, it was likely that the colony's military leaders actually read them and attempted to employ in combat what they learned. European warfare had indeed made inroads in the New World, particularly in Connecticut, through a variety of means such as imported texts, military experience abroad, and written communication with the Old World.

Connecticut's settlers in fact had prepared to confront the threat from European powers. Hostile neighbors threatened that colony more than others in New England because it was on the frontier with the Dutch New Netherlands and astride two potential invasion routes from French Canada—the Hudson and Connecticut River valleys. As the population centers of Plymouth Colony and Massachusetts Bay Colony became more removed with the westward advance of the frontier, Connecticut's populated settlements remained threatened by the Dutch and French. The Indian threat also affected Connecticut more than the other New England colonies, with the Narragansetts to the east, the Nipmuck and River tribes to the north, and the Delaware and Iroquois leagues to the west.

The evidence of fortifications in Connecticut's colonial records enables an expansion of Geoffrey Parker's assertion that "in America as in Asia, however, isolated fortresses proved of limited use. They served to create a safe environment for trade and a defense against low-intensity threats, but they could not resist a major assault."[45] Although European forces did not attack Connecticut's defenses directly during the seventeenth century, the colony implemented European artillery fortresses to deter them and prepare for potential attacks. Fort Saybrook, at the strategic mouth of the Connecticut River, deterred the higher-intensity threat of New York governor Andros's invading force, and the earliest garrison there, prior to the Pequot War, had fired cannon at a Dutch ship to prevent a landing.[46]

The Dutch also had threatened Connecticut in the Eastern Niantic conspiracy of the early 1650s. In 1665, 1667, and 1673, Winthrop, Jr., believed that the Dutch would raid the colony's coast, and Connecticut leaders assisted the English colonists on Long Island against an invading force from Manhattan in 1673–74.[47] This command consisted of a "small vessel of six guns wth

300 men," a considerable force of European infantry for the New World at the time, justifying Winthrop's fears.[48] Militia forces led by Connecticut's Fitz-John Winthrop defeated the Dutch in battle, and the English won a number of other skirmishes.[49] As part of the war settlement, England regained control of Manhattan. Dutch settlers near Albany, however, continued to undermine English rule during the Great Narragansett War by supplying the hostile coalition with powder and ammunition.[50]

New France was the English colonists' greatest threat in the decades following 1676; it was even a threat to Connecticut's security as early as the mid-1660s, despite the French being temporarily allied with the English.[51] Although technically partners, the competition of European powers on the colonial frontier, far removed from the halls of Versailles, Whitehall, Binnenhof, and El Escorial, held sway in the Americas. Governor Winthrop was suspicious of French interaction with the Algonquian peoples to the north of Connecticut, worrying that France's Indian allies, with or without European forces, would use their war against the Mohawks as an excuse to attack English settlements.[52] Winthrop regarded this threat grave enough to ready his militia on one occasion.[53] He sent Connecticut cavalry in a joint expedition with Massachusetts forces "to discover the way toward Canada, whether passable for horse, as also to get good intelligence of the motion of the French Army . . . [which was] pretending against the Mohaques."[54] Winthrop also noted "the strange march of a French army in the very depth of winter fro Canad, wch alarmed all our inland plantations."[55] This invasion marked the continuation of the long French and allied Indian war with the Iroquois confederacy. The governor probably was reacting to the 1665–66 campaign against Mohawk villages that utilized soldiers of the Carignan-Salieres Regiment—the first deployment of substantial European regular forces to northeastern America.[56] England considered the French in Canada a serious-enough threat to order an invasion, although Winthrop ultimately avoided committing Connecticut troops to a Canadian expedition, proposing instead an attack on the French Caribbean islands.[57]

In 1669 John Mason believed strongly enough that the French were attempting to ally with the southern New England Indians, including the Mohegans, Pequots, Niantics, and Narragansetts, that he ordered Owaneco to bring in some of his followers' muskets.[58] Archaeologists have discovered a large number of Jesuit rings at Narragansett gravesites from this period, signaling an economic, and possibly a cultural, relationship between the French and indigenous southern New Englanders.[59] During the Great Narragansett War, the French supplied the coalition with powder and ammunition, and agents at Pocumtuck (Deerfield) reportedly encouraged attacks.[60] They also instructed the coalition to spare the English mills and meetinghouses because a three-hundred-man French army, with extra ammunition for the Indians, would travel down the Connecticut River in the spring to reinforce the uprising, and that the French navy would blockade Massachusetts Bay. The agents even exhibited letters to the Indians, the contents of which supposedly confirmed the operation.[61] Philip probably met with Monsieur Normanville outside of Boston prior to the conflict. The French agent's role in the war was complicated, however, as he later tipped off the English that the upper Connecticut River groups were massing against them.[62] That a Frenchman could travel in a country rife with violence and racial tensions also indicates that the Indians viewed the French favorably compared to the English and hence had a more nuanced understanding of European politics than the English often had of tribal dynamics.

The boast partially materialized as intelligence arrived before the Connecticut War Council in the fall of 1675 indicating a French influence in the war: "From such a common enemie, whoe are sayd to be encouraged by the French who supply them with ammunition great store, some have been seen amongst them lately as we are Informed, & promise them in the Spring great assistance of men & ammunition."[63] Just prior to the defeat of the hostile coalition, Governor Andros coordinated a response with Mohawk sachems to French encroachment into the Mohawk and Lake Champlain River valleys, though the connection to the Great Narragansett War remains vague.[64] Although a direct French attack never materialized at any time during 1675–76, the English colonists' fears proved justified when combined Indian-French forces attacked New England a decade later and repeatedly thereafter during the French and Indian wars.

Unsurprisingly, Connecticut settlements responded to the European threat by building fortresses with elements of Continental design. During the early modern era, engineers designed defensive works to absorb the power of artillery fire with earth and provide defenders with overlapping fields of fire against assaulting forces.

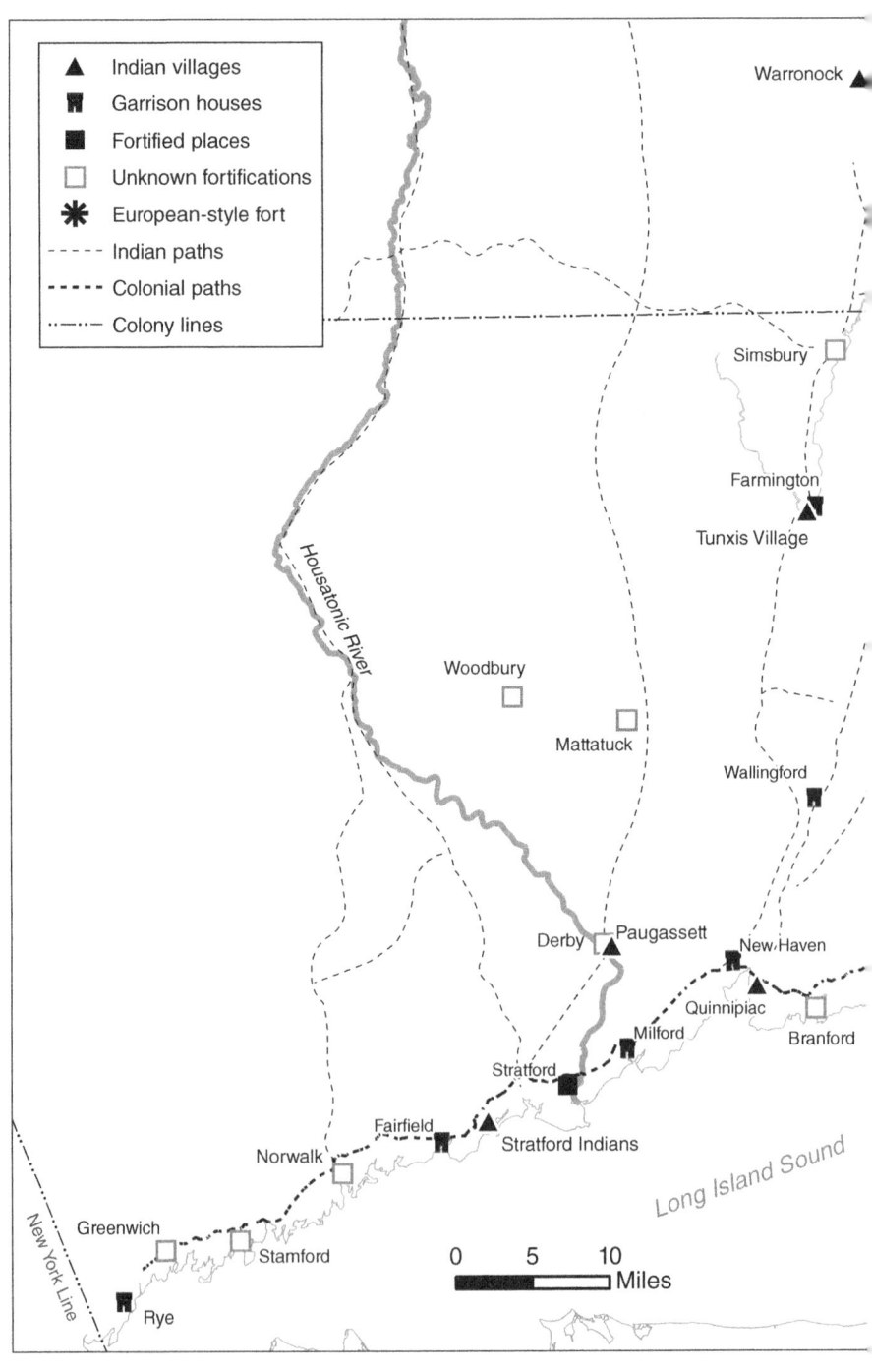

Connecticut garrison defense. Map by Bill Keegan.
© 2014, University of Oklahoma Press.

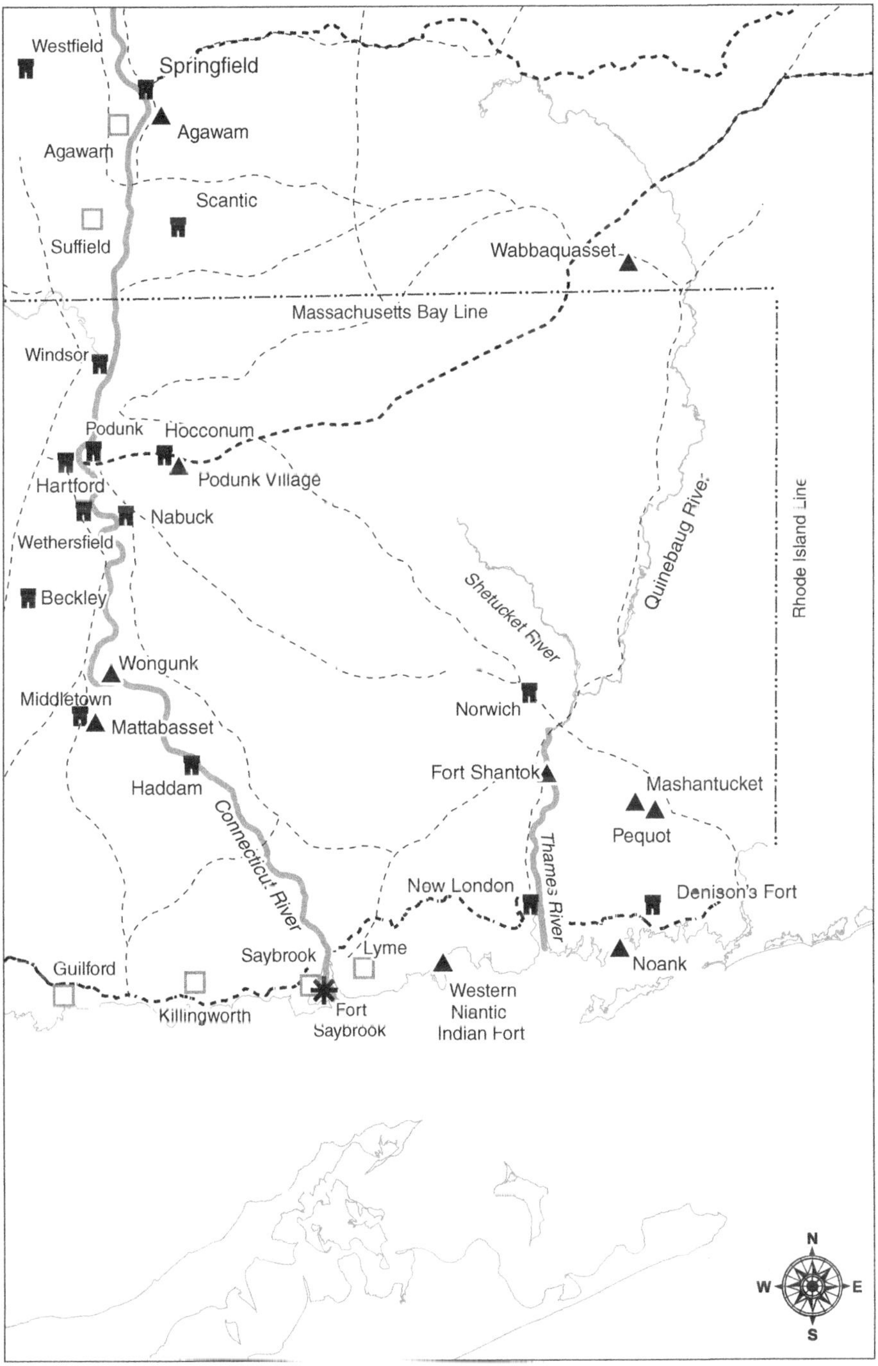
Westfield
Springfield
Agawam
Agawam
Scantic
Suffield
Wabbaquasset
Massachusetts Bay Line
Windsor
Podunk
Hocconum
Podunk Village
Hartford
Nabuck
Wethersfield
Beckley
Quinebaug River
Rhode Island Line
Shetucket River
Wongunk
Middletown
Mattabasset
Norwich
Haddam
Fort Shantok
Mashantucket
Pequot
Connecticut River
Thames River
New London
Denison's Fort
Saybrook
Lyme
Guilford
Noank
Killingworth
Fort
Saybrook
Western
Niantic
Indian Fort
N
W
E
S

These angled, mostly earthen structures, unlike the tall, vertical stonewalls of the Middle Ages, boasted "thick [sloping] walls, broad moats, and geometrical bastions."[65] The War Council directed that colony defensive sites adopt this geometrical pattern and incorporate the "flanker" design as well.[66] Authorities designed these fortifications with moatlike ditches; mutually supporting "flankers" with interlocking fields of fire; wooden palisades reinforced with earthen mounds; sally ports; ramparts lined with platforms, from which garrisoning troops could fire down upon the enemy; and fields of fire cleared for observation around the entire position out to effective musket range.

Artillery augmented key defensive positions in major towns such as Hartford and New Haven and at the strategic mouth of the Connecticut River at Saybrook. Fort Saybrook sported bastions, and the original Windsor fortification boasted "an irregular parallelogram" and ditches, both strongholds thus featuring components of geometric design.[67] The Fort Saybrook had always been a major colonial position, and Connecticut forces improved it over time. The original fort burned down in the mid-1640s and was rebuilt closer to the water's edge due to the elimination of the Pequot threat after 1637. The initial site controlled the narrow causeway to Saybrook Point, but after the Pequot War English settlers developed the area, obviating the purpose of covering the causeway with cannon fire. The fort's new position allowed for cannon to achieve greater range and accuracy for controlling the mouth of the Connecticut River.[68]

By the onset of the Great Narragansett War, the post had deteriorated. Shortly after Andros's departed after threatening Fort Saybrook, the War Council on 19 July 1675 ordered Captain Bull to Hartford "to receive some Instructions about renewing the fortifications upon the place." He was to leave only sixteen to twenty men in garrison there. Even with this tiny force, the fort still depended on local towns to provide for it as Bull was "to give notice to Lime & Kennelsworth to be in all readynes to assist Seabrooke upon Call."[69] A few years after the war, the Crown ordered a survey of the English colonies, and Connecticut's report reveals that the local towns even then still provided for the fort:

> 6Q: what castles and forts are within your corporation and how situated and fortified and what stoares and provisions they are furnished with.

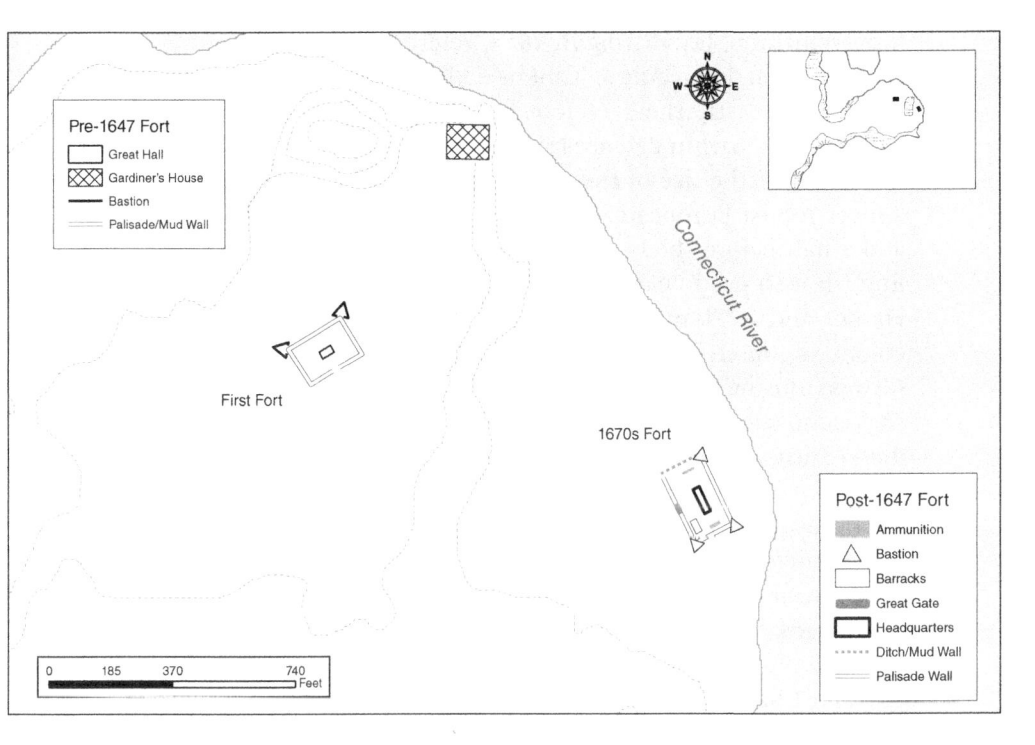

Evolution of fortifications on Saybrook Point. Map by Bill Keegan. © 2014, University of Oklahoma Press.

> Answ: we have one small fort with[in] our colony which is at the mouth of the Conecticutt River; at a place called Saybrooke, and our stores of provision are but slender we having townes about it that can carry provision to it upon all occasions.[70]

Fort Saybrook continued to exist as a key fortification through the nineteenth century.

Connecticut fortified other critical areas in addition to Saybrook Point. The fifth clause of the laws of New Haven Colony, before it was incorporated into Connecticut in the early 1660s, required that elected officials maintain "Works and Fortifications" within its boundaries.[71] New Haven's leadership also warned against insurrection, specifically a scenario in which rebels would seize the fortification, platform, or "great Guns" in the town itself.[72] There was discussion of fortifying the meetinghouse as early as 1654 as well as using this artillery as a warning signal in the event of armed threats.[73]

John Winthrop, Jr., writing in 1673, referenced New Haven's fortifications when describing a "captaine Manig" who "fell downe fro the wall of the castle there 16 foot high."[74] Since colonists referred to strongpoints within defenses that were more than wooden palisades as "castles," the use of the term signifies that at least remnants of a more robust European-style defense were in place as late as a year and a half before the outbreak of the Great Narragansett War. The English also used "castle" to refer to the main defenses at Boston Harbor and at Plymouth proper. In the case of Massachusetts Bay, colonists constructed their fortification in the harbor as an artillery fortress meant to contest other European warships from entering. Massachusetts Bay's court used the terms "castle" and "castle soldiers" during the Great Narragansett War, ordering garrison troops there to pay taxes at the same rate as its cavalry troopers, since such duty presumably was of a safer and more elite nature than service in the infantry or dragoons.[75] The colonists thus erected the fortresses at Saybrook, Plymouth, and New Haven, which they also described as "castles," to combat and deter European forces, though in the latter two, there was a measure of deterrence against Indians as well. Both Fort Saybrook (after the Pequot War) and Boston's Castle Fort underwent redesign exclusively to combat Europeans since these works commanded key water approaches that only naval forces could exploit.

In 1675, however, serviceable fortifications did not exist at New Haven. A town meeting on 24 September debated where to build such defenses (as well as repairing the artillery).[76] In October, after the War Council ordered extensive fortifications built at key locations, New Haven decided: "Upon debate of these things it was propounded and ordered that at ye ends of ye streets & at ye fouer angles thos fortifications or places of shelter against ye shott of an enemy should be set up as ye committee shall appoint, and ye persons in ye Towne to work freely at it until they wer finished." Residents also agreed to continue fortifying the meeting house and to clear out brush up to a half mile from the town square to prevent "skulking" Indians before the defenses could be completely established.[77] Settlers outside of New Haven proper in the nearby vicinity of "Stony River and the South end" applied to the town's fortification committee for their own defenses, although it is unclear if the colonists constructed any.[78] When Connecticut came under attack in March 1676, the committee arranged for more-advanced fortifications, including breastworks and ditching, ordering the young and the old alike to contribute to their construction.[79] As in other towns, New Haven's defenses do not appear to have been completed by the end of the war. A number of meetings returned to the issue of fortifications, but even the prodding of the town's committee did not result in completed palisades, though the settlers finished many individual elements of the works.[80]

Seventeenth-century New Englanders allowed their defenses to slip into a state of disrepair, anticipating a trend in U.S. history. As has often happened in following centuries, peacetime in early colonial America ushered in policies resulting in the enervation of martial assets, only to have to rebuild the same infrastructure during crises. This fact reveals the colonists' inherent fear of the oppressive nature of standing forces, which they had experienced in Stuart England, as well as an inherent dislike of the high taxes necessary to pay for unused military apparatuses during peacetime. The European-artillery fortresses at Boston, Plymouth, Saybrook, and New Haven repeatedly fell into disrepair and disuse, only to be reconstituted when threats of invasion or uprising surfaced. The use of the traces of these works gave New Englanders a head start in reconstruction, however, instead of having to begin fresh each time. This was especially the case in Connecticut, where settlers originally built more forts because of the colony's tenuous position on a frontier adjacent to the Dutch, the French, and the Pequots (until 1637), Narragansetts, Delawares, and Iroquois. The Dutch threat was especially dangerous as the skirmishes on Long Island confirmed, so the colonists focused on building fortifications along the coast.[81]

The traces left at Saybrook, New Haven, Hartford, Windsor, and Stratford where evidence exists of pre-1675 fortifications—translated into a military advantage for the colonists during the Great Narragansett War. This benefit was redoubled because of the generally concentrated nature of Connecticut's population along the shoreline and the Connecticut and Thames Rivers. In 1675 the coalition's focus on Massachusetts Bay and Plymouth allowed the colonists' to rebuild their defenses from the previous generation of fortifications.[82] This reprieve was a significant factor in Connecticut's later success.

Although scant primary-source evidence exists, Hartford's defenses probably were rebuilt along an original trace described by

Noah Webster in an early history of the town: "When Hartford was first settled . . . the main street was laid out very wide, and nearly a mile in length. At each end a fort was built: that at the north end was near the house now occupied by the descendants of Col. Talcott; that at the south was on or near the side of the late south school house, at the forks of the road—one leading to Wethersfield, the other to Farmington. The Garrison could see from one fort to the other."[83] The town's original defenses thus would have corresponded to Plymouth's defenses, with the main avenue of the latter town roughly the maximum range of an artillery piece of the time period. Most black-powder weapons of the era, regardless of how large the caliber, the amount of charge, or training of the cannon crew, did not fire accurately at over one thousand yards.[84] Hartford's settlement pattern thus corresponded to the range of the guns so that the cannon could traverse the town from one end to the other, at least at maximum effective range, should a portion fall into enemy hands. The developed nature of these original defenses corresponded to the Dutch threat, for they too maintained a fortress in Hartford for over a decade after the arrival of the English. Hartford likely revived some of its defenses, at least the strongpoints, along these old traces during the Great Narragansett War as the War Council, headquartered there, demanded advanced works for all of the major towns in the colony.

The Windsor colonists from Plymouth originally constructed palisades around the town in the irregular pattern described above. The name of the main thoroughfare—Palisado Avenue—which crosses the Farmington River near its confluence with the Connecticut River, reflects the defensive posture of the first settlement. Having observed a portion of the original town trace, the terrain slopes down to the Farmington River on the south and a meadow on the east, creating the effect of a ditch; the settlers constructed their outer palisades on the top of this high ground. It was efficient for them to utilize the natural terrain instead of placing the original town in an area where they would have had to dig a defensive ditch. The colonists realized the strategic importance of fortifying the area that controlled the confluence of two significant rivers in central Connecticut. They probably borrowed the general concept of the defenses observed at Plymouth and built a castle-strongpoint defense, complemented by an encompassing wooden palisade and the ditchlike structure of the natural terrain.

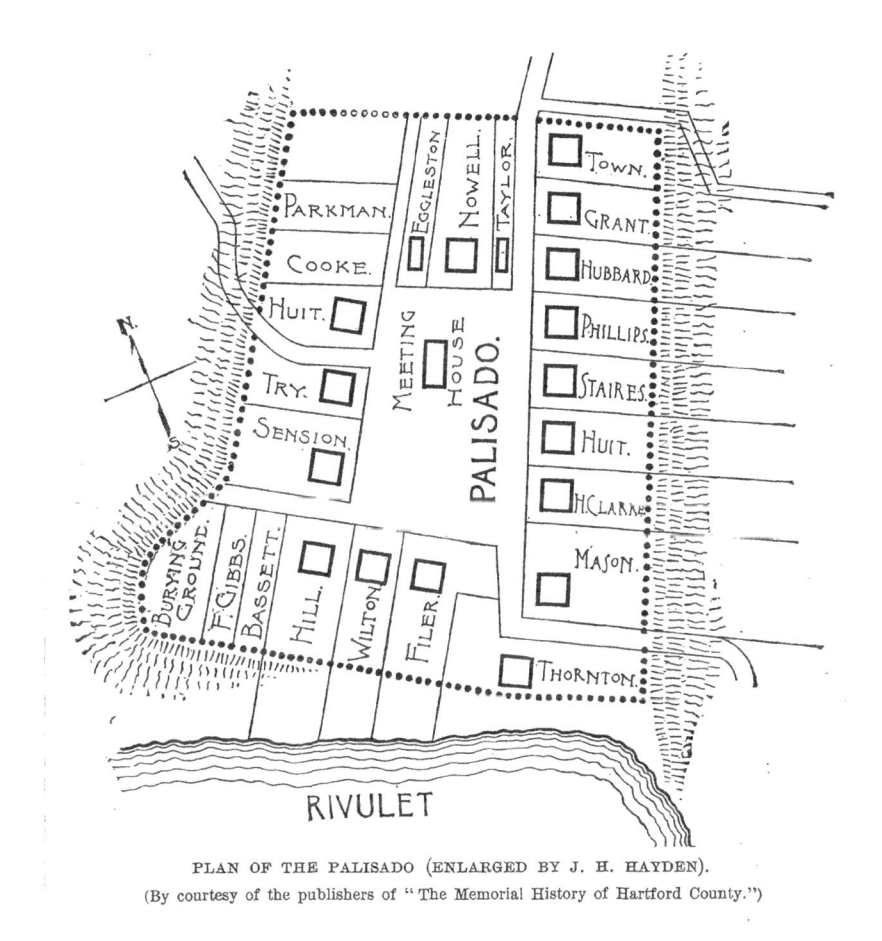

PLAN OF THE PALISADO (ENLARGED BY J. H. HAYDEN).
(By courtesy of the publishers of "The Memorial History of Hartford County.")

Stiles's drawing of Windsor fortification plan.

With the outbreak of war in 1675, Windsor had long outgrown the restrictive palisade model, but perhaps the colonists revived the old trace as an inner defense and refuge. Henry Stiles related that the local colonists worked on a "stone fort," which was really a garrison house with a flanker. Town leaders excused Windsor men from training to work on this structure. There was also reference to a large gun on a carriage that the men repaired during the war.[85] As colonists mounted such guns at strongpoints, Windsor likely reconstituted some form of such a structure after the war began. Whatever constituted the town's defenses, hostile Indians did not attempt an assault, even though they burned the outlying portions of what was then Springfield (now Suffield), Connecticut, a mere six miles away. The Springfield colonists had abandoned Suffield, however, prior to its destruction and sought to resettle it after the cessation of hostilities: "The Settling of suffield having been some Time obstructed by the War with the Indians; which necessitated such as were there to remove the last year, and put a stop to many others that were coming to that Place, And Whereas, Thro the favor of God in scattering the Heathen, and giving us some Quiet, there is hope of resettling there."[86]

The town of Stratford in Fairfield County also relied on past traces. On the coast and near the Dutch, Stratford relied on more than the traditional "palisadoe" defense. Like New Haven and other significant coastal settlements, Stratford built a castlelike structure to mount its few guns within the network of wooden palisades. Palisades alone could not mount cannon, and the guns were one of the first items that town leaders considered in planning. Stratford was on the frontier with the unsettled bounds of southwestern Connecticut, and as recounted, intelligence indicated suspicious Indian activity in the area at the time of the Great Narragansett War. Stratford followed the War Council's orders for towns to reconstitute their defenses, utilizing perhaps the original trace.[87]

The Stonington settlement also had a significant fortress for colonial America, boasting a strongpoint within the palisades on the property of Captain Denison. The fort was twenty-five rods in length at its longest point and more than 410 feet total. This was a significant fortification, located on a spur commanding the surrounding low-lying farmland and a crossing point of the Pequotsepos Creek. Denison's farmstead abutted the works, but no other settlements were located within the palisades. Besides for defense and intimidation, the colonists used the Denison fort as a rallying point for offensive operations in the same way as the Pequot's Mohantic Fort (described below).[88]

The towns' execution of the War Council's orders varied by locale. As with Wethersfield and others, New Haven's fortifications were "still incomplete when the war ended."[89] Into March 1676 the "fortefication" at Milford, for instance, was only one-third complete, and the town's leadership complained of the citizens' unwillingness to build it. Thomas Topping, one of the leaders, actually confiscated town-members' goods when they failed to turn out for fortification detail, using the War Council's previous order

Archaeological dig at Denison Fort site.

as justification. Topping also mentioned that the "stockadoe line" was under dispute by members of the town committee, while others complained that the Indians would simply cut through it.[90] Hostile forces actually tried to burn down the part that was completed, and one might assume that this propelled the colonists to work with more diligence.

Even with unfinished defenses, Connecticut towns were more defensible than they had been before the war, complete with the European design elements of geometric patterns, flankers, and ditches. By the end of the war, the forts at Saybrook, Hartford, New Haven, Stonington, Windsor, and Stratford had extensive works similar to, though smaller than, European artillery fortresses, while Wethersfield, Milford, Farmington, Simsbury, Fairfield, and other towns erected palisades to some degree of completion.[91] The inhabitants of Fairfield "strongly fortified" their town, having previously erected a "fence" (meaning palisades) against the Dutch, and probably reconstituted this trace in 1675–76.[92] Still other towns relied on fortified garrison houses, including Haddam, New London, Norwich, Rye, and Wallingford. At the latter, the Reverend Street's house was a garrison and Nathaniel Merriman's barn was chosen as another with flankers.[93]

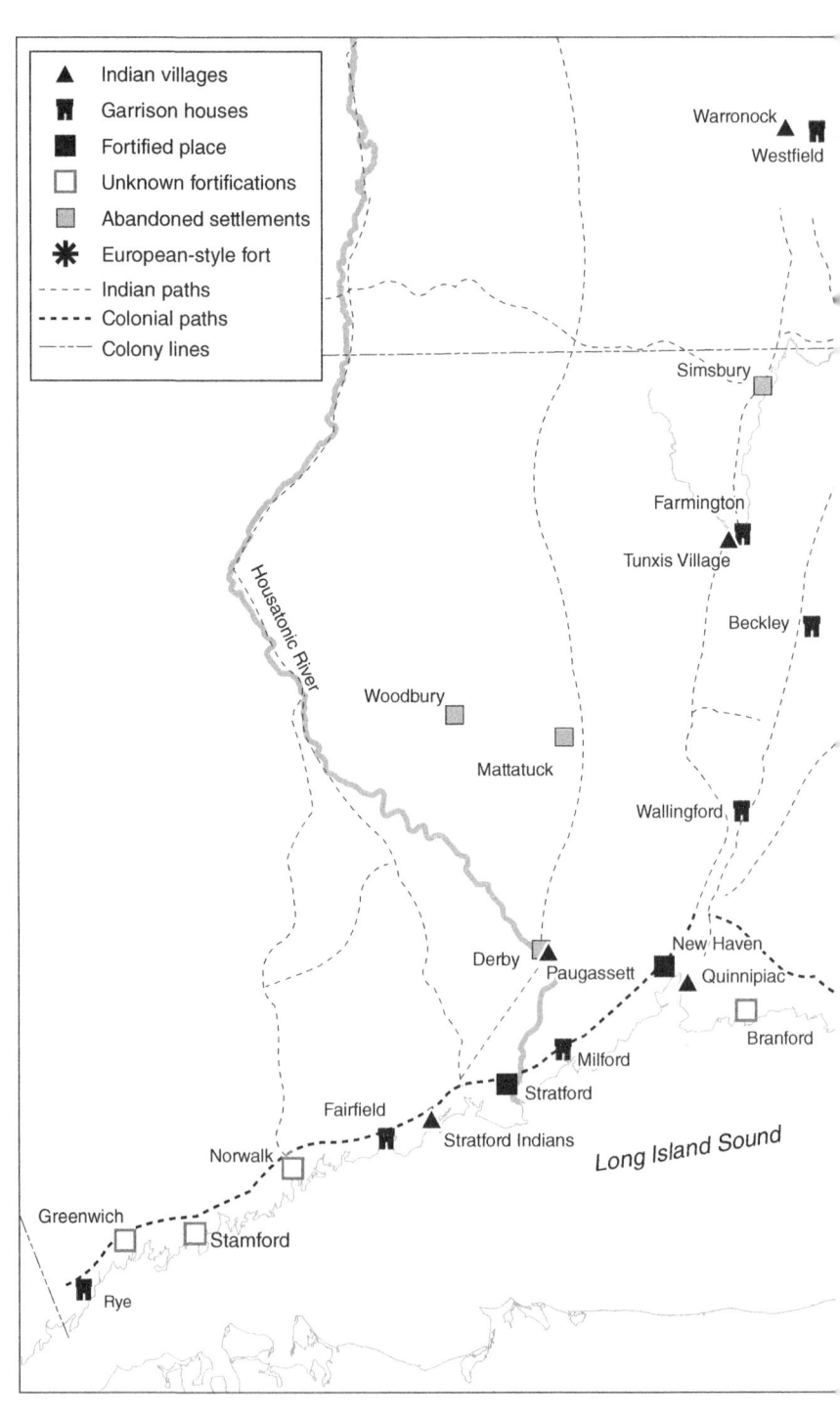

Connecticut transition to fortifications from garrison defense.
Map by Bill Keegan. © 2014, University of Oklahoma Press.

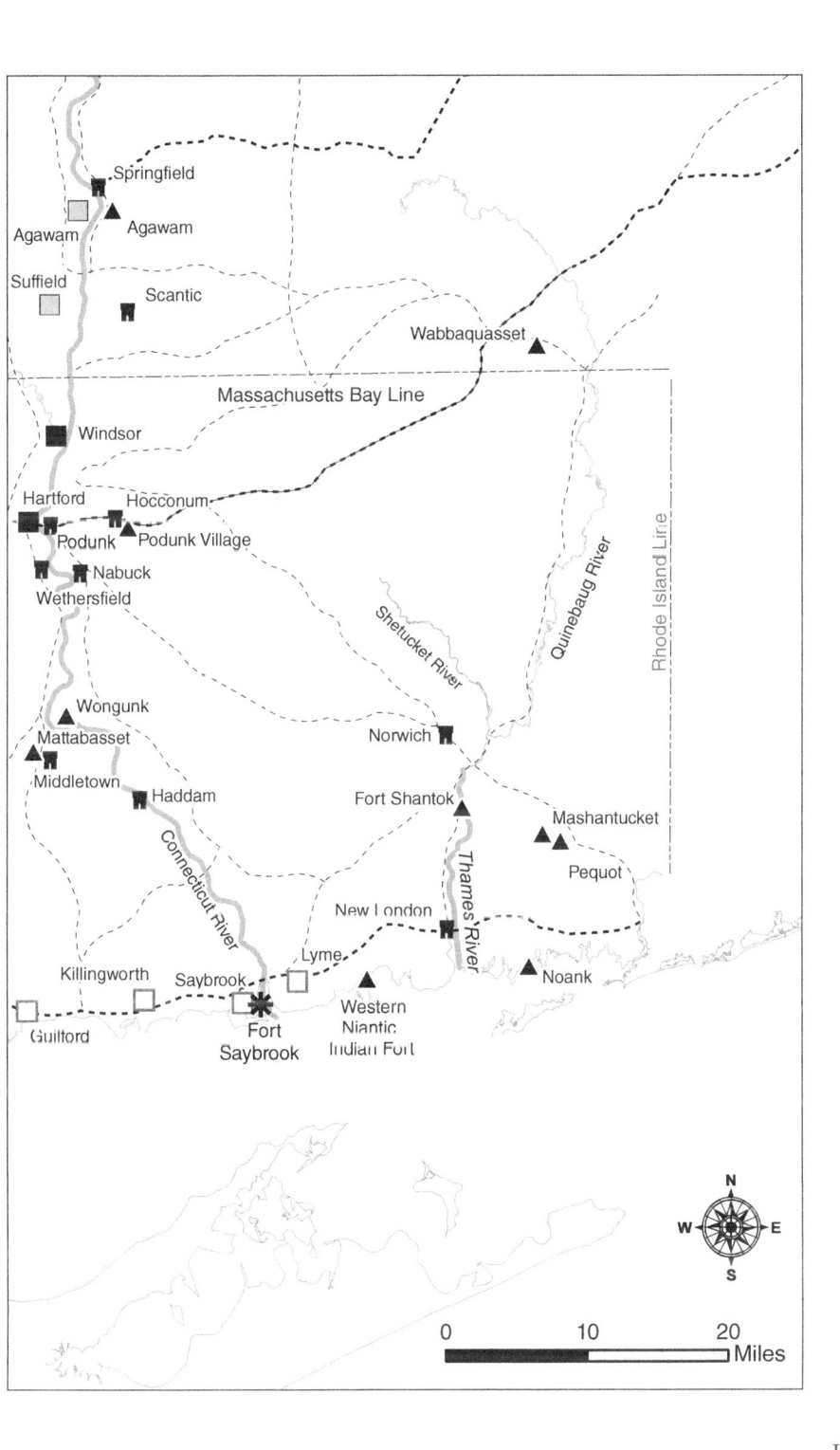

Reverend Street Garrison House, 2013. Courtesy Tom Trask and James Warren.

In the cases of New London and Norwich, multiple garrison houses created interlocking fields of fire, each in supporting positions around the outer perimeter of the towns.[94] Many settlements that still relied on garrison-house defense alone, however, risked the destruction of property that occurred in other colonies with similar defenses. Given its relatively small population, residents had heavily fortified Connecticut by mid-conflict. By 1676, it had become virtually an armed camp, and the number of fortifications per density of population was comparable to some areas of Europe. This system assisted in deterring major attacks during the hostile coalition's winter–spring offensive.

Residents abandoned indefensible frontier settlements, sometimes with the consent of Connecticut's leadership as in the cases of Derby and Simsbury.[95] Settlers also abandoned Woodbury, Mattatuck (later Waterbury), and perhaps other outlying settlements during the war.[96] Abandoning towns had a net-positive defensive effect, similar to fortifying them. Not only did this practice protect lives and removable property, but it also allowed authorities to concentrate limited resources on towns that were more defensible. It also enhanced the contiguous pattern of the colony's settlements, which was a major security problem elsewhere in New England. But these actions essentially meant that Connecticut's western and northwestern frontier had been abandoned. Perhaps in some small measure this was a victory for the hostile coalition, but the military operational effect was to increase the colony's overall security.

Though the other New England colonies relied more on garrison-house defense than Connecticut, in scattered instances they also employed robust elements of European methods. The main work at Plymouth and the Castle in Boston Harbor retained elements of European-artillery fortresses, while scattered references suggest that there were other advanced constructions. One Captain Henchman wrote to Governor Leverett discussing the completion of a southeast flanker of the fort at Pocasset Swamp.[97] Beyond Connecticut, however, advanced fortifications were an exception. Rhode Island employed garrison-house defenses, and many of its residents subsequently evacuated to Newport on Aquidneck Island.[98] The Rhode Island War Council's order to abandon Warwick and Providence and remove to Newport during the spring offensive epitomized the ineffective nature of the garrison-style defense.[99]

Connecticut's policy toward the local Indians augmented its physical defenses by preventing intelligence on structural weak points and operational patterns from falling into enemy hands. The colony utilized European methods observed directly in England or communicated across the Atlantic as well as taken from available military texts. The longevity of New England's first generation ensured that Connecticut's experience in the early Pequot War influenced its security posture, and the colony's war leaders also relied on their experiences against the Dutch and during the English Civil Wars. These factors provided the basis for a defensive triumph, yet it took sound managing of events and intelligence, along with an active defense, to translate these underlying factors into victory.

CHAPTER 5

THE DEFENSE OF CONNECTICUT

Connecticut's deliberately moderate policy toward the local Indians and construction of adequate defenses based on the European model were inseparable—one was ineffective without the other. The colony enacted a number of self-defense measures and incrementally increased them as it became apparent that King Philip's rising would spread from a local conflict to a New England–wide war. One of the first measures that the Connecticut General Court took was to ensure proper wartime leadership with the creation of the War Council, which first convened on 14 July 1675.[1] Facing the dual hostile threats of Philip and New York governor Andros, the court granted the council wide powers, preauthorizing all of its decisions that were consistent with the colony's charter. The council originally consisted of the governor, deputy governor, "assistants" (other colony leaders), Captains Benjamin Newbery and Samuel Wells, Mr. John Wadsworth, and Mr. Richard Lords, although the court later added additional members. The group needed a quorum of at least five members to vote, with the governor or deputy governor always present to convene it.[2] The War Council's ability to make effective and timely decisions was impressive especially given the slow movement of information by messenger.

The council reflected the gender norms of the rigidly patriarchal and hierarchal Puritan society of the seventeenth century. Puritan New England's concept of masculinity mirrored to a large degree the societal customs of midcentury England. To be truly a man meant embodying upright Puritan-Protestant Christianity and engaging in military activities for the defense of his community as his station in life required. Leaders bore the heavier responsibility of appearing beyond reproach in all manner of social interactions.[3] A lack of surviving sources detailing the War Council members precludes a closer examination of gender norms and its effect on their decision making. Massachusetts Bay's and Plymouth's leadership would have operated within a similar masculine framework, though some differences were likely, given Connecticut's relatively humane policy concerning Indians during 1675–76.

The other New England colonies also established war councils soon after the outbreak of hostilities. These were of like composition as Connecticut's, though Plymouth allowed more members than its Puritan sister colonies until streamlining its body late in the war.[4] New York, serving as an interesting counterpoint to New England, also prepared for the violence to spill over its borders. Governor Andros's central management of the royal colony was the major difference between its war council and those to the east. Andros appointed New York's council, and the eldest member became the acting governor and president of council in the governor's absence; this body also served as the colony's highest appellate court and cabinet, after 1691 becoming a legislative body "concurrent with the General Assembly."[5] Thus, New York's polity was structured for less internal dissent.

While Andros was a field-grade officer and veteran of Continental conflicts, the New England colonies lacked strategic and active military experience at the deliberative body level, those responsible for implementing military policy and command and control. The United Colonies attempted to coordinate policy and strategy (though without Rhode Island's input). Each colony also maintained its own general court and war council, which caused friction with the regional authority when attempting to coordinate New England–wide policy and strategy. The United Colonies' deliberative body disagreed on many issues, such as the invasion of Narragansett territory, to which Connecticut governor Winthrop objected. Connecticut and Massachusetts Bay were also at odds over campaign objectives in the upper Connecticut River valley. This episode did not make for smooth operations there or lead to sound relations between the colonies.[6]

Where the United Colonies struggled to manage conflict, Governor Andros was a deliberative body of one, having personally appointed councilors who would support his decisions when he took to the field. This was the situation early in the conflict when he attempted to make good the Duke of York's charter for the royal colony by invading Connecticut, and after failing at this, coordinating for supplies to be sent to staunch royalists in New London, Connecticut, Rhode Island, Martha's Vineyard, and Nantucket (the islands were then New York territory). The governor then met with Indian leaders across Long Island to ensure their loyalty and later visited Albany to gain support of the Iroquois by establishing the Covenant Chain. This agreement would greatly influence the course of Indian-colonial relations on the Eastern Seaboard and in the Ohio Country for more than a century, and hence the development of North America. During Andros's absence, the New York War Council did his bidding.[7]

In addition to the leadership styles and experiences of individual councilmen, differences such as population density, settlement patterns, and geography also affected each colony's war effort and its council's ability to manage the conflict. These factors combined to create a subculture for each war council that transcended the macro-Puritan culture of 1675.[8] Connecticut's War Council maintained the easier task of managing the war effort than Massachusetts Bay's executive body because of advantageous physical conditions. The hostile coalition also did not target Connecticut early in the war, which allowed the colony's leaders more time to implement policies to bolster security. With its population settled more densely along major rivers and Long Island Sound, Connecticut more readily established advanced defenses. The colony also abandoned outlying settlements vulnerable to possible coalition raids. Connecticut's major offensive focus was along the upper Connecticut valley until the entry of the Narragansetts into the war. Its primary line of communication with these Massachusetts Bay towns thus corresponded to the valley's north–south orientation, facilitating rapid communication on or along the river. Rivers served as the superhighways of the era, and the proximity to the Connecticut aided the speed of transmitting and receiving orders from the colony's headquarters at Hartford. This increased the War Council's ability to manage affairs and stay abreast of the military situation. As is often the case with terrain features, however, the Connecticut River valley also served as an invasion route for the hostile groups.

New York contained advantageous terrain for managing a conflict, such as the waterways of Long Island Sound, the East River, and the Hudson River valley. Governor Andros used these to further his diplomatic efforts and to influence the crisis in an advantageous way for his colony, keeping it out of the war. Besides Connecticut, the other New England colonies lacked such a neat strategic corridor. Massachusetts Bay's council had to administer far-flung settlements along the upper Connecticut and elsewhere that were not geographically contiguous with the main population centers that arced around Boston. It also lacked a solid east–west line of communication centered on a terrain feature that would allow for effective management of its war efforts in the western theater in the same fashion that the Connecticut River valley allowed Connecticut to command and control its seat of the conflict to the north. With estimates placing Massachusetts Bay Colony at about three times the size of Connecticut's population of nearly 12,000 people, managing the latter was a simpler task for councils of roughly equivalent size.

The colonies faced the endemic seventeenth-century problems of poor communications and lack of infrastructure, which hampered conflict management. Although a lack of a "military orders process" for the time period would have rendered a larger council less effective than in modern times, simply having more assistants to communicate with field leaders and transmit orders would have aided in this mission. Massachusetts Bay's War Council had the most difficult task of any in New England, for it was roughly the same size as its counterparts yet had to manage and lead a much larger population with a disparate settlement pattern and a lack of advantageous terrain. The council was thus unable to manage its war effort effectively. In turn, this burdened Massachusetts field commanders with higher-level decision making, requiring experienced subordinates who could have translated the unclear or absent intent of the council in Boston into their campaign and battlefield decisions. Massachusetts lacked such seasoned field officers, especially after the hostile coalition killed Captains Beers and Lathrop, two of the colony's experienced "Indian fighters," two months into the war.

How leaders, particularly on the war councils, defined their roles in conflict management also affected performance. Plymouth's council, for instance, was loath to direct its overall war effort and therefore authorized town councils to act as they deemed fit.[9] Defining its conflict-management duty in a more decentralized fashion, the war council concerned itself only with greater Indian policy and military-personnel issues.[10] Plymouth's self-imposed command-and-control restriction created a campaign guidance vacuum for its field commanders. It was not until late in the conflict, on 7 June 1676, after the hostile coalition already had devastated the colony, that the government sought to streamline its procedures by authorizing a small group of leaders to make emergency decisions for the colony without deliberation by the full assembly.[11] Large decision-making bodies are useful for representative politics but can act as a retardant in military matters that demand decisive action. Plymouth's relative lack of battlefield success reflected, in part, this failure at the highest levels of command.

Connecticut utilized a smaller war council than Plymouth from the beginning of the war, leading to a more cogent and efficient command process. The council's ability to make effective and timely decisions, even with terrain advantages, was impressive given the slow communications of the era. It also made more invasive lower-level decisions, for instance, detailing even which roads Connecticut troops would patrol and where many of the field forces would concentrate their efforts.[12] In the spring of 1676, Governor Leete contacted Major Talcott to "offer Two things to your consideration first that you march wth your Forces Intire thorow the country to Hadly takeing Nipschosuck in your way or to com from Nipschosuck at the wabaquassuck country hither & so up the country or els thar your selfe wth about Two Hundred of our English & one Hundred of the most trusting Indians March up hither & leave Capt Denison wth th rest of the English & Indians to doe what they [document ripped] able In those parts."[13] Certainly, more experienced leadership would have chafed under such micromanagement, but Majors Treat and Talcott both appear to have lacked combat experience, though both were savvy military administrators and politicians. Political acumen and military organization cannot be underestimated in New England militia culture, in which members of the trainbands (militia) had a voice in unit affairs. Both leaders tolerated the War Council's meddling, tacitly acknowledging their lack of campaign-level military experience. Whereas Massachusetts Bay and Plymouth delegated responsibility to inexperienced field officers (in the latter case even very inexperienced town committees), contributing to their forces' defeat in the field, the Connecticut War Council attempted to overcome its higher commanders' lack of operational experience by issuing detailed directives. The lack of campaign-level field leaders across the colonies should not be confused with Connecticut's experienced junior field commanders, who performed well at the tactical level, managing those issues directly related to combat. Connecticut also had considerably fewer forces in the field, rarely over one hundred men at any one time, while Massachusetts had well over that number operating across its more geographically expansive colony.[14] At the outset of the conflict in late June 1675, Massachusetts already had three hundred infantry and eighty cavalry in action.[15]

Connecticut leaders also had experience from managing the earlier Pequot War. Many junior participants of that conflict survived as town leaders during the Great Narragansett War. Although this did not necessarily translate into experience in the field, it did in such ways as generally dealing with Indian conflict. This focused the War Council's tasks on important actions like maintaining friendly relations with local Indians that furthered the colony's war effort.

Connecticut's General Court prior to the formation of the War Council began managing the conflict at the onset of hostilities by sending military reinforcements to the border nearest the fighting; this force consisted of thirty dragoons and ten "troopers."[16] In addition to bolstering the local militia in southeastern Connecticut, the court warned other towns to prepare for their own defense. It repositioned troops in the southern coastal settlements, where suspicious Indians were thought to be marauding.[17] On 16 July 1675 Uncas sent a warning to colonial leaders that the Narragansetts would soon join with Philip.[18] The War Council, then in session, reacted by dispatching Captain Bull to "secure the borders" along the southeastern frontier. After the threat of a Narragansett uprising dissipated for the time being, the council disbanded these forces. Unsurprisingly, given Connecticut's history of cooperation with the Mohegans, the council directed Bull to enlist that group to support his mission.[19]

In defensive operations the allied Indians were effective in disrupting hostile forces within the colony. "Likewise the Pequods and Mohegins . . . proved a good Guard to New London, Norwich, and the River's Mouth," related a contemporary writer of the conflict.[20] The Mohegans and Pequots contributed their unique tactical skills to the active defense of Connecticut. An enemy can thwart the best-laid defensive plans that lack an active presence to maintain the initiative and keep the adversary off balance, especially one that utilizes irregular tactics and can strike virtually anywhere at any moment. The mainstay of the Connecticut war effort in this regard was the alliance with the Mohegans and Pequots, who maintained the best military skills of any of the Indians in southern New England (further discussed in chapter 6). The colony's friendly Natives conducted reconnaissance and search-and-attack missions. These forces operated in much the same way as colonial scouts during later colonial wars with the French and their Indian allies:

"defensive scouts operated 'on the backs of the towns'; . . . first, they had to look for signs of enemy raiding parties, usually revealed by their tracks or campsites, and warn the towns; second, they protected the inhabitants while they performed their labors; third, they pursued the enemy after they had struck; and finally, they ambushed known trails and fords used by enemy raiding parties and Indian fishing sites."[21] Allied Indians scouted the passes through difficult terrain where the hostile groups infiltrated the colony, such as gaps through ridges and the fords across the numerous rivers and creeks. These warriors would have also reconnoitered places that offered enemy bands protection from the elements, such as the leeward side of hills and ridges.

Attacking forces would consolidate for an assault near their objective, and the allied Indians would have attempted to prevent this from happening or at least alert the colonists to the enemy's presence. The Mohegans, Pequots, and Western Niantics conducted these active-defensive operations in the same ways that they conducted offensive operations in Narragansett country and in western Massachusetts. They proved adept at locating enemy war parties on the enemy's own lands, which was partially a result of women, children, and the elderly impeding the mobility of larger elements. Locating small bands of warriors unimpeded by noncombatants, however, proved more difficult, and such groups ranged Connecticut throughout the war.

By 5 August an emergency meeting of the council—it was annotated that they met close to one o'clock in the early morning—determined to put the colony on full alert by calling up significant numbers of dragoons in all of the counties.[22] Intelligence from Major Pynchon at Springfield, Massachusetts, precipitated this decision. The conflict had spread to the western Massachusetts Bay settlements, some of which bordered Connecticut. These new dragoon forces could be termed "hourmen," having been ordered to muster in an hour's time after an alarm (as opposed to the minutes required of the minutemen of Revolutionary War lore). These troops were used both for the active defense of the colony and for offensive operations in the other colonies. The soldiers from this call up remained on duty through the Great Swamp Fight, and the council utilized various elements of this force throughout the war.

The War Council, in addition to raising troops, determined to increase the security of Connecticut's towns and highways as it became apparent that enemy forces were within the colony itself. There was by that time clear-cut intelligence of the enemy's presence, more so even than the initial warnings about local Indians acting suspiciously in early July and the warning by Uncas that the Narragansetts near the Hockanum River should not be trusted.[23] Fearful of Philip's rumored advance on Norwich, the council on 24 August commissioned sachem Joshua (Attawanhood) of the Western Niantics to intercept them.[24] Reacting to hostile activity, it later ordered Major Treat back to Connecticut, when on 31 August 1675 a hostile band fired at Christover Crow between Simsbury and Hartford and the following day at John Coalt near the "North meadow" of Hartford.[25] The council commanded that his dragoons reconnoiter along both sides of the river and from Windsor to Hartford.[26] With Treat's recall, the hostile coalition was thus able to achieve temporary success without directly attacking Connecticut's settlements, isolating the Massachusetts towns on the Connecticut River through the execution of feints and demonstrations in the rear of Connecticut forces deployed upriver.[27] Although this precipitated a temporary withdrawal of forces, it remained indecisive, for the colony's troops always returned to offensive operations. Ultimately, this was the coalition's dilemma: it needed to undermine Connecticut's offensive operations by attacking the colony itself, but Connecticut's defenses proved too strong by the late winter of 1676, when the coalition was at its strongest inside the colony.

On the first of September, the War Council ordered each plantation to maintain a night watch in addition to the quarter of each town's militia that stood guard during the day. The council then dictated that parties working in the fields must consist of at least six armed men and stipulated that colonists should conserve their ammunition for combat.[28] With hostilities increasing upriver in Massachusetts Bay, on 4 September the council arranged a system of guarding the main roads in Hartford County, where each major settlement sent out a two-man patrol on reconnaissance along major routes of travel to the next major settlement. The towns would alternate each day, hence the patrols were sent out from opposite directions in turn: "[t]hese men to be taken out of the guard of each towne, and to be upon theire worke by sun an hower high in each day."[29]

After the coalition's near destruction of Springfield, the council on 5 October ordered that each town designate safe areas for its women and children and to identify sufficiently fortified garrison houses. At the same meeting members ordered the inhabitants of central and northern Hartford County to deposit their maize east of the Connecticut River.[30] Four days later residents sighted hostile Indians on that side of the river, but it is unclear if the colonists had already transported their grain as directed. The council again employed allied Indians in a defensive role, sending Joshua and Tomsquash "beyond the mountaines" into eastern Connecticut to search for the "strange" Indians who had been observed there.[31] On 11 October it ordered "Flankers placed in or neer the outside houses of the towne, so as they might be able to command from Flanker to Flanker round the towne."[32] Here, the War Council directed the colonists to utilize their European militarily strengths.

By early November 1675, with hostile forces ranging in all of the New England colonies, Connecticut directed the establishment or improvement of fortifications. The War Council thus increased the defense of the colony based on its perception of the enemy threat. Although incomplete in some instances, elements of European-style fortifications were the end result of this incremental increase once it became clear that hostile forces were able to devastate colonies utilizing only a garrison defense. When the Narragansetts entered the conflict, the threat became greater to Connecticut. Indeed, the colony began to transition from garrison houses to a system of fortifications during November while planning for the preemptive attack on Great Swamp. The colony's white population immediately following the conflict (October 1676) only numbered 2,303 landowning men.[33] Probably fewer than 2,000 additional males were capable of bearing arms in an emergency, essentially the old, the young, and the marginally incapacitated. In a crisis indentured servants and slaves could be armed. The high proportion of fortifications to population made the colony a more difficult target for the coalition.

Connecticut's defensive success can be partly attributed to the deterrence factor of their stout fortifications since the Indians' "cutting off way of war" did not normally include assaulting positions that would cause high casualties and the coalition lacked artillery. Wayne Lee recounts the case of a Creek war party lurking outside of a fortified Cherokee town waiting for an opportunity to attack, but ultimately the sound defenses deterred it.[34] As in this instance, war parties usually opted for softer targets or situations that they could exploit to their advantage. This was the case in Connecticut, with enemy bands "skulking" around the colony's towns, committing random acts of violence on the periphery but never conducting a major attack on a population center. Such an assault would have been too costly for the coalition without local intelligence or a colonial mishap that would have tipped the odds in their favor.

The pace of construction on the fortifications was not what the War Council had anticipated. By 22 November 1675 the council authorized the creation of town fortification committees to impress citizens, if volunteers were not forthcoming, along with beasts of burden.[35] This failure to supervise the construction of fortifications until three months after the coalition was active on the northern frontier and harassing Connecticut's settlements can be attributed to the fact that the English were farmers first, soldiers second. During these months, it was harvest season in southern New England, and the bounty was needed to maintain the colony during the long winter months ahead as well as to supply the field forces during the projected winter campaign. Viewed from this perspective, the council's priorities seem reasonable. The council can also be credited with not overreacting to the threat, and it had done something, namely ensuring that the residents employed a garrison defense throughout the colony.

When the threat to the colony increased as spring approached, Governor Andros sent intelligence to Connecticut obtained from two freed English captives "affirm[ing] that the said North Indians, at the said Rendezvous, in a vapouring Manner, declared, that their Intent was, first to destroy Connecticut this Spring."[36] At this time authorities also received intelligence that the coalition was planning to strike the colony once the rebel Indians had broken their winter encampments. After Major Treat led Connecticut forces into Narragansett country as part of the joint effort to subdue that hostile group, the War Council ordered on 28 December 1675 that the inhabitants of Hartford, Wethersfield, and the Windsor plantations east of the Connecticut River repair to their garrison houses, take in their provisions, maintain a vigorous guard, and scout the nearby woods.[37] As part of a "vigorous" guard, the colonists utilized natural terrain features such as hilltops to augment town watches and to pass messages between settlements. Towns named local hilltops and ridges after these guard posts, such as Guard Hill and Watchhouse Hill in Stratford and Sentry Hill in Norwich.[38] Lamentation Mountain, at the time on the Wallingford town boundary but now in present-day Berlin, also served as a lookout near the Belcher garrison house, although it was unclear if this post existed during the war.[39] Unlike the forested state of Connecticut's rural areas today, colonists deforested key terrain surrounding the towns for grazing and firewood, which also allowed the guard posts on the high ground to keep watch on the surrounding countryside.

The War Council's advice to repair to garrison houses proved prescient when, at the end of January 1676, Major Palmes relayed intelligence that hostile forces had split into smaller groups and were lying in wait "downwards" from Nipmuck country.[40] The council ordered friendly Indians, along with two Englishmen, to scout the eastern side of the Connecticut River from Hartford to Springfield on 10 February.[41] This was the council's reaction to continued intelligence that hostile forces would attempt large-scale attacks on Connecticut as well as to the recent killing of the two men on the Shetucket. A few days after Cohas's band badly wounded William Hill on 18 February at Hoccanum, the council ordered the inhabitants on the east side of the Connecticut into their garrison houses, each with a guard of at least six men.[42] A short time later an unknown number of friendly Indians and one hundred colonial soldiers were enlisted to "clear" the eastern side of the river.[43]

Reacting to additional threats, especially against Hartford, the council ordered that town, New Haven, and other large towns "to compleat and lyne their stockades and flanckers with a ditch and brast worke."[44] The colony was now facing the gravest danger to its existence since the Pequot War and reacted by erecting more-formidable defenses boasting elements of European fortresses. On 16 March the council ordered towns to increase the number of night-watch guards around daybreak and to scout the nearby woods on horseback. It also advised Mr. Fitch to convince the Mohegans and Pequots to "draw off as many of the enemie as may be" near Norwich.[45] Four days after the burning of Simsbury in late March, the council took the extraordinary step of disbanding some of its forces in the face of this extreme danger, sending New Haven and Fairfield County soldiers back to their towns.[46] These troops also conducted reconnaissance along their route of march back to their respective communities. The council thus opted for a defense of fortifications at this time instead of maintaining a large standing army to systematically hunt down the enemy war parties. After the burning of Simsbury, the board ordered Norwich leaders to "endeauour to send out the Mowheags and Pequots in a sculking manner to suppress the enemie."[47] By using the term "skulking," the council believed that the allied Indians would be able to defeat the enemy warriors operating in Connecticut with their own tactics.

The absence of recorded entries in the War Council's journal for almost two months confirms that the significant threat during the early spring dissipated soon after the killing of Canonchet in early April and dropped off almost entirely by late summer. In June the council advised the training of men and boys in the handling of firearms, including boys under the age of sixteen. This expanded the pool of potential soldiers, considering that Connecticut forces were operating throughout western Massachusetts and Narragansett and Nipmuck lands. The council also advised that the training consist of marksmanship.[48] This was an important change from standard English tactical training. Through the American Revolutionary War, British and colonial forces did not have a command for "take aim," instead relying on "level."[49] In this instance, the New England colonists adapted to their new military environment, particularly one in which opponents rarely faced each other in organized ranks; without taking aim, it would have been difficult for anyone to draw a target on a hostile Indian. These were the final entries concerning the defense of Connecticut. On 19 August 1676 Hartford disbanded its forces altogether after it became apparent that the colonies had largely defeated the hostile confederacy.[50] Combined allied Indian and colonial forces continued, however, to carry out mopping-up operations.[51]

Demonstrating ingenuity and adaptation, the Indians also constructed European-style fortifications. The Narragansett defenses at Great Swamp had characteristics of European design. This elaborate fort, deep in the heart of a swamp outside of what is now West Kingston, Rhode Island, was equipped with a flanker and a blockhouse.[52] William Hubbard describes the design as "a Kind of Blockhouse right over against the said Tree, from whence they sorely galled our Men that first entred . . . [the colonial soldiers] presently beat the Enemy out of a Flanker on the left Hand."[53] Another contemporary account relates that "the Indians had built a Kind of Fort, being Palisado'd round, and within that a Clay Wall."[54] The clay wall was either a supporting structure for the palisades or an inner defensive structure common in European fortifications at the time. The fort was so well designed that a combined army sustained the worst colonial casualties of the war in taking the position.[55] Only after repeated sallies across a fallen piece of timber at an unfinished portion of the works were the colonists able to gain entry. They had been fortunate during the battle, given the advanced state of the Narragansett defenses. A renegade who had deserted his comrades guided the English army to the Great Swamp.[56] The swamp was also frozen over, allowing the colonists to maneuver, where they normally would have been channeled onto a narrow trail.[57] In addition, the portion of the fortification that they happened upon was unfinished.[58] Even with good fortune, the colonial army achieved only a pyrrhic victory at Great Swamp because the Narragansetts had employed modern fortification techniques.

The Narragansetts also appeared to utilize a European-style fortification known as "The Queen's Fort," named for Sunk Squaw (Quaiapen). This fort was so well hidden in the remote wilderness that the complete works were not completely discovered until sometime after the war. Its exact specifications remain unknown, and the debate surrounding its purpose continues.[59] Nineteenth-century writers, however, concluded: "The builders taking advantage of huge bowlders, laid rough stone walls between them, making a continuous line. 'There is a round bastion or half moon on the northeast corner of the fort, and a salient or V-shaped point, or flanker, on the west side.'"[60] The Narragansetts here briefly fired on colonial forces advancing to Great Swamp.[61]

A firsthand account details how after Great Swamp the Narragansetts regrouped "twenty Miles farther into the Country, to some Rocks where we could not get at them without much Danger," although the English army eventually "beat the Indians from the foresaid rocks" some weeks later.[62] This was the Queen's Fort, which in fact was approximately fifteen miles from Great Swamp using straight-line distance.[63] In the early colonial era, colonists measured distances by the windy trails without reliable maps, accounting here for the difference in distance.

A third European-style Indian fortress existed in Narragansett country during the war, only seven miles from Great Swamp in what is now Charlestown.[64] When compared to the other two strongholds, the design of this fortress was the most obviously geometric in construction, and mystery has shrouded its origins and utility during the Great Narragansett War.[65] Recent archaeology, however, indicates that the Eastern Niantics constructed the fort and had occupied the site precontact. Archeologists view the structure as less military in nature and more as a means to control the wampum trade and house wampum and other goods.[66] This seems at odds, however, with their own findings that demonstrate that the defensive characteristics of the site increased during the conflicts of the seventeenth century.[67] It is likely that the Charlestown fort was part of an earlier chain of fortresses meant to protect both the Narragansetts and the Eastern Niantics from attack, though protecting wampum and other goods certainly would have played a role in their considerations. Generally, historians have considered the site to be Ninigret's main Eastern Niantic fort at the time and was supposedly where Captain John Mason, Jr., confirmed the sachem's neutrality during the Great Narragansett War.[68] The colonists granted approval for Ninigret's men to bury the dead the day after the attack on Great Swamp, indicating that the Eastern Niantics were located in force in the area and may have come from here.[69] Although the Narragansetts did not control this fort, the Eastern Niantics have often been considered part of that group and in any case were closely related. Ninigret exercised power over certain elements of the Narragansetts during the interwar years, further clouding the issue.

Thus, the Narragansetts fortified their villages earlier than Connecticut transitioned from garrison to full-scale fortification defense and possessed more-advanced defenses than nearby Rhode Island settlements employed throughout the entire war. In proportion to its population and the size of its territory, the Narragansetts employed a defense in depth not dissimilar to many European states of the time period. Other Indian defensive systems indicate that this was not unprecedented in the New World. Lee's description of the Tuscaroras' and Cherokees' use of fortifications, with or without knowledge of European military techniques, was an additional case of Indians utilizing European-like designs: "the Tuscaroras . . . were using bastioned palisades and partially squared walls."[70] When the European threat increased, they increased their use of fortresses, building "generally one per village. . . . Some of these were more sophisticated than others. . . . [A] larger [European] threat would require a more concentrated defense."[71]

The Narragansetts and Tuscaroras thus employed a defense-in-depth method, where there were alternate positions, or forts, to fall back to if an enemy captured one or more of the others. They thus forced invaders to move deeper and deeper into enemy territory, extending supply lines and making them more vulnerable to attack. Similar to some of the Tuscarora fortifications, the fort at Great Swamp was incomplete when the English invaded.[72] Even with incomplete works, the Narragansetts understood how to integrate modern defenses with the local terrain. Since warriors from Queen's Fort fired on the colonial column marching to Great Swamp, the fortification thus commanded the trail. At the Charlestown site, the fortress was strategically situated to command the landing at the harbor.

The fortification at Great Swamp also utilized local terrain inside the dense swamp. One wonders what additional works were never found that were part of the Narragansetts' defensive posture. A contemporary report actually claims that the Indians from Great Swamp sheltered five miles away after the attack before reaching the Queen's Fort.[73] Another claims that "fresh" warriors "out of an adjoining swamp" nearly turned the tide of the battle when they arrived to reinforce Great Swamp.[74] The Narragansetts and Niantics certainly constructed the forts themselves, although it remains unknown if any Europeans assisted them. The Indians of Connecticut also employed fortresses with elements of Western design. The Pequot fort of Mohantic on the Mashantuckett Reservation consisted of such elements, though it was more of an offensive position (as discussed in chapter 6). Although the design of some Indian forts remains uncertain, it is clear that the Natives of southern New England, as elsewhere on the Eastern Seaboard, utilized European-style defenses.

Connecticut's effectiveness in defensive operations allowed the colony to remain free from major attack, as it was not a lack of hostile attention that allowed its residents to escape unscathed. The coalition devastated other New England colonies and conducted major attacks within miles of the Connecticut border. Contemporary commentators willingly attributed some of this defensive success to the allied Indians, though their accomplishments were obscure. Their known achievements outside the colony reflected their martial prowess within: "with their simultaneous objectives of warning, protection, pursuit, and ambush," allied Indians were very useful in the active defense.[75] Active scouting complemented the colony's advanced fortifications.

Unconventional forces, such as those employed by the hostile coalition, normally attack less-well-defended areas to inflict

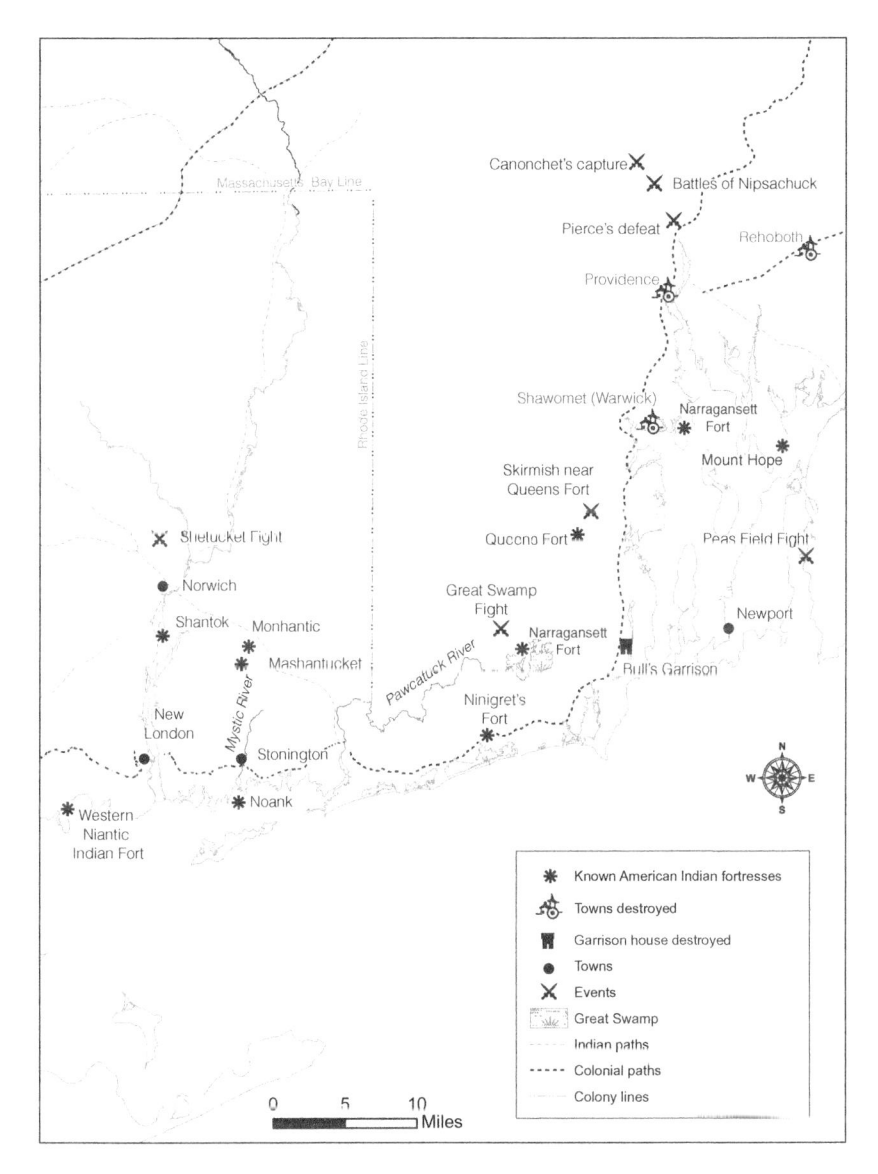

Narragansett country and Indian forts. Map by Bill Keegan.
© 2014, University of Oklahoma Press.

maximum damage without a corresponding risk to their own men. These tactics corresponded with the Indian's "cutting off way of war." Enemy activity never scored major successes because Connecticut became more secured by the time the Narragansetts entered the war (and for the number of other unique characteristics of the colony discussed). Its leaders ordered measures for self-defense after learning of the outbreak of hostilities in Plymouth Colony and took measured steps thereafter to ensure their colony's safety. Once the enemy largely disbanded into smaller war parties after breaking winter quarters, it would have been difficult for them to attack after Connecticut transitioned from a garrison defense to one based on elements of European-style fortifications.

Bands of mainly seven to nine Indians harassed lone settlers or small groups but could not carry out large-scale attacks on well-fortified towns. When larger war parties operated in Connecticut, they also failed to carry out substantial attacks. Combined groups of hundreds of warriors could have devastated Connecticut towns, largely unfortified until mid-autumn 1675, but the coalition lacked the support of local Indians, and focused other areas of New England instead. Had large-scale attacks occurred during the period of June–November 1675, judging from the other colonies' experience, most of Connecticut's garrison strongpoints would have survived, but the hostile forces would have destroyed the nongarrisoned portions of settlements. The threat of major attacks on Connecticut was very real because of its proximity to the Massachusetts Bay towns on the Connecticut River.

The War Council took advantage of Connecticut's more advantageous terrain and settlement pattern, especially compared to Massachusetts's situation, acting decisively from the onset of the conflict. It more actively managed the conflict than Plymouth Colony's council, providing detailed orders to inexperienced commanders. These officers willingly accepted this direction and carried out successful operations. An active defense augmented the colony's advantages of contiguous settlement patterns and the resulting concentrated population. The colony's unique policy of moderation toward local indigenous groups cemented all of these factors into a viable defensive apparatus. Even with a strong system of defense and happenstance that worked in the colony's favor, offensive operations played a decisive role in Connecticut's success. Without complementary defensive and offensive operations, the hostile coalition would have ultimately penetrated the colony's defenses. Connecticut's offensive operations kept the hostile groups off balance and maintained the colony's initiative during the war.

CHAPTER 6

"To Prosecute the Enemie Wth All Vigor"

Connecticut's Offensive Operations

Pushing forward with all speed they came upon two Narragansett sentinels, on the crest of a small hill, who fled in panic down the further slope, past the place where Canonchet and a few of his men, were lying at ease. The English, following close at their heels, were almost upon the camp when another sentinel, rushing among the startled Narragansetts, called out that the English were upon them. . . . Canonchet himself ran swiftly around the back of the hill to get out of sight on the opposite side, but, seeing the Niantics and Mohegans in close pursuit, he threw off his royal belt of wampum. Recognizing immediately from these articles that the fugitive "was the right bird," the friendly Indians and a few of the English followed with renewed zeal. Forced by his pursuers toward the river, through which his only way to safety lay, he rushed into the stream, but his foot slipped, and falling heavily into the water, he wet the priming of his gun. His pursuers were upon him before he could recover himself.

Connecticut's victory during the Great Narragansett War hinged on the colony's offensive operations against the hostile Indians, such as this raid carried out in early April 1676 against the coalition's primary war leader, Canonchet.[1] The success of Connecticut's field forces proved an effective combination with Connecticut's defensive efforts, and the colony's moderate Indian policy set the stage for both offensive and defensive operations. Connecticut's English-Indian forces remained undefeated in the field and with only about sixty soldiers killed in action or later dying of wounds, suffered far fewer casualties than those of the three other New England colonies.[2]

The other New England colonies also understood the necessity of offensive operations, but they usually failed to locate the enemy and suffered terrible setbacks in the process. This was the case with both Captain Richard Beers's defeat and the battle at Bloody Brook. At the latter battle, Captain Samuel Moseley's company, riding to the sound of the guns, almost was destroyed in turn but for the arrival of Major Treat's mixed Connecticut force. Plymouth Indians aided the colonists at Pierce's Fight, but even their presence did not prevent defeat.[3] At Sudbury the coalition annihilated Captain Samuel Wadsworth's men. During the return march from Turner's Falls in spring 1676, Massachusetts Bay forces were all but wiped out.[4] These failures demonstrate a qualitative difference between Connecticut units and the other New England contingents despite their shared English-Protestant culture and military background.

These defeats shocked New England's colonists because they had perceived themselves for decades as militarily superior to indigenous groups. What went wrong? As discussed in the introduction, almost all historians agree with Patrick Malone's assessment in *The Skulking War of War* that the colonists' martial ineptitude derived from a failure to adopt the Indians' "skulking" tactics until the spring of 1676, at which time the tide turned against the hostile coalition. The vast majority of English soldiers, however, did not adopt skulking, or a "cutting off way of war," a finding at odds also with John Grenier's description of the colonists' developing a "First Way of War" in 1676. This is a particularly American-centric view, as Grenier himself points out, when describing similar British tactics of the mid-eighteenth century. The colonists prior to the Great Narragansett War were also well schooled in the art of extirpative warfare. The English relied on this experience in America when facing a threat similar to that posed by Irish insurgents. Their extirpative warfare, however, differed from the Indian tactics that Grenier attributes to Benjamin Church, and those employed by Connecticut's Captains Denison and Avery.[5] While few colonial-Indian raids devolved into the extermination described by Grenier, most operations were merely meant to disrupt the coalition's operations. Too few colonists beside Church, Denison, and Avery, however, adopted Indian tactics for this explanation to be plausible, and even in their units, the English rarely fought like Indians on the battlefield.

Guy Chet, contrary to other historians, attributes Wadsworth's and Pierce's defeats, and the costly colonial victory at Great Swamp, not on the failure to adopt skulking tactics but on the abandonment of the European-style "tactical defensive."[6] The initial failure of the colonists, however, had less to do with adopting Native tactics or abandoning European methods and more with the lack of competent allied Indian support. For the English to remain on the tactical defensive, the hostile Indians would have had to decide to stand and fight; otherwise they could refuse battle as they often did, when they did not perceive an advantage. Hostile war parties demonstrated a selectivity of targets associated with their "cutting off way of war," choosing to fight pitched battles against Captains Wadsworth and Michael Pierce after identifying that both commands were isolated from friendly units and at a tactical disadvantage in relation to the terrain. In Pierce's Fight, the hostile band led by Canonchet, "above 500 Indians, who in very good Order, attacqued [Pierce's command]. . . . The Indians were as thick as they could stand, thirty deep." Once surrounded, Pierce arranged his men in either a circle or two lines back to back, presumably to maximize volley fire. Another account remarks that the Indians, "upon [Pierce's] Approach . . . drew into Order, and received his Onset with much Difficulty."[7] The Narragansetts, far from skulking, massed their fires against the captain's trapped formation. Pierce had not abandoned a linear European tactical defense but misinterpreted the local terrain. At Sudbury, Wadsworth's men actually kept the enemy at bay with conventional tactics and only broke formation after the Indians set fire to the battlefield. Both colonial defeats resulted from superior Indian tactical performance and the English forces' failure to employ competent allied Indians. Chet also argues that "one has to condemn General Winslow and his officers for criminal optimism" in their decision to abandon the defensive and attack the Narragansetts at Great Swamp with a less than desirable logistics base, potentially outnumbered "deep in enemy territory," and in the dead of winter.[8] Winslow could be praised, however, for maintaining the initiative, utilizing the element of surprise (poor weather can be an advantage as well as a disadvantage), employing intelligence from an Indian informer, and understanding the strategic necessity of employing his combined army before it disintegrated due to infighting.

Michael Howard argues that military historians can make ready judgments because their subject matter often identifies clear-cut winners and losers.[9] When conceiving such a judgment about Connecticut, the colony's numerous battlefield victories and the absence of defeats indicates that its forces performed more effectively than its New England counterparts. Connecticut conducted successful offensive operations primarily because its allied Indians were more numerous and tactically superior to those of the other colonies.[10] Its dragoon-heavy English forces also overcame some of the limitations inherent in the military organizations of not only the other New England colonies but early modern European armies in general. Comparatively, Connecticut employed better-led mobile forces, mustering more volunteers who represented a greater cross section of society.

As a result of these factors, the colony's forces were more combat effective than others in New England, demonstrating that Old World military skills were useful in certain circumstances in the New World. These capabilities were not suitable, however, for bringing the hostile Indian forces to battle. By accomplishing this mission, Connecticut's Indian allies actually rendered useful the Old World military skills of the dragoons, which otherwise would have been incongruous with the American battlefield. Only a small number of mainly Connecticut colonists—Plymouth's Benjamin Church was a rare exception—adopted irregular Indian warfare to a degree of effectiveness, which allowed them to conduct successful raiding in conjunction with indigenous forces. Even then, English troopers in these contingents rarely mimicked their Indian allies. As society and culture influence military systems, such as with European design influencing colonial fortifications, so the Indians derived their fighting ability from their lifestyle of hunting and moving quietly and rapidly through the wilderness. It would have been difficult if not impossible for Englishmen to develop the same skills during the war. The colonists required time to develop "skulking" tactics, and this transition would have been nearly impossible during the fifteen-month period that marked the Great Narragansett War. Anthony Clayton discusses the difficulties inherent with woodland fighting in *Warfare in Woods and Forests*—particularly a lack of visibility for fields of fire and dampness hindering early modern weapons' function—for trained, professional armies, and one can surmise the obstacles for part-timers trying to develop such skills.[11] Even with the success of these joint war parties operating in Indian fashion, the tactical division of labor, in which Indian and colonist both performed tasks that he did best, solidified military cooperation. These factors led to Connecticut's victories in the field and the disruption of the hostile forces' war effort. The moderate treatment of the colony's Native groups also served as the foundation for offensive operations—it otherwise would have been difficult to recruit trustworthy Indian allies. Connecticut maintained the initiative with offensive operations by forcing the coalition to protect its noncombatant population and logistics base.

Conventional military doctrine dictates that wars are not won on the defensive. This held true for Connecticut during the Great Narragansett War. The success of the colony's active defense would not have been enough to keep at bay indefinitely the hostile coalition if not for effective offensive operations. The colonists and their Indian allies never would have defeated the coalition if the latter remained unmolested in their territory. Hostile groups ultimately would have exploited a weak point in Connecticut's defenses in accordance with the Indian's "cutting off way of war." The colony avoided defeat at home and achieved success abroad by attacking the hostile groups in their own country. Connecticut's attacks caused the coalition to react to its operations. Its field forces, ably assisted and in many times led by its Indian allies, disrupted the coalition's operations and forced the confederate peoples to guard against the colony's search-and-destroy missions in order to protect their noncombatant population and logistical base. Stephen Eames, although writing about a later period in colonial history, describes the utility of the kind of offensive operations employed by Connecticut during the period 1675–76 as "threefold: to disrupt the economy of the Indians, to intimidate Indian raiding parties with the presence of provincial soldiers on their invasion routes, and to destroy warriors through ambush and battle."[12]

Historians have omitted or downplayed Connecticut's successes. Harold Selesky contends that "Connecticut soldiers were cautious and unskilled, and were never able to trap the enemy."[13] Even without a culminating victory to end the war, the combined Connecticut-Indian forces did have notable successes. These included rescuing the garrison of Northfield and Moseley's command at Bloody Brook; defending Northampton, Hadley, and Hatfield (operational offensive though tactical defensive); sharing in the pyrrhic victory at Great Swamp; capturing Canonchet; wiping out the Narragansett Quaiapen's band; and defeating the fleeing remnants of the hostile coalition on the Massachusetts stretches of the Housatonic River.[14] Connecticut's soldiers were thus not incompetent, particularly in the more traditional forms of European warfare of garrison defense and assault and when operating with allied Indians. Chroniclers of the conflict and contemporary historians alike, while lamenting English fighting ability, misinterpret the purpose of the New England militias. The only fair measure of a military formation is actual battlefield performance, considering the unit's expected missions and quality of training. Militia units had a limited scope of missions that concentrated on a European foe, failing to anticipate an improvement in Indian tactics since 1637, and thus trained accordingly.

Militiamen prepared to fight like Europeans against an enemy who would accept battle, exchange volley fire, and maneuver in a like manner—in other words, European forces or other colonists. With three Anglo-Dutch wars and hostilities against the Catholic monarchies during the period of Atlantic settlement, the English colonists practiced for battle within the same frame of reference that they had employed in fortification building: against other Europeans in the New World.[15] They forecasted a limited conflict, for the significant logistical problems that would face a European invader, even from a bordering colony, entailed challenges that only the rare commander overcame in America. This was the era that historians have termed "limited war" even in Europe because of the negative effect that Vaubanian fortresses and logistical challenges had on offensive operations. Although it appears that colonial leaders planned to fight limited wars, they may simply have benefited from the formidable geography and lack of infrastructure in the New World. During times of conflict, however, New England's leaders did temporarily increase military readiness. Colonists there found standing armies anathema given recent experience with Cromwell and the New Model Army, and there was the historic English opposition to expensive military apparatuses during peacetime that required higher taxes.

Force projection from across oceans remains problematic even with twenty-first-century technology, let alone for those carrying out such operations with the military capabilities of 1675. Even if the neighboring Dutch in New Amsterdam had invaded Connecticut—the most likely military threat to the colony and the one that its residents feared most prior to the Great Narragansett War—their forces would have had to occupy a harbor or to seize, build, and garrison roads and other strongpoints with a force that Holland would have had to provision from across the Atlantic.[16] The manpower needed to garrison a line of communication from the captured port of New Haven, for example, to the capital of Hartford, and having to fight the Connecticut militia and its Indian allies along the way, simply would not have existed without a sizeable commitment from the Dutch Republic's far-flung empire. The logistics required to feed and clothe men in the field for a prolonged campaign would have been problematic at best. Provisioning the horses that pulled the wagon trains and the siege artillery alone would have been a logistical nightmare. A decade after the Third Anglo-Dutch War, a single horse in William III's army digested eighteen to thirty kilos of fodder *daily* during combat operations in the Netherlands.[17] A similar intake of calories for horses in an invasion of Connecticut would have crippled the effort. During the Great Narragansett War, Captain Appleton twice warned Boston that without provisions for his horses, he would have to suspend field operations because the colonists' harvest of hay had been disrupted by the war.[18] For the Dutch of the mid-seventeenth century, the benefit of defeating, subduing, and occupying a hostile Puritan-English and Indian population, with little tangible political and economic benefit, simply did not justify the cost. In fact, a large-scale European invasion of New England never occurred from any quarter during the seventeenth century.

The training of the New England militia also reflected a striking lack of offensive capability. Trainbands were a self-defense force; during times of crisis, the colonies formed special field units recruited from, and in addition to, the town militias. These forces lacked the numbers and field artillery necessary to reduce Dutch or French strongholds in the New World, and New Englanders had lived with a tenuous peace with local indigenous groups for the vast majority of the seventeenth century. The Puritans and Separatists exhibited a penchant for nonviolent arbitration, submitting competing land claims between English colonies, Indians, and other Europeans to London or establishing local agreements many times acceptable to all parties.[19] In terms of colonial competition, land in the New World was abundant and the population was sparse. When flashpoints occurred, in addition to the issues of legitimacy described above, it was due to local population pressures on traditional Indian or European territory or competition over dwindling economic resources (for example, wampum or fur) that could not readily have been abandoned without real or perceived political, economic, or cultural loss. Weather, terrain, resources, and the lack of infrastructure limited offensive options in the New World, taxing armies with limited manpower.

The reality of "strategic consumption," when disease and combat as well as garrisoning lines of communication literally consumes an attacking force, was at play throughout the military history of colonial America.[20] Often exacerbated by military incompetence, strategic consumption inflicted its campaign-terminating calculus during the wars between England, France, and the Indians on the operations of Fitz-John Winthrop (1690), Francis Nicholson (1709), Edward Braddock (1755), and James Abercromby (1758). Louis-Joseph de Montcalm's successful campaign for Fort William Henry (1757) might have gone further if not for the killing of some of the fort's inhabitants by his Indian allies.[21] Additionally, strategic consumption afflicted the Revolutionary War campaigns of William Howe (1776), John Burgoyne (1777), and Charles Cornwallis (1780–81). The rare successful offensive campaigns of Jeffrey Amherst and James Wolfe (1759) and George Washington and Jean-Baptiste de Rochambeau (1781) depended on significant naval power from Europe as well as unique local circumstances and temporary advantages.[22] In his defense of Quebec and reflecting the belief of other North American military leaders in weather and terrain as defensive "force-multipliers," Montcalm reasoned that his French forces would hold off the British invaders long enough to allow for the Canadian winter to do the rest.[23] If not for Wolfe's daring assault, greatly aided by the Royal Navy and *perfect* weather conditions, New France's best ally—winter—would have carried the day. These *two* successful operations were exceptions to the rule of limited war as most European campaigns failed during this period. Generally, Europeans and North American colonists failed to project sufficient military power to overcome natural conditions in the New World during the seventeenth and eighteenth centuries.

A full century before the British victory in Canada, the New England militia of the mid-1600s needed only to maintain a capability to oppose a threat even less technologically advanced than Wolfe's state-of-the-art armada and well-trained regular infantry. Standing ground and delaying an invader would have been sufficient to allow for casualties, distance, terrain, and weather to terminate the operation. The trainbands did not need to drill extensively to fight European-length conflicts because a war against Westerners— the primary threat identified by the colonists before the Great

Narragansett War—in seventeenth-century New England would have been inherently limited.

This was the actual threat that English colonists faced from the Dutch, when a three-hundred-man contingent of marines sent from New Amsterdam attempted to capture Connecticut's settlements on eastern Long Island in early 1674 during the Third Anglo-Dutch War.[24] Fitz-John Winthrop led the local militia forces in defeating the Dutch in one skirmish, and though undocumented in surviving records, the English seem to have defeated the invaders in others engagements as well.[25] Connecticut's militia had served its purpose in this limited operation, even against regular Dutch soldiers. The threat particularly suited a population of part-time soldiers, lacking the opportunity to train to a higher degree of military proficiency because of the requirements of their primary occupations.

Military unpreparedness, however, to combat a non-European threat was a significant weakness in the New England militia system. This was magnified by an overconfidence about potential Indian conflicts. In some circles the Pequot War reinforced perceptions of English military dominance over the indigenous population. Massachusetts Bay and Plymouth Colonies' limited experience during this conflict led to misconceptions about Indian martial prowess. The Native populations' adoption of the flintlock and its subsequent incorporation into their tactical system took many colonists by surprise in 1675. Viewing history backward, it seems obvious that the Indians would transition to firearms during the interwar years of the mid-seventeenth century, but this was not a certainty. The Choctaws of the American Southeast maintained the bow and arrow and used it with greater effect than those Native groups armed with muskets.[26] At the Battle of Nipsachuck, about a quarter of Philip's warriors still armed themselves with bows and arrows.[27] Without allied Indian support, New Englanders were unprepared to fight an adversary armed with the latest military technology.

The replacement of the matchlock with the flintlock and the gradual disappearance of the pike—without the introduction of the socket bayonet until the turn of the century—left European-style armies in a state of tactical flux during the period 1675–76. Pikes, primarily a defensive weapon, had little utility against an Indian foe who did not field cavalry, and thus the militia did not employ these weapons during the war. The colonists predominantly used swords to close with the hostile Indians. Connecticut's General

Court armed conscripted dragoons with swords to fight the Dutch, along with a belt and muskets, less than two years before the Great Narragansett War.[28] At Turner's Falls the colonists used swords to dispatch Indians hiding in the river bank, while Connecticut ordered every tenth man marching against the Narragansetts at Great Swamp armed with axes instead of swords, indicating most were armed with the latter weapon.[29] Europeans utilized swords in battle, especially with the cavalry arm but also with dismounted infantry. One captain wrote about his experience in the English Civil War at the Battle of Naseby: "The Foot on either side hardly saw each other until they were within Carabine Shot, and so only made one Volley; ours falling in with Sword and butt end of the Musquet did notable Execution, so much as I saw their Colours fall, and their Foot in great Disorder."[30] As in such battles in the mother country, swords played an important role in New England combat as well.

Many European militias and some armies throughout the early modern era were no better trained than New England militias. The poor military readiness in Europe accounted for the multiple reforms of the period, from the Dutch reforms to Cromwell's New Model Army. As one colonist quipped in the American South, a "Planter who keeps his Body fit for service, by Action, and a regular Life, is doubtless a better Soldier, upon Occasion, than a Company of raw Fellows raised in England."[31] This man had a point when considered against the backdrop of the especially limited type of warfare in North America. This argument can only be taken so far, however, for to employ American part-timers during the occasional open-field battle of this era would have led to their destruction.

Although less well trained than some European counterparts, the New England militias could conduct the basic tactics of the time period: volley fire and simple maneuver to a more advantageous position on the battlefield in the face of the enemy. It was not a matter of eschewing European tactics, as Chet would have, or Malone's theory of belated adaptation, rather, the New England militia's lack of early success was a case of the coalition refusing to accept battle on Western terms. The only tactical countermeasure in field operations, barring a mistake on the part of hostile warriors, was to employ competent allied Indians in sufficient numbers in an attempt to force the enemy to battle. This was the very countermeasure that Connecticut employed from the beginning of the Great Narragansett War. The addition of competent Native allies made relevant traditional European tactics in the New World. This in combination with those few colonists who did adopt the "cutting off way of war" led to Connecticut's successful offensive operations.

Mobility also played a critical role in the colony's success. Connecticut soldiers were almost always mounted during field operations, a significant difference between them and other New England soldiers. Connecticut answered a survey of the king's colonies from 1679, noting, "For the present in our last warres with the Indians we found drageones to be most usefull, and therefore Improved about 300 of them in the service to good success."[32] The colony employed smaller numbers in the field than Massachusetts Bay, allowing its force to consist almost entirely of dragoons. At the outset of the conflict, Massachusetts already had three hundred infantry and eighty cavalry deployed into Philip's territory.[33] It went on to raise many more men to defend its far-flung settlements and search for hostile parties. By contrast, enough mounts were available in Connecticut because that colony's campaigning force was relatively small.

The General Court at various times mandated that the dragoons either arm themselves with long arms or return to the dismounted militia companies.[34] This indicated that the colonists considered the dragoons to be a more elite arm of service, holding infantry in comparatively lower esteem. Dragoons were most likely drawn from the middle-class segment of the population. The lower classes would have been less likely to know how to ride horses and, similar to the outcasts of some of Massachusetts Bay's field forces, would have been unable to afford to arm themselves. Kyle Zelner reveals this situation in Massachusetts, where local militia committees drafted men from the lower segments of society, including criminals and drifters. Even those Essex County towns that employed a force more representative of their populations sent their less-desirable members on dangerous field missions outside of the towns, keeping men connected with town leaders safely at home.[35]

Connecticut pressed at least some of its soldiers, including dragoons, but there were many volunteers as well.[36] Volunteers outnumbered pressed troops on some occasions, such as during the raid into Narragansett country that captured Canonchet, and Massachusetts Bay leadership later lauded these men.[37] Standing in stark contrast to the muster roles of the Essex County militia, prominent families in Connecticut came forward for field service. Town leaders Nathaniel

Merriman of Wallingford and John Mason of Norwich lost sons at the Great Swamp Fight, and the son of Stonington's Lieutenant Minor also served in the field.[38] Connecticut authorities, encouraged by the success of these volunteers, urged Massachusetts Bay also to raise volunteers and to offer them plunder as an incentive.[39] Connecticut established more equitable means of reimbursing the service of both pressed troops and volunteers, but the colony's forces originally experienced lax discipline with rivalries over payment and spoils.[40] The volunteers—whether for duty or monetary reward or both—provided the colony with a force that was qualitatively superior to those that mainly employed pressed soldiers.

Drafted Massachusetts soldiers likely served as dismounted infantry without possessing the skills to ride or the means to arm themselves as dragoons or cavalry. That colony lacked the resources to provide mounts for all of its men, even if it wanted to employ a dragoon-heavy force. Zelner makes the case that the low morale of these pressed soldiers led to poor unit performance on the battlefield, and in fact the record of Massachusetts Bay and Plymouth's forces did not improve until later in the war, when both colonies employed more volunteers and allied Indians.[41]

Connecticut's troops appear to have been better motivated and undertook more successful operations, usually in conjunction with drafted soldiers. This point can only be taken so far, however, as Zelner has demonstrated only a correlation between pressed troops and poor battlefield performance. There are many factors in war in addition to motivation that achieve victory, and throughout history units of drafted soldiers and even malcontents have performed admirably. It would also be a mistake to assert that the upper classes of New England or any society would make better soldiers, this too failing a consistent test of history.[42] Connecticut forces performed better than their Massachusetts Bay counterparts because of a combination of factors discussed here, including higher mobility, superior leadership, and most importantly, the employment of more and better allied Indians.

Performing missions without Indians, however, was not beyond the capabilities of Connecticut's troops. Dragoons riding to the relief of Springfield, for instance, did not require an Indian escort; the allied Indians moving on foot did not reach the town until early the following morning.[43] The coalition never ambushed Connecticut forces even on such occasions as this, while hostile groups frequently surprised other New England troops. William Harris of Rhode Island, in the late summer of 1676, detailed: "Recently, however, Connecticut has greatly cleared these coasts of Indians, having this summer slain or captured five hundred Indians, and lately the principal squaw sachem of the Narragansetts."[44] New Englanders did not completely forget the service of these men. Massachusetts Bay governor Thomas Hutchinson observed in the eighteenth century that "the brave action of the Connecticut volunteers have not been enough applauded."[45]

Connecticut envisioned operations differently than Massachusetts Bay and even Plymouth (Church excepting) or Rhode Island, much to the benefit of its field operations. Massachusetts captain Samuel Appleton's feud with Connecticut forces operating on the upper Connecticut River exemplified this operational divergence. When Massachusetts allowed Major Pynchon to resign his post as commander after his great personal loss with the burning of Springfield, it thrust Appleton into an unenviable position. The hostile coalition had reduced colonial holdings in western Massachusetts Bay to the towns of Hadley, Hatfield, Northampton, Westfield, and the remaining buildings of Springfield. This not only disrupted the harvest but also caused overcrowding and food shortages in the remaining towns, which had to provision to some extent nearly one thousand soldiers and allied Indians as well as horses. Major Treat was more experienced than, and outranked, Appleton, though the United Colonies had agreed to a Massachusetts officer as commander in the region. The captain also rightly acknowledged that he was unprepared to perform diplomatic duties with the well-organized and talented Connecticut War Council. Further, the poor line of communication with Boston hampered the transmission of orders and resupply.

Appleton's vision of his mission, under pressure from local settlers, entailed garrisoning the towns by dividing up his roughly five-hundred-man contingent, which Connecticut forces occasionally bolstered to a combined strength of eight hundred colonists (the number of allied Indians varied as described below). He feared that if he sallied out in force against the hostiles, they would march on his rear and destroy the unprotected towns. The Massachusetts Bay War Council tried to ease the captain's anxiety by allowing him to rest his soldiers in the towns when not on field duty, but it also directed him to use local settlers for garrison defense. Appleton never embraced that idea, in actuality, acting contrary to Boston's orders by garrisoning the towns as his primary mission, sallying out only when local intelligence dictated the presence of enemy forces.

Appleton's conception of operations placed him squarely at odds with Treat and Connecticut's council, which favored aggressive field operations, employing the Pequots and Mohegans as scouts for actionable intelligence. The captain, however, sought to integrate the Connecticut troopers in garrison, mainly at Westfield and Springfield, nearer their home colony for resupply, though he also intended to scatter some among the upper towns. Connecticut predictably interpreted the United Colonies orders in a manner conducive to its own operational framework. The colony chided Appleton for his garrison-centric campaign plan, threatening to withdraw its soldiers because they were being utilized in a manner contrary to the United Colonies' orders. Complicating Appleton's negotiating position was that he relied on Connecticut to make up for his shortfall of supplies, among these, a shipment of ammunition from Hartford arriving at the height of fall campaigning in the theater. Acting on intelligence of enemy parties threatening its headquarters at Hartford and later Norwich, the War Council finally withdrew the bulk of Treat's forces. Those remaining, under Captain Nathaniel Seeley, refused to obey Appleton's directives, precipitating a serious crisis in operations. This predicament foreshadowed future friction between Connecticut and the rest of New England for the remainder of the war and with the northern conflict that Massachusetts continued to fight after 1676. This disagreement also presaged the downfall of the dysfunctional United Colonies, which had been formed for the purpose of Puritan collective defense, specifically to deal with a potential war with the Narragansetts, emerging from their conflict with the Mohegans. When viewing events since 1637 through the prism of the Great Narragansett War, the Puritan squabbles over operations come more clearly into focus.

Friction within the Puritan coalition reflected not only differing conceptions of how to campaign against an elusive enemy but also the status of resources and security postures. Connecticut favored aggressive field operations, though in the fall of 1675, this did not lead to victory on the upper Connecticut River. This in part was attributed to the colony's allied Indians operating outside of their normal range between the river and Narragansett Bay. That Connecticut had the option of aggressive action also reflected its luxury of time to prepare for home defense, which Massachusetts Bay did not have. Drawing upon its experience during the Pequot War, the colony established an operational framework with which to fight Indians. And its leaders' were confident in managing military matters, with the recent Dutch threat. The most important martial difference between Connecticut and the other New England colonies that permitted an offensive-minded war plan, however, was the colony's employment of large numbers of competent allied Indians.[46]

Fitz-John Winthrop advised his younger brother, Wait, at the outbreak of the war concerning the use of these allies: "The Pequot & Monhegen Indians may be of very good use if securely managed, & will be useful to send out in partyes or march at a distance from ye body to clere up any suspitious places."[47] By employing these warriors in significant numbers, Connecticut leaders facilitated more-effective operations than their colonial counterparts. Allied Indian forces nullified the coalition's advantage in "suspitious places," difficult terrain, and anywhere the enemy could ambush the less-experienced English: "& if you desire & must speke with the Naroganset sachems, it will, I beleive, be best to appoint them a place in some open ground, to prevent yt treachery & surprise wch they use in dark & mountaynous places, & is always to be avoyded, for ye security of yor men, who may easely be cut off by such disadvantages."[48]

The allied Indians' ability to "clere up any suspitious places" in large part prevented Connecticut forces from suffering a single ambush during the entire conflict. The hostile Indians surprised other colonists even when they employed Native allies, such as at Brookfield and in the defeats of Beers, Thomas Lathrop, and Peirce. Hostile forces ambushed Plymouth's renowned Indian fighter Benjamin Church on two occasions. If not for the fortunate evacuation of his force by a Rhode Island naval patrol during one of those episodes, Church would not have survived to publish his account of the war.[49] While lauding the Mohegans and Pequots' contribution to the war effort, Harris implies that some of the other colonies' "allies" even acted treacherously.[50] The policy of employing Indians in a complementary role to its English forces was a product of both Connecticut's experience during the Pequot War and its leadership's moderate disposition toward the local groups. While many historians have noted the utilization of Mohegans and Pequots from the beginning of the conflict, there has been little examination of how they were employed and why they proved qualitatively superior to Indians of the other colonies.

Although the Pequots and Mohegans shared the same Algonquian culture with the other New England Indians, Connecticut's allies had a reputation for being the fiercest groups east of Mohawk country. Fierceness, however, does not translate into competence on the battlefield. Though morale is a factor in successful operations, the "spirit of the bayonet" has been proven throughout history to be less important than sound tactics and superior leadership. The Pequots and Mohegans appear to have been dominant over other indigenous groups for a long period of time, at least through the Great Narragansett War, surviving attacks by numerically superior hostile coalitions. Miantonomi acknowledged that the Pequots were qualitatively better fighters than his Narragansetts, which an English author of the 1620s attributed to the latter groups' preoccupation with wampum manufacturing at the same time the Pequots dealt in violence.[51] The relative improvement of Narragansett fighting ability against the Mohegans in the decades following 1637 was likely due to the large number of Pequot captives that they incorporated. Another factor that could explain Pequot combat superiority was the group's interaction with the Mohawks.

The Pequots' sphere of influence adjoined that of the Mohawks (also known as the "man-eaters"), which was not the case with the Narragansetts. Pequot territory and the nearby Mohegans virtually formed a barrier, albeit largely uninhabited, between Narragansett country and Mohawk raiding parties. The Pequots' relative proximity to the Mohawks probably coincided with western Connecticut's otherwise inexplicable vacancy. West from the Farmington and Quinnipiac Rivers—with the Quinnipiac only inhabited in significant numbers near New Haven—there was an absence of indigenous groups to the territory of the Wappinger on the Hudson River. The Paugussetts were the closest Native group to this uninhabited area, situated on the banks of the Housatonic and Naugatuck Rivers west of New Haven, and groups also occupied the upper stretches of the Stratford and Stamford Rivers near southeastern New York. Indians inhabited the remainder of Connecticut much more densely, particularly around rivers and on Long Island Sound. There was no geographic or environmental hindrance preventing groups from settling west of the Farmington and Quinnipiac Rivers, and a Native renaissance in fact occurred in the northwestern portion of Connecticut in the following century.[52] Historian John De Forest argues that the Mohawks somehow ensured that Connecticut's western regions remained uninhabited but offers little evidence to support this claim.[53] During the Beaver Wars of the mid-seventeenth century, the Iroquois confederacy conquered huge swaths of territory east of the Mississippi River, destroying, displacing, and subjugating numerous Indian groups.[54] The same occurred during the precontact epoch in western Connecticut, the Quinnipiacs later explaining to the colonists that they were caught in a vice between the Mohawks and the Pequots, which forced them to disperse and greatly reduced their numbers.[55] This suggests that western Connecticut represented a demilitarized zone between the two powerful Native groups.

It also indicates that contact between the Pequots and Mohawks occurred in this region. Indeed, as the "keepers of the eastern door" of the Iroquois Confederacy, the Mohawks were active in other parts of New England, warring against the nearby upper Connecticut River Indians at the end of the 1650s. They launched a devastating assault against the Pocumtuck main fort at Deerfield and raided other groups all the way to Massachusetts's Merrimack River. A few years later the Mohawks fended off an assault upon one of its fortresses by a coalition of Massachusetts groups out to avenge this earlier invasion. The Mohawks utterly defeated that coalition, ambushing the force on its retreat back to New England.[56] A close relationship between the revived Pequots and English settlers beginning in the 1650s, however, prevented similar attacks east of the lower Connecticut.

The uninhabited region of western Connecticut was a buffer zone, where neither the Pequots nor the Mohawks sought to antagonize the other. Anthropologist Steven LeBlanc contends that "farmers, or similarly organized tribal people, develop buffer zones between their territories. . . . Since crops are vulnerable to destruction by an enemy, and since egalitarian farmers have limited ability to organize boundary defenses, tribes tend to leave areas of unfarmed land between competing groups; . . . these buffer zones are essentially fallow fields."[57] Citing the example of the conflict between the Yumans and Maricopas of the American Southwest, he argues that Indians utilized buffer zones "as a means of survival" by allowing "societies to avoid being constantly in conflict."[58] This theory lends credence to the de-facto buffer zone between the Mohawks' and Pequots' spheres of influence. It also elucidates the Pequot-Mohegan combat superiority in southern New England as that of frontier peoples in contact with a people known to be aggressive fighters.

There were other significant groups in the area to the northwest of Connecticut, such as the Wappinger confederation of the Delaware cultural group and the Mahicans farther to the north on the Hudson River. Perhaps the Pequots confronted these groups as well, but it is certain that the Mohawks influenced areas west of the Connecticut River, where two elder Mohawk statesmen made their rounds each year, exacting tribute.[59] The Pequots and Mohegans also faced the possibility of a two-front war against the Mohawks and Narragansetts, a threat unknown to other New England Indians. The Pequots would not be the first people in history to develop dominant military tactical skills when confronted with two potent enemies on its flanks. Alan Gallay asserts that geopolitical conditions were the primary cause of the martial dominance of some tribes in the American South, and the same situation factored in to the Pequot-Mohegan qualitative superiority.[60] These peoples were in an unenviable geographic position that forced them to become the capable warriors that their reputation implied.[61]

Connecticut employed large numbers of allied Indians relative to colonial soldiers—a significant difference from the other New England colonies. Leaders like the Winthrops maintained confidence in the colony's Indian allies, whom they believed would win the war in its early stages: "I am apt to think that our indians would bring in Philip if we had order to send them out beyond Narrogansett espetially if he be com on this side Seconk River as the report is."[62] The Mohegans almost proved Winthrop right when they assisted Massachusetts troops at Nipsachuck. The engagement occurred during the Mohegans' return march from pledging their loyalty to the Massachusetts court. Only Captain Daniel Henchman's hesitation denied the allied forces the victory, ending a short conflict that rightly could have been termed "King Philip's War."[63]

In August 1675 eighty Pequots and one hundred Mohegans were searching for Philip's forces in western Massachusetts Bay Colony, and the War Council soon sent another thirty allied Indians under Joshua to join those already in the field.[64] On 5 September, after the council learned of Beers's defeat, it sent one hundred Mohegans and Pequots to search for hostile warriors in the beleaguered western stretches of Massachusetts Bay. An additional combined force of colonists and allied Indians, commanded by Captain John Mason, Jr., was sent there a day later to link up with Major Treat.[65] The Connecticut field commander, with sixty Mohegans (and likely some Pequots), saved Moseley's command at the Battle of Bloody Brook after the captain attempted unsuccessfully to relieve Captain Lathrop's company. The allied Indian contingent represented 40 percent of Treat's entire force.[66]

After the Mohegan-Pequots returned around 24 September, the War Council called them back to duty four days later and on 7 October claimed to have over 100 allied Indians operating upriver in Massachusetts.[67] At Great Swamp 150 Mohegan and Pequots formed nearly one-third of Major Treat's expeditionary force, accompanying 315 colonial soldiers.[68] In January 1676 the council ordered the major, whose command was regrouping in Connecticut following that battle, to ensure that the English properly identified allied Indians with markings in future operations to prevent friendly fire incidents, a concern of the council throughout the war. An unknown number of Connecticut Indians accompanied the colonial army into Nipmuck country in the late winter (as recounted by John Stanton below). In the early summer of 1676, some 200 allied Connecticut Indians joined 240 English commanded by Major Talcott and invaded Nipmuck country, composing 45 percent of the Connecticut force. In early July 1676, in one of the final major actions of the war, a large expedition under Talcott defeated Quaiapen. On 8 July the War Council again ordered the major to lead an expedition into Narragansett country for "mopping-up" operations.[69] The Mohegans, Pequots, and other allied Indians assisted the colony, especially in multiple expeditions into Narragansett lands, although Connecticut did not always record their exact numbers.

Allied Indian numbers influenced Connecticut's offensive success. Although they did not outnumber Philip's forces by themselves, when combined with Connecticut colonial forces, the number of allied Indian forces made a difference both qualitatively and quantitatively. Massachusetts Bay and Plymouth employed smaller numbers of Indians, with only twenty, for example, present at Captain Pierce's defeat.[70] There were only a handful of allied Indians with the Massachusetts Bay militia at the ambush outside of Brookfield.[71] At the war's outbreak, one of Massachusetts Bay's initial expeditions included a paltry five or six friendly Indians.[72]

Even if Connecticut forces did not achieve a war-ending victory by employing larger numbers of qualitatively superior warriors, they achieved notable successes in the field and completely avoided the disasters that plagued the other colonies.

With the most tactically proficient Indian force in New England deployed in relatively large numbers, how did Connecticut Colony actually utilize the allied warriors on the battlefield? John Stanton provided a rare description of tactics and operations during the winter campaign in west-central Massachusetts revealing that the Pequots and Mohegans not only remained dominant on the battlefield in 1676 but also served in a variety of other capacities:

> [The] Enemey fled before the army and in the persute those pequets indienes did very good serves: we slew in all neere about fower score persons and followed them neare about thre score and ten mille the enemies having noties of our armyes aproching the sachems fleed and their wimen and Chilldren and lefte sixtye pe Kom tonk Indians and three hundred fitteing men to waylay the army by the amboscadoes but weare by the providence of god timly discovered by our endyins they wounded five endglish men in the reare of the army after they weare beaten in the fronte by our Endelish and our endyians we slew at that time five of the uplanders and killed on[e] of there Chefe Captaines and the same day tooke the towne and badyed there all night the next day burned the towne and then morchet to the metropolitente glace and found it deserted so fiered nere five hundred widgwames this scalpe cared by the beorer was a endyion of greate accounte and was taken by with 25 persanes more by the pecaits Indians upon there retirneign home after they ported with the Endglish.[73]

Allied Indians acted primarily as scouts and flankers, as the Pequots ferreted out the enemy ambush in this battle.[74] Flankers ranged on the sides of formations when the colonists expected enemy contact during movement, attempting to prevent any ambush by denying the enemy the element of surprise. Scouts moved farther afield of the main body than flankers, searching for the enemy as well as a viable route of march, including alternate routes if obstacles were encountered. This was to avoid unnecessary halts, always a risky proposition in enemy territory. Moving bodies of troops are much more difficult to locate and attack then those that are stationary in unfamiliar terrain.

During battle, the best employment of the Indians was through "cutting off way of war" tactics while the English provided the firepower. The Indians would circle around the hostile forces' flanks while the main colonial body moved forward in a standard European assault. The "cutting off way of war" often "took the form familiar to us as the 'Indian way of war.' . . . [A]fter the first exchange of fire individual warriors 'took to the trees,' firing and moving, while each group tried to surround the other in the classic half-moon style that would negate the cover of a single tree."[75] There are accounts of hostile forces attempting to circle around the colonists' flanks, and Connecticut's field commanders employed their own Indians in the same way. They also likely used the warriors as skirmishers in front and on the flanks of the English main body, capitalizing on Indian marksmanship.[76]

Stanton's passage above also indicates how the allied Indians and Connecticut troops cooperated. The Pequots fought "in the fronte" with the English, suggesting that they were engaged in the main battle, not just as flankers and scouts. This type of employment reveals that the warriors could fight as main combatants. As with the battle Stanton recounted, the vast majority of Connecticut English did not adopt Indian tactics even when in smaller groups, fighting instead like Europeans, while their Indian allies normally fought according to the "cutting off way of war." The surprise and destruction of Sunk Squaw's Narragansetts, for instance, saw the implementation of the allied warriors as the hammer to flush out the Indians from difficult terrain into the waiting anvil of the colonists, undoubtedly in standard linear formation.[77] The English simply charged through the camp and pursued the surprised Narragansetts during the attack on Canonchet's band. These three episodes, together with Bloody Brook, Great Swamp, and the battle on the upper Housatonic, do not indicate that the colonists practiced the "cutting off way of war" in any meaningful way. Rather, they demonstrate the effective combination of traditional English and Indian tactics.

The colonists did not depend on allied warriors to assault fortified positions such as at Great Swamp, drawing perhaps on the experience of combined operations during the Pequot War. Michael Oberg claims that the Indians were "unfamiliar with attacking fortified positions," but it was far more likely that they *chose* not to attack them.[78] Allied Indians had accompanied the English at Mystic Fort and Fairfield Swamp during the Pequot War and at

Great Swamp during the Great Narragansett War, and they clearly would have observed the rather simplistic English tactics of cordoning off and then assaulting the objective. As Wayne Lee points out, the Tuscaroras of the South easily adapted to English fortification building and counterengineering, and the Cherokees drew their own lessons from accompanying colonists during the campaign against the Tuscaroras. Indians chose not to attack fortified positions as portrayed in the example of a Creek war party that gave up after observing a well-fortified and vigilantly guarded Cherokee village. It was not a matter of skill or courage, but Native groups simply could not replace casualties due to relatively low birth rates (as well as the cultural factors discussed).[79] The New England Indians did play a role, however, in combined operations in which colonial forces attacked fortified positions. The allied warriors normally led the English forces to the enemy, then served as an outer perimeter as the colonists conducted the assault. They also helped defend fortifications by using their marksmanship skills, firing from the parapets at Northampton and Hadley.[80]

Lee describes another role that Connecticut's allies served during the conflict:

> The real value of indigenous aid was a kind of strategic intelligence that informed the English of who the enemy was, where they were, how to get there, what their probable intentions were, and keeping that kind of information up-to-date over time. Despite difficulties in achieving set-piece battles, English military leaders nevertheless often focused on finding and destroying their enemy's military forces, and to do so they sought surprise—while avoiding themselves being surprised. Since the native inhabitants knew the landscape more thoroughly and also usually had more intimate connections among other locals, it was they who were most able to provide the up-to-date information necessary to achieve surprise.[81]

The Indians' identification of enemy forces was especially critical given the high level of intermarriage between Native southern New Englanders and the splintering of groups, with varying degrees of loyalty to the colonists. Connecticut's area of offensive operations essentially covered three theaters outside of the colony's borders: Narragansett country in Rhode Island, the upper Connecticut River valley in western Massachusetts, and Nipmuck country in central Massachusetts. Allied Indians identified the theater location of enemy groups, guiding the implementation of Connecticut's limited military resources.[82] Connecticut forces also targeted and eliminated key enemy leaders, such as Canonchet, hampering severely the coalition's ability to conduct operations.

Colonial and Indian cooperation in the war first occurred at the Battle of Nipsachuck, when the Mohegans supported Massachusetts forces. Owaneco's band was returning to Connecticut from swearing allegiance to the English at Boston and assisted in the transitory cornering of Philip during his flight to the Nipmucks. It is interesting that Massachusetts Bay failed to learn from this near victory that the employment of competent allied Indians contributed to battlefield success. At Nipsachuck Philip's band delayed the English for a few hours, fighting while low on powder and allowing time for their noncombatants to evacuate the area. This fierce delaying action came at a cost, resulting in twenty-three warriors killed in action from Philip's command, including some of his primary captains.[83]

At Bloody Brook Major Treat's Connecticut dragoons, accompanied by Mohegans, saved Captain Moseley's command. Moseley, prior to the major's arrival, had himself attempted to relieve Captain Lathrop's combined force of Essex County militia and Deerfield recruits, which hostile Indians had ambushed earlier in the day. The standard account of the battle claims that Lathrop's men had failed to consider security in their dispositions. During a picture-perfect late-summer day, Lathrop had sallied out with much of the Deerfield garrison to transport crops to the garrisons to the south that had swelled with the arrival of Massachusetts's militia. His column included lumbering supply wagons loaded with corn, which decreased his rate of march. The captain led his command down a winding cart path south of town, through the deep wilderness of the surrounding countryside. As the column crossed Muddy Brook (known thereafter as Bloody Brook), hostile warriors lying in concealment revealed their presence with terrifying war whoops and then unloosed a fusillade into the ranks of the surprised colonists. The Indians ripped Lathrop's column to shreds, killing nearly all of his men, then scalped their victims and pillaged the wagons.[84]

While this combined force of upper Connecticut River Indians, Nipmucks, and Wampanoags quickly overwhelmed Lathrop's entire column, it is less clear as the narrative claims if the captain failed to effectively command. As a Pequot War veteran, Lathrop was familiar with "the cutting off way of war." He also was aware of the presence of hostile groups in the area because he had shared command during the Battle of Hopewell Swamp nearby and knew of Beers's recent defeat.[85] Deerfield itself had been attacked on 1 September, with seventeen houses burned, and on 12 September, when Indians infiltrated the town and ambushed settlers traveling between the two garrison houses.[86] Under such circumstances, it is highly unlikely that Lathrop would allow his soldiers to stack arms in the carts and not consider security for the route of march. A more plausible explanation is that superior numbers quickly overwhelmed his men on the narrow path, perhaps silently disposing of flankers in the morass, before the captain could deploy into a suitable defensive formation.[87] Successful Indian attacks on forces led by capable commanders are ubiquitous in American history. For instance, Indians defeated the proficient Robert Rogers (of Rogers's Rangers fame) on the outskirts of French Fort Carillon (later Fort Ticonderoga) during the French and Indian War and George A. Custer, who was one of the Civil War's most competent cavalry commanders, at the Little Bighorn. Indians also preferred to attack when the opposing force was crossing watery terrain, a maneuver that experienced military leaders throughout history have feared.[88] Various examples of this preference abound in early New England history, including the destruction of Lathrop's and Pierce's commands as well as the Pequots' counterattack on Mason's company as it crossed a creek while returning from Mystic Fort during the Pequot War.[89]

Captain Moseley attempted to rescue Lathrop, and as testament to the strength of the enemy forces, the hostile Indians surrounded his pirate volunteers. Moseley had more time to react than Lathrop, however, and he employed his troops in European fashion by maintaining formation, firing volleys, and assaulting the enemy.[90] His volunteers performed better than the Lathrop's impressed Massachusetts militia even without the "skulking tactics" employed by his enemies. Moseley also maintained the advantage of not falling into an ambush. But he lacked allied Indians and the numbers necessary to drive off the enemy, who continued to busily strip Lathrop's dead.

Where Moseley's command failed to drive off the hostile band, Treat's Connecticut forces succeeded with the assistance of the allied Mohegans and Pequots. Either the hostile coalition conducted a fighting withdrawal at Treat's approach or the Connecticut force drove the warriors from the battlefield. There were no reports of friendly fire incidents from Moseley's command accidentally targeting the allied Indians. Thus, Treat moved his English troops directly forward to link up with Moseley, keeping his Indian forces on his flanks. This maneuver would have ensured that the Massachusetts men could see friendly units moving onto the battlefield while helping prevent them from accidentally targeting the Mohegans and Pequots. Serious combat did occur between the English and allied Indians and the hostile groups, as Secretary Allyn reported to Wait Winthrop that the Pequots had performed well and had avoided casualties, though they suffered bullet holes through their clothing.[91] Treat perhaps attempted to envelop the enemy force with his Indians by maneuvering on its flanks and attempting to block its escape. The situation was ripe for the major to exploit battlefield chaos, the hostile Indians distracted by stripping the dead as well as the ongoing engagement with Moseley's command.

One can imagine the scene upon Treat's arrival. Smoke from black-powder weapons blanketed the battlefield, a veritable shroud of death, while savage screams from both sides added to the tumult of musketry and the shrieks of the wounded and dying. His colonists dismounted a short distance from the field and marched into action. Connecticut troopers carried their flintlock muskets, wore broad-brimmed campaign hats or open-faced helmets, and quilted vests. The detachment unfurled the militia flag of the colony, resembling the old London trainband flags of the English Civil War and reminding the command of its proud lineage before battle.[92] Treat's troopers delivered volleys and methodically advanced across a battlefield strewn with the impediments of the dead and dying. Meanwhile, the Mohegans and Pequots, colored brightly in war-paint hues and adding their war whoops to the din of the fighting, harassed the enemy flanks. That the fresh Connecticut troops did not pursue the enemy was uncharacteristic of Treat, who had been pushing for more aggressive operations. This indicated that the Connecticut forces were too exhausted to exploit their battlefield success. It was the first engagement for many of the Connecticut men, having only operated to draw off the garrison from Northfield. There, they had first witnessed the aftermath of the horror of battle and atrocity, observing the desecrated colonial bodies from Beers's defeat.[93] Yet they had not experienced combat firsthand, and this perhaps was part of Treat's calculation not to pursue the hostile Indians into the wilderness, having driven them from the field at

Bloody Brook. Dusk was also approaching, which undoubtedly influenced the major's decision not to pursue. But darkness had already fallen on the victims of New England's bloodiest battle since Mystic Fort, some thirty-eight years earlier.

The Connecticut troops at Bloody Brook and other engagements would have maneuvered on the battlefield in the same fashion that was standard for mid-seventeenth-century European forces. Troops in the English Civil Wars had adopted earlier Dutch and Swedish tactics, which Connecticut commanders Denison and Fitz-John Winthrop would have observed and other officers would have read about in military tracts. The standard maneuver was by battalion, pitting pikes in the middle with ranks of musketeers of varying depths flanking them. As Connecticut combat men were dragoons and pikes remained in New England armories during the war, they dismounted at Bloody Brook, becoming musket-bearing infantry, and then methodically marched across the battlefield using standard tactics for the time period.

The main basis for maneuver was the countermarch. A standard deployment of musketeers was for two or more ranks to march ten paces in front of the main body. Coming to a halt, the first rank would fire while the second rank made ready. The first rank would then pivot to the rear, countermarching in the gaps between the rear ranks, a maneuver that Maurice of Orange first copied at the beginning of the seventeenth century from texts describing tactics of the Roman legions. The follow-on ranks would then march through those who had just fired, and the infantry would repeat this process across the battlefield. In order to perform this maneuver, officers would have formed their musketeers into "open order formation," creating the space necessary for countermarching. This tactic required drill, and the New England militia rehearsed this maneuver during exercises on the town greens ubiquitous to the region. That there were no accounts of friendly fire incidents, as described as occurring often in the English Civil Wars, was a testament to the degree of proper training for Connecticut's field forces.[94]

The Great Swamp Fight on 19 December 1675 demonstrated that allied Indians could outperform the colonists during more conventional operations. During the deep winter, Governor Winslow of Plymouth led a combined colonial force of more than one thousand soldiers against the Narragansetts, to that point the largest army ever assembled in New England. After staging his force in Rhode Island

and initially skirmishing with the Narragansetts, Winslow employed a turncoat member of the tribe named Peter to lead his expedition through the snowy wilderness to a huge morass in present-day West Kingston. The Narragansett stronghold was in the center of this vast swamp, but fortunately for the colonists and their Indian allies, the extreme winter had iced over this obstacle, and penetration was possible where it would not have been weeks earlier.[95]

Following standard practice, the allied warriors, including Pequots, Mohegans, and Niantics (both Eastern and Western), formed the outer perimeter of Winslow's army, while the English assaulted the stronghold. The Narragansetts inflicted many casualties on the colonists as the soldiers tried to rush single file across a fallen log into the fort, a blockhouse concentrating enfilading fire on this narrow approach.[96] At this defile the crash of musketry drowned out the cries of the wounded and the exhortations of the officers. Although some of Connecticut's most experienced captains led the assault, the colony's forces here suffered most of their casualties for the entire conflict as the Narragansetts destroyed the initial wave of assailants. Among the casualties were four company commanders.[97] English forces elsewhere located an unfinished entrance and poured through, relieving the pressure at this critical point as the bruised Connecticut forces finally made their entrance into the stronghold.

Once inside the fort, a more conventional battle ensued, with the English and Narragansetts exchanging fire while facing each other, European fashion, mere yards apart. This played to the strength of the colonists' training in volley fire, though the Narragansetts continued the fight until the English set fire to the wigwams.[98] Although many enemy warriors made it out—only forty were killed in combat—around three hundred noncombatants were killed in the inferno or by the outer perimeter of allied Indians when trying to escape the flames.[99] Some English blamed this ineffective cordon for allowing so many warriors to escape; indeed the Eastern Niantics, closely related to the Narragansetts, failed to target their kinsmen.[100] By failing to do so, they attempted to maintain their allegiance to the English while avoiding direct participation in the shedding of kin blood. The Mohegans and Pequots, however, the latter perhaps in revenge for the Narragansett participation at Mystic, were more effective in killing the Narragansetts than even the English.[101] Their warriors on the outer perimeter scored targets of opportunity on fleeing Narragansetts, who would have been illuminated in the dusk by the fire of the wigwams to their rear. The English also destroyed a blacksmith's forge, further limiting the Indians' ability to repair weapons and fashion flints.[102] Great Swamp was a pyrrhic victory for the colonists, resulting in relatively few warriors killed, the deaths of many Narragansett women and children, their subsequent suffering of the now exposed and hungry survivors, and the Narragansetts joining the hostile forces.

In late summer 1676, after the allied Indians and the English had shattered Philip's coalition, Major Talcott led a Connecticut contingent against the fleeing bands. His force was described as "consisting of some five or six hundred men, English and Indians.... These are very diligent, hardy, bold, valiant men, habituated and hardened to that duty, and incensed by the barbarous inhumanity they have heard of and the evidence of which they have seen in the form of the English bodies they found in the woods."[103] Talcott located a refugee group on the Housatonic River, near what is now Sheffield, Massachusetts. His plan reveals something of the tactical wherewithal Connecticut forces had developed during the conflict.

Talcott dismissed some of his English troops and all of the horses for lack of provisions and proceeded on foot with roughly sixty soldiers and about the same number of Indians. He divided his force into two bodies: an assaulting force crossed the river to attack the refugee group already on the western side, while a supporting element was to fix the enemy with volleys from across the river once the assault had commenced. The Housatonic must have been narrow at this juncture because of the limited range of the flintlocks and the fact that the supporting force quickly pursued the enemy after crossing the river. One of the refugee Indians, who was fishing early in the morning, detected the assault force as it approached his camp and gave the alarm. The major's supporting unit unleashed a volley and then also became the assault element as the designated attacking force never reached the camp in time to play a significant role in the action. The lone Indian fisherman prevented the entire encampment from succumbing to the onslaught.[104] In this engagement Connecticut troops were confident enough in their tactical prowess and in the ability of their allied Indians to send a portion of their force home with all of the horses in the face of the enemy. Talcott afterward maneuvered without maintaining contact between his divided columns—an action fraught with danger given the hostile forces in the immediate vicinity of his command.

Complementing the larger expeditions launched by Majors Treat and Talcott, smaller raiding parties kept Philip's confederates off balance in their own territory, maintaining the element of surprise. One of Captain Denison's expeditions captured Canonchet and Captain Church's men killed Philip.[105] Denison argued for the use of small units in a letter to Connecticut's War Council:

> the enemy we may not seeme to Give them any time of retreat or firther calling not slip any opertunities or advantages as God shall put into our hands: former neglects may be a suffetiant Caution: The missing of times being nessary now honored Gentlemen the maine question will be in what way to prosecute the war whether by our intire bodys or by smaler parties: as to which I have formerly declared my [crossout] foolish apprehensions and my readiness to secur God and the country with a [unreadable] force, being sensable that a smale forces will move with more speed and secrey then Greater bodyes for the sirprisall of the enemy and without by sirprisalls, we shall Doe but little Good upon the enimy: exsperience teacheth that if the eminy bee either alarmed or have intelligence; owar bodyes must be content with litell suckses.[106]

The raiding forced the hostile bands to maintain constant vigilance and to change locations frequently. This disruption of village life lowered morale in the hostile confederacy, particularly with the Narragansett bands, which were the frequent targets of Denison's and Avery's raids. Repeated strikes also prevented the Narragansetts from planting new fields and returning to caches of supplies and their warriors from refitting in terms of weapons maintenance, ammunition acquisition, and supply replenishment. Governor Hutchinson related that the raids "sunk and broke their spirits, and seems to have determined the fate of English and Indians, which until then was doubtful and uncertain."[107]

The raiding parties often linked up at the Pequot stronghold called Mohantic Fort at Mashuntucket, unearthed recently on the present-day Pequot reservation. The fort's dimensions of roughly 58 x 52 meters was too small for the entire Pequot population to inhabit, but positioned on a hilltop and protected on two sides by a swamp, it offered defense against sudden raids. Mohantic was designed to maximize flanking fire from small-scale bastions on each corner, with the length of the walls corresponding to effective musket range. The excavation has revealed a blacksmith's forge and

Model of Mohantic Fort. Courtesy Mashantucket Pequot Museum and Research Center.

a large number of flints for muskets, indicating that allied Indians, and perhaps colonists as well, refurbished weapons there.[108] Within the relative protection of the fort (Mohantic was not designed to withstand a deliberate siege), raiding parties coalesced and outfitted for expeditions into Narragansett country. These raiding parties were shaping operations for the larger expeditions and proved critical to Connecticut's victory.

The militia leader Thomas Minor reported linking up with allied Indian forces at Mashuntuckett for numerous expeditions into Narragansett lands. Sergeant Minor was promoted to lieutenant of dragoons on 3 November 1675 at the youthful age of sixty-seven. His diary indicates that he was at "Meshuntapit" and "Meshuntup" at the end of October and again at the end of November, although this was prior to his raiding activity (the Narragansetts would not overtly join Philip's coalition until December). Minor probably was urging the Pequots to continue fighting and, at the end of November, coordinating for allied Indian support of the Great Swamp expedition. On 7 March 1676, however, he recorded meeting at "Meshuntupit" again, this time presumably to raid into Narragansett country, from which he returned on the thirteenth. Minor campaigned again from 28 March to 4 April. Although the starting point for this expedition is unclear, the lieutenant had been at Norwich, Connecticut, the day that the expedition departed. Mashuntuckett was less than twenty miles from Norwich and on a route into Narragansett country, so perhaps Mohantic was the rendezvous for Connecticut forces. This was Captain Denison's expedition that captured the Narragansett leader Canonchet, a raid into Rhode Island that included seventy-nine colonists and a body of Indians that were detached from Major Talcott's larger force in western Massachusetts.[109]

Unlike Talcott's force, Denison's party was only large enough to defeat smaller enemy groups, like Canonchet's band, or to harass larger bodies. Denison and Avery undertook a number of successful raids, but this one was the most successful of all, capturing perhaps the hostile coalition's most capable war leader. The capture and execution of Canonchet was the singular victory of the war: "The news of this defeat, when it came, doubtless astonished and troubled them more than anything that had befallen them since the war began."[110] After this raid, the War Council ordered Denison and Avery "to prosecute the enemie wth all vigor," and Minor detailed that the command rendezvoused at "Meshuntupit."[111] This expedition returned to New London on 29 April, having killed nearly eighty Narragansetts.[112] Once again on 9 May, a raiding party of English and allied Indians launched an expedition into enemy country from "Meshuntuck" and returned to Connecticut from Providence, Rhode Island, on 15 May. In July another army marched out of "Mashantuckset" into Narragansett territory, the second major expedition of that month. These two operations were larger than the usual small-scale raids. Even though the war in Narragansett country largely ended afterward, it was clear that smaller expeditions—mostly launched from Mashuntuckett during the spring—not only weakened the hostile bands through attrition and by eliminating key leaders but also disrupted their logistical base.[113]

Connecticut's success did not depend on the adoption of Indian methods of fighting, and it is far from clear if any colonists utilized such tactics on the battlefield, even in Denison's and Avery's small contingents. Instead, Connecticut's military alliance rested on an effective division of labor. This was not lost on the colonists' "Indian allies who see and say that it is they who overtake the enemy, otherwise how could the English overcome those they cannot catch or come near to kill, who still outrun them whenever they wish."[114] The battles noted here demonstrate that the allied Indians and the English each performed military functions according to their own battlefield strengths. The Indians mainly conducted scouting, flanking, marksmanship, and pursuit, while the English delivered disciplined volleys and assaulted fortifications. If the colonists could fight in the same fashion as their allies, and the warriors had the same willingness to storm fortifications, then it is difficult to imagine the alliance surviving differences over land, religion, and sovereignty that had strained relations during the interwar years. Generated from the hard reality of frontier warfare, mutual respect for military skills on the battlefield buttressed the mutually beneficial colonial-Indian alliance in Connecticut.

Colonial leaders understood that the key to ultimate success was to employ warriors and soldiers to complement each other. From 1675 through the spring of 1676, Major Treat was the colony's commander in chief. Although he reportedly was sought after because he "knew how to fight the Indians," there is no indication that Treat experienced actual combat before the Great Narragansett War.[115] He began his military career as "the chiefe military officer [of Milford] for the present to order ye military affaires of that towne."[116] Respected as both a military and political figure, he was instrumental in settling Newark, New Jersey, where his statue still stands. Treat abandoned Connecticut during the annexation of New Haven Colony, a union that he found objectionable. He eventually returned to the colony, and during the Third Anglo-Dutch War, Treat served as commander of New Haven County's militia and second in command of all Connecticut forces.[117] As described, during the Great Narragansett War, he led expeditions along the Massachusetts Bay stretches of the Connecticut River, rescuing Moseley's command and defending Northampton and Hadley. When leading Connecticut's expeditionary force at Great Swamp, Treat was nearly killed when a bullet passed through the rim of his hat. Always leading from the front, he was the last Englishman to leave the Narragansett fort as the commander of the rear guard.[118] Treat utilized allied Indians in large numbers, avoiding the ambushes that repeatedly plagued the forces of the other colonies.

When Connecticut selected Treat as deputy governor in the spring of 1676, John Talcott replaced him and enjoyed even more successful operations than his predecessor. Talcott employed large numbers of allied Indians as well, and his operations finished off the Narragansetts as an effective fighting force by mid-July. Weeks later the major defeated remnants of the hostile coalition fleeing New England in the engagement at the Housatonic described above. Although neither Treat nor Talcott appeared to have combat experience prior to 1675, their general leadership experience, willingness to submit to detailed orders from the War Council, cooperation with Indian allies, and administrative abilities all contributed to successful operations.

Connecticut often called upon certain officers, such as Captains Denison and Avery, to lead Indian forces. Captain John Mason, Jr., was another such leader before he was mortally wounded at Great Swamp. Secretary Allyn related to the Massachusetts council that "Captn John Mason in whome they take greatest content" had to be sent for to lead the Indians because they refused "to move farther without some of our English to conduct & direct their motion."[119] Lieutenant Minor's son Samuel served as an interpreter for the English and allied Indians.[120] As Wait Winthrop urged his father, "they will [not] think much to go so far and com back againe without doing anything."[121] Connecticut leadership understood that the mismanagement of Indian forces could lead to their disillusionment.

Indian leaders also advised the colony's leadership. Uncas urged offensive operations outside of the colony so that "the enemyes hearts will be weakened or damped, The Indian friends hearts encouraged, to fall in with the English."[122] Motivated from the beginning by his own policy goals and standing within the Mohegan Native group, Uncas was also advocating a course of action favorable to his personal objectives. This was another attempt in a decades-long quest to influence English policy for his own benefit and that of his followers, but the advice was prescient nonetheless. Without diplomatic go-betweens who could straddle both English and Indian cultures like Mason, Jr., and Uncas, the Connecticut alliance would not have generated as much battlefield success.

Connecticut's English allies failed to employ the same effective leadership. Some Massachusetts Bay and Plymouth officers, though veterans of the Pequot War, led their commands into ambushes, and the hostile coalition severely defeated others in a number of actions. Not only failing to employ sufficient Indian allies, some colonial leaders such as Captain Moseley even committed atrocities and acted undiplomatically, driving friendly or neutral groups into Philip's camp. Massachusetts Bay condoned this behavior by not immediately removing him from command. This unethical conduct was counterproductive in a campaign attempting, in part, to coax hostile Indians to surrender and to join with colonial forces. Although by conflict's end, Massachusetts Bay and Plymouth had adopted Connecticut's model of volunteer troops complemented by sufficient allied Indians, the earlier failure to do this and the immoral conduct toward many groups, described above, extended the conflict by several months.

Connecticut conducted more successful offensive operations than its New England allies because the colony paired sufficient numbers of qualitatively superior allied Indians with its English dragoons. Its superior led, mobile forces consisted of more volunteers, who better represented the colony's population than the forces employed by the other New England colonies. Allied Indians brought the hostile forces to battle so the English troops could bring their military assets to bear. Small bodies of joint colonial-Native forces, fighting in irregular style, assisted in shaping Connecticut's major offensive operations. These elements in concert created a potent offensive capability, allowing the colony to maintain the initiative, which proved decisive against the hostile coalition. Indian and English leaders realized early in the conflict that Connecticut forces would never defeat the coalition with defensive operations alone. Leaders from both Connecticut's English and Indian ranks stepped forward to serve each other in a time of mutual danger. Although a culminating battle with the coalition never occurred, Connecticut forces disrupted the hostile groups' logistics base, keeping the enemy on the run and defeating them in combat whenever possible. Led by experienced officers, Connecticut Colony emerged largely unscathed from New England's bloodiest war, in large measure due to the effectiveness of its offensive operations.

Conclusion

Connecticut triumphed in the Great Narragansett War by capitalizing on its relationship with local Native groups, while the other New England colonies sustained devastating losses and achieved only a pyrrhic victory. The colony's unique policy and the generally good relations between settlers and local Indians set the stage for both successful defensive and offensive military operations, but the traditional narrative of the conflict has focused on King Philip and omitted Connecticut's success. My analysis of the colony's role in the war questions long-held assumptions about the conflict. This includes the standard naming convention of "King Philip's War," which should be replaced with the more accurate "Great Narragansett War," allowing for the violence of 1675–76 to be better integrated into a long century's framework of indigenous groups attempting to adjust to European arrival. Connecticut's military role highlights the effective use of European military skills in the New World, often in combination with more plentiful and competent Indian allies than the Native forces of the other New England colonies. The English never adopted a "skulking way of war" in 1676, for only a miniscule number of colonists fought in any way resembling Indians and never as effectively. What proved effective were smaller joint Indian-English patrols utilizing the strong suits of both English and Indian military culture. Connecticut's War Council and military leadership also more efficiently managed the conflict than the leading men of its sister colonies. Given the similar background of all of New England's Puritan leaders, this phenomenon demonstrates the limitations of macrocultural explanations when records on individuals are scarce. Connecticut's story in the Great Narragansett War establishes a paradigm for historians to consider military operations in the early colonial Atlantic world from the perspective of sound relations with local indigenous groups and the employment of certain European principles of war in combination with allied Indian forces.

The causative factor in Connecticut's victory was its leaders' identification of good relations with local groups as the essential element of military success. These men, such as Governor Winthrop, Jr., and his sons, then fostered this relationship, demonstrating a nuanced understanding of the nature of the conflict. Critically, Indians in the colony accepted this policy of neutrality or active alliance, spurning the leadership of Native groups hostile to the colonists of southern New England. The decades of intermittent warfare between the Mohegans and Narragansett-led coalitions greatly influenced these groups' decisions on whether to support the colonists. The War Council and the General Court repeatedly cautioned local English leaders to observe productive and just relations with their Indian neighbors. They depended upon friendly local Indians' knowledge of the hostile coalition, given the difficulty in even identifying, let alone fighting, the colonists' adversaries. Hostile raiding parties operating in Connecticut proved difficult to identify using overly simplistic "tribal" delineations. By maintaining positive relationships with neighboring Indian communities, the colonists prevented critical intelligence about the vulnerabilities of their daily lives from falling into the hands of the coalition. Without the intelligence necessary to formulate military operations, the hostile Indians, though having infiltrated the colony's defenses at various times, were unable to execute large-scale attacks upon major settlements. The policy with the local Natives thus served as the foundation for Connecticut's success in the war.

The legacy of the Pequot War influenced Connecticut's handling of Indian policy. Governor Winthrop, Jr., and a number of other veterans of that earlier conflict—including by 1675 many town leaders—experienced firsthand the necessity of maintaining positive relations with local groups as well as utilizing allied Indians during military operations. Winthrop, Jr., and others utilized their European experience and remained abreast of global military developments. Fitz-John and Wait Winthrop, George Denison, and John Mason, Jr., the second generation of Connecticut leaders, inherited these lessons from their predecessors through correspondence and bequeathed military texts. They also relied on their own military and diplomatic experiences with both Indians and Europeans when acting during the Great Narragansett War.

Even given positive relations since 1637, it was not predetermined that Connecticut indigenous groups would support the

CONCLUSION 175

colony, nor were the years between the Pequot War and the Great Narragansett War a linear progression for good colonial-Indian relations. Any number of episodes could have led to war between Connecticut colonists and local Native groups, including the Mohegans, and it was never certain that various episodes of infighting between opposing colonists and their Indian supporters would not result in an armed standoff or worse. The nonlinear nature of the relationship between individuals and factions, both Indian and colonial, infused the interwar years with uncertainty, increasing the chance of violence between factions. In the end, Connecticut supported Uncas and the Mohegans and the reconstituted Pequots against outside Indian threats and during internal colony feuds. This consistent policy, carried out on the personal and governing levels, set the stage for effective relations during the crisis of 1675-76.

Connecticut's Indians almost exclusively avoided supporting the hostile coalition. Little evidence survives to illuminate why this was the case, but for the larger groups, such as the Mohegan and Pequots, there were economic and political factors that tied them to the colonists. The Connecticut River Indians, the Tunxis of the Farmington River valley and the scattered peoples of west and southwestern Connecticut, also chose largely to support the colonists or remain neutral. Local relations held sway in places like Hartford, Wethersfield, Middletown, and Norwich, where colonists and Indians, spurred on by local relationships, cooperated for matters of security and sustenance. These relationships existed, though the "why" largely has been lost to history. The presence of armed allied Indians operating in conjunction with a well-led English force of dragoons to carry out an active defense likely deterred other groups from joining Philip. Connecticut's overall defenses, on average more robust by midwar than that of other colonies, perhaps dissuaded local Indians from joining with Philip as well.

Connecticut remained on the frontier of New England throughout most of the seventeenth century, facing threats from the Dutch, French, and various Indian groups to a greater degree than its sister colonies. This partially resulted in its different viewpoint concerning the primacy of sound relations with local indigenous groups—thus, good relations pivoted on practicality coupled with fair mindedness. The combination of Indian and European threats solidified the policy of maintaining local Indian support and hence denying intelligence to an enemy, either Indian or European. It also led Connecticut to consider matters of security more often than its neighbors, resulting in robust frontier defenses early in its history. Over time, Connecticut allowed these defenses to deteriorate, but the skeleton traces, as well as the concept behind such works, did not erode completely by the Great Narragansett War, resulting in a military advantage. The trace of past defenses along with the Indian coalition's initial designation of Connecticut as a secondary objective bought critical time for colonial leaders to reorganize its latent military potential. The devastating preemptive strike against the Narragansetts in late December 1675 had a similarly disruptive effect, granting Connecticut further respite.

When the Narragansetts entered the fray, the nature of the war dramatically changed. Even after the Great Swamp Fight, that group retained more political and military clout than any other single people in the region. With the addition of Narragansett power, the hostile coalition now retained the capability of destroying all English settlements save the well-protected strongpoints at Boston, Plymouth, Newport, Hartford, New Haven, and Fort Saybrook. Narragansett leaders quickly overshadowed Philip, whose role as war leader remained murky at best even before the English drove the Narragansetts into his ranks. The early designation of the war as Philip's misidentified the leadership of the hostile coalition and clouded its intended military targets by downplaying the Narragansetts' role. Connecticut's primacy in the war as a potent military force and a target for hostile forces becomes evident when viewing the conflict as the "Great Narragansett War." This places not only Connecticut in its proper historical context but also links this conflict to the overall postcontact American Indian struggle for adaptation to new cultural, economic, and military influences in the region.

The Narragansetts had a significant, decades-old feud not only with the Mohegans and remaining Pequots but also with their colonial Connecticut supporters. They repeatedly had gone to war since 1637 in an attempt to thwart burgeoning Mohegan power emboldened by Uncas. Connecticut leaders continually disrupted these efforts. The Narragansetts would have desired nothing less than extirpating their mortal enemies and their colonial supporters once they openly joined the war in 1676. Unfortunately for the Narragansetts and the rest of the coalition, Connecticut already had reconstituted much of its defenses and had undertaken field operations for months before the Great Swamp fight, leading to a well-prepared joint military effort between the English and their allied Indians. The Narragansetts, however, having their main village surprised and destroyed at Great Swamp, adjusted their military operations to account for noncombatants—now without shelter and starving in the harsh New England winter—and had no choice but to flee farther away from Connecticut's borders to Nipmuck country for refuge.

Any chance of the Narragansetts exacting revenge ended in early April 1676, when the colony's combined Indian-English force ambushed Canonchet, the one Indian leader with the clout and ability to lead a concerted effort against the Narragansetts' most hated colonial adversary. As might be expected with the loss of a competent leader, the hostile coalition now struck at the most exposed settlements in the three other New England colonies. These targets were less of an operational and logistical challenge for the coalition than Connecticut's stout defenses, which were augmented by the underlying relationship with its local Native peoples. The other colonies had, by this time, interned peaceful Native groups and committed other atrocities, losing the support of friendly and neutral local Indians, and suffered the bloody consequences. The Great Narragansett War quickly degenerated into a fight of endurance in which the Indian coalition had little chance of succeeding by the late spring of 1676, given its battle losses and inability to generate food and ammunition. Ironically, given the success of the coalition's winter–spring offensive—despite Mohawk intervention at the behest of New York's governor Andros—there was no hope of restoring antebellum relations with the English. Thus, the operational success of the coalition led to strategic failure by subverting the possibility of a true peace accord. Afterward, many hostile warriors opted to fight to the death, while others attempted to flee or joined the English. Some warriors did surrender to face execution, slavery in Bermuda, or indentured servitude in New England.

While its sister colonies showed almost no mercy to any Indians, Connecticut's moderate policy reflected the beliefs of the Winthrops, Masons, and others in the good treatment of indigenous groups. The actions of Connecticut colonists, though not uniformly ethical, compared favorably to the heavy-handed treatment and outright atrocities committed against Indians by civil and military leaders in the other colonies, such as Captain Moseley.

The Massachusetts General Court sanctioned the imprisonment of Praying Indians on Deer Island, and the governor of the colony accepted Moseley's actions without punishment. Plymouth Colony enacted a similar policy of imprisonment for a local Native group on Clark's Island in Plymouth Harbor. This undoubtedly set an unethical standard within those colonies for subordinates, indicating that such behavior was acceptable to the colonial civil leadership. It is difficult to imagine Winthrop, Jr., sanctioning a field commander's execution of an Indian woman, particularly in the manner of having her torn apart by dogs. The governor even objected to hostage taking from the Narragansetts and the preemptive invasion of that people's territory, even though it was sympathetic to, and passively aiding, Philip.

Connecticut colonists, Mohegans, Pequots, and other allied bands, drawing on experience from the Pequot War and conflicts in the intervening decades, successfully merged their two dissimilar fighting styles into a formidable complementary frontier-military system. The Indians performed tasks that best suited their military strengths, while the colonists largely executed those tasks that they were trained to perform. A handful of colonists adopted the "cutting off way of war," and their joint expeditions with friendly Indians complemented larger "search and destroy" missions.

Connecticut's allies were qualitatively superior tactically to the other New England Indians. The Indians of southern New England feared the Pequots most of all groups save the Mohawks, and the closely related Mohegans and remaining Pequots after 1637 continued their successful martial tradition. One can attribute Pequot-Mohegan fighting ability to their geographic position, located between Mohawk raiding territory to the west; the large, powerful Narragansett group to the east; and the assorted Nipmuck bands to the north. A state of constant conflict against formidable peoples likely honed Pequot-Mohegan tactical prowess.

Refining military skills abroad during the English Civil Wars and against the Dutch at home benefited Connecticut's English leaders, including Fitz-John Winthrop and George Denison, leading to success in the Great Narragansett War. Conventional warfare during the conflicts did not always translate directly into frontier fighting, but the basics of military organization and leading men in the difficult circumstances of battle proved beneficial. Generally employed in complementary fashion, Connecticut's Indian allies performed missions at which they excelled—reconnaissance, flank protection, security, and exploitation—while the colonial troops focused on garrison and fortification defense, delivering disciplined volleys, and assaults on fortified enemy villages and encampments. This system worked because this "division of labor" focused on the strengths of these respective military cultures. The tactical failure of the other New England forces through most of the conflict was not a matter of their failing to adopt the "skulking war of war" or the product of the erosion of European fighting skills. While there is no debating that a handful of colonists developed better wilderness tactics as the war progressed, they could not mimic the Indian way of life—the cultural basis point from which indigenous military skills derived. Both sides retained a natural advantage in the realm of their traditional tactics. Connecticut's combination of English troops with competent allied Indians proved lethal against the hostile forces. While these combined forces sometimes failed to locate the enemy, they were never ambushed in the field and never lost an engagement.

Connecticut's field forces were not "a rabble in arms," which sometimes characterized the military formations of the other colonies. Connecticut employed more volunteers, who were motivated by principle or bounty (or both) to serve. It also engaged competent field commanders, such as Majors Treat and Talcott. Connecticut's field forces were dragoons, riding to battle and then dismounting to fight. The better mobility of these troops was an advantage over those of the other colonies, which often employed infantry formations that inherently were less mobile and thereby easier for hostile groups to ambush. New England militia trained to combat a transitory threat, as European powers of the seventeenth century lacked the power-projection capability necessary for prolonged campaigns. They needed only to hold out long enough for time and weather to take effect in reducing an invaders' logistics and personnel capability, which would inevitably force the intruders to withdraw. Thus the militia's training was adequate for the inter-colonial situation that they were anticipating, but it can be legitimately criticized for failing to prepare for a possible conflict with hostile Indians. New England forces in 1637 had dispatched the Pequots, who like most groups of the period remained unfamiliar with gunpowder technology. This victory created a false sense of security among the English, who largely failed to anticipate Indian adaptation of firearms into traditional Indian tactics by the 1670s. The cooperation of Connecticut's Indian allies with its own English forces, however, negated the general lack of preparation for Indian warfare that afflicted the other colonies.

Employing the techniques of the European Military Revolution, Connecticut employed elements of continental fortifications in a more widespread fashion than the other New England colonies. Settled on the frontier bordering a hostile Dutch colony and confronted with more numerous Indian neighbors of dubious loyalty, Connecticut had arranged for its own defense in a highly systematic way. Original fortifications at Saybrook, New Haven, Hartford, Windsor, and other towns boasted defenses with elements of European design. The settlements retained the trace of these fortifications, even if colonists allowed the original works to fall into a state of disrepair in the years after 1637. During the Great Narragansett War, after the colony's leadership ordered the transition to more-robust defenses in October 1675, the towns with dilapidated structures had a base on which to reconstitute their defenses. This was not uncommon in early American history, as exemplified by "The Castle" in Boston Harbor, which repeatedly lapsed into a state of disuse only to be resurrected again during times of military crisis. Emerging here was American unwillingness, based on English precedent, to maintain standing military forces and structures during periods of peace. This theme continued on and off again in American history through the emergence of the United States as a superpower post-1945. (Considering the current drawdown of U.S. forces in the Middle East and Southwest Asia with the concomitant reduction of army brigades, there appears to be a return to this pre–World War II tradition.) In addition to fortifications, Connecticut also employed both colonial and Indian scouts to augment its defenses, on some occasions combining these forces to patrol the colony. This active defense prevented hostile Indians from coalescing to attack Connecticut settlements.

The colony's security relied upon the military decision-making ability of the War Council. Indicating that subcultures existed within New England's white-male Puritan war councils, Connecticut's council issued more detailed orders than those of the other colonies, demonstrating a willingness to dictate operations and tactics to its field leaders. Although experienced at the diplomatic and military-administrative levels, Majors Treat and Talcott lacked campaign and combat experience. Both men obeyed the council's orders and probably required this detailed military guidance. Connecticut's advantageous terrain, contiguous and dense settlement pattern, and smaller population numbers all contributed to the council's ability to manage the conflict while aiding the defensive operations of its military forces. The other New England colonies' war councils lacked either the willingness to direct military affairs for inexperienced field leaders or the advantageous terrain, settlement pattern, and population density that aided defensive military operations and eased the burdens of managing the conflict.

By utilizing an active defense with rebuilt elements of European-style fortifications, both rendered effective by the Connecticut's moderate policy toward the local indigenous groups, the colony prevented the bloody attacks that occurred elsewhere in New England. Massachusetts Bay, Plymouth, and Rhode Island all suffered devastating losses, primarily by failing to secure the support of their local Native peoples. Once hostile forces won the allegiance of such groups located near English settlements, they obtained the local intelligence necessary to plan and conduct offensive military operations. This was the situation at Swansea, Brookfield, Northfield, Deerfield, Northampton, and Springfield. The hostility of local Indians toward these towns largely surprised the settlers, who were unprepared militarily to deal with the hostile coalition. Their incredulity resulted from poor policy toward local groups as well as cultural deafness to the underlying issues of identity, sovereignty, legitimacy, and land that angered the Indian population.

The colonists' difficulty in identifying friend from foe in such situations was compounded by the fact that traditional "tribal" political breakdowns, largely an English creation based on European political norms of grouping peoples, did not readily apply to early colonial Indian delineations in southern New England. Indigenous communities reflected a high degree of intermarriage and hence kinship loyalties, resulting in mixed communities, the formation of which accelerated after friction with European economic and cultural factors. Connecticut avoided these issues by maintaining stable neighborhood relations, thereby denying the critical local support hostile forces required to carry out large-scale attacks. By considering what the colonists and allied Indians contributed militarily to the war effort, along with Connecticut's moderate policy toward local groups, an explanation becomes possible for the colony's ability to remain unscathed at home during the war and suffering less than other New England forces on the battlefield.

The cooperation between the Connecticut Colony and its Indian allies and their mutual respect in military affairs did not exist elsewhere in New England, especially at the outbreak of the Great Narragansett War. Forged during the Pequot War and the interwar years, the synergy of the Indian "cutting off way of war" with traditional European tactics into an effective military system proved vital to Connecticut's success during the conflict and the enduring nature of the Connecticut-Mohegan-Pequot alliance. The colony's moderate policy, however, made this system possible and became the critical factor in its success. This policy, largely disseminated and obeyed by Connecticut's English communities, though unshared by the other Puritan colonies, created the framework for successful military operations during the Great Narragansett War. Considering events of 1675–76 through the lens of local relations, a new methodology emerges for the examination of warfare during the early colonial era in the Atlantic world and beyond.

Notes

Abbreviations Used in the Notes

CWS   Connecticut Colonial Records, Colonial War Series, ser. 1, vol. 1, Connecticut State Library, Hartford, microfilm.
EBC-CSL   Eva Butler Collection, Connecticut State Library, Hartford.
EBC-ICRC Eva Butler Collection, Indian and Colonial Research Center, Old Mystic, Conn.
IS   Connecticut Colonial Records, Indian Series, vol. 1, Connecticut State Library, Hartford, microfilm.
PRCC   J. H. Trumbull, ed., *The Public Records of the Colony of Connecticut, from April 1636 to October 1776 . . . Transcribed and Published (in Accordance with a Resolution of the General Assembly)*, vol. 2 of 15 (Hartford, Conn.: Brown & Parsons, 1850–90).

Introduction

1. Leach, *Flintlock and Tomahawk*, 234–35. Leach's solid but dated work remains the authoritative account of "King Philip's War."
2. This description is based off of my extrapolation of Leach's account of the incident.
3. Mandell, *King Philip's War*.
4. Virginia's Opechancanough's Rebellion in 1622 cost the English at least one-third of their population, more fatalities per capita than the English colonists suffered in the Great Narragansett War. Alfred A. Cave, "Anglo-Indian Relations," in Gallay, *Colonial Wars of North America*, 31.
5. Combatants on both sides also killed women and children. For losses, including the hostile coalition's destruction of seventeen towns, see Mandell, *King Philip's War*, 137. Also see Leach, *Flintlock and Tomahawk*, 243, 247; and Ellis and Morris, *King Philip's War*, 288 (both of which claim the destruction of thirteen towns). While the Ellis and Morris account is dated, it remains useful because it was written before modernity largely changed the landscape of New England with paved roads and other changes to the natural environment, hence their detailed account provides an important analysis of terrain that no longer exists. Ellis and Morris were also members of the Connecticut Historical Society, and the editor of their book, Henry Stiles, also authored *The History of Ancient Windsor, Connecticut*.

6. John Brodhead, "London Documents," vols. 1–8 of Brodhead, Fernow, and O'Callaghan, *Documents Relative to the Colonial History of the State of New York*, 3:240–44. This monetary sum represents colonists' individual losses and does not include government expenditures.
7. Hubbard, *History of the Indian Wars in New England*, 15. Lepore uses this quote in *Name of War* to analyze the remembrance of the war in American history.
8. Selesky, *War and Society in Colonial Connecticut*, 31.
9. Hew Strachan, *The First World War* (New York: Penguin, 2003), xv.
10. Leach, *Flintlock and Tomahawk*, 241; Temple and Adams, *History of the Town of North Brookfield*, 36–38, 74. The authors make an unconvincing case that the war should have been titled the "Quabaug and Nashaway War." Ibid., 99n1. Chapter 2 below examines Philip's role in the war.
11. In addition to Lepore, Jean M. O'Brien in *Firsting and Lasting* articulates how nineteenth-century New England historians wrote Indians out of their accounts by perpetuating the falsehood that they were extinct.
12. B. Church, *Diary*; T. Church, *History of King Philip's War*; Hubbard, *Narrative of the Troubles with the Indians in New England*; Mather, *Brief History of the Warr with the Indians*. Leach cites Hubbard, Mather, and (especially) Church in one-fifth of his book.
13. Leach, *Flintlock and Tomahawk*, 228; Grenier, *First Way of War*, 33. I consider operations and tactics in chapter 6, examining in part Grenier's argument about Church's campaigns.
14. Pulsipher, *Subjects unto the Same King*, 128, n44. Although Pulsipher names a "Narragansett War" phase of King Philip's War, she maintains the standard narrative's focus, including "Massachusetts" in the titles of a third of the book's chapters.
15. Eames, *Rustic Warriors*, 15.
16. Schultz and Tougias, *King Philip's War*, 51 (quote); Leach, *Flintlock and Tomahawk*, 88.
17. Mandell, *King Philip's War*, 75.
18. Historians acknowledge the friction between the Narragansetts and the English in the years from the Pequot War to King Philip's War and then abruptly transition to the Philip narrative for the period 1671–75. Mandell refers to the prewar Narragansett tensions as a "Cold War with the Narragansetts." *King Philip's War*, 19. Pulsipher, over the first hundred pages of *Subjects unto the Same King*, also addresses this growing hostility. I make explicit to the conflict of 1675–76 the centrality of the Narragansetts' rivalry with the Mohegans and their English patrons, seating it within the larger postcontact crisis in the region.
19. Selesky, *War and Society in Colonial Connecticut*, 31. Leach argues that "Connecticut . . . throughout the war had shown the greatest skill of all the colonies in dealing with friendly Indians." *Flintlock and Tomahawk*, 227. He then highlights some of Connecticut's defensive

measures and a number of offensive operations, but his book lacks specific detail because of its broad focus on all of the New England colonies. Robert J. Taylor mostly defers to Leach for Connecticut's role in King Philip's War. *Colonial Connecticut*, 79. He offers an impressive political synopsis, including the colony's confrontation with Governor Edmund Andros of the Royal Colony of New York. Richard A. Radune acknowledges the success of Indian and English raids launched from eastern Connecticut. *Pequot Plantation*, 189–233.
20. Selesky, *War and Society in Colonial Connecticut*, 17–32. Brian Zawodniak notes how Connecticut's better treatment of local groups facilitated its gaining Indian allies. "Connecticut in King Philip's War," chap. 6.
21. Selesky, *War and Society in Colonial Connecticut*, 20.
22. Oberg, *Uncas*, 180. Oberg details Uncas's relationship with the Connecticut's colonists. Mandell acknowledges that Connecticut sought to maintain the support of the Pequots and Mohegans at the outbreak of the war. *King Philip's War*, 60–61, 68–69. While he finds it surprising that the Pequots would join with the English after 1637, I explain this rapprochement in chapter 1.
23. Chapter 1 briefly discusses precontact warfare in southern New England and also describes the effect of disease on the Indians' diplomatic framework.
24. J. Drake, *King Philip's War*. Jean M. O'Brien argues that the English attempted to integrate the Praying Indians into the English social order of seventeenth-century New England, which over time, led to literal dispossession by degree of Native American landholdings. English conception of landownership and dominance of the "legal system," combined with the Indians' somewhat mobile society to disinherit Indians to the point where they became so marginal within New England society that they were written into the historical narrative as extinct. This in turn benefited white American land claims and created the rationale for continued oppression, although the Indians resisted in creative ways to maintain an existence to the present day. *Dispossession by Degrees*, 212–13. O'Brien expands her Natick thesis to other tribes in New England and the United States in *Firsting and Lasting*.
25. Alden T. Vaughan argues in *New England Frontier* that the Puritans had good intentions though they often blundered in their dealings with native New Englanders, while Francis Jennings maintains in *Invasion of America* that Western colonists were intent on oppressing Indians with European-style feudalism. John Grenier claims that the New England colonists waged "extirpative war, what today's soldier's term unlimited warfare, manifested by the destruction of enemy noncombatants and their agricultural resources." *First Way of War*, 21. I discuss the issue of extirpative warfare below. Stephen Saunders Webb contends that Puritan racism drove a genocidal war against the New England Indians. *1676*, 353–54.
26. Pulsipher, *Subjects unto the Same King*, 113, 117.

27. "Frontier" here refers to the colonists' perception of political boundaries between Connecticut and the territory of other colonial entities and Indian groups. I believe this term best describes border areas because the Puritan colonies squabbled with each other, as well as the apostate Rhode Island and Royal New York colonies, over land claims and charters.
28. Malone, *Skulking Way of War*, 120, 128; Ellis and Morris, *King Philip's War*, 56; Hirsch, "Collision of Military Cultures," 1210.
29. John W. Hall discusses in *Uncommon Defense* the issue of feigned alliances. Also see Tiro, "Dilemmas of Alliance," 215–34.
30. Grenier, *First Way of War*, 34; Mandell, *King Philip's War*, 109; O'Brien, *Dispossession by Degrees*, 61; Melvoin, *New England Outpost*, 116–21; Philbrick, *Mayflower*, 332; Richter, *Ordeal of the Longhouse*, 135; Anderson, *War That Made America*, 13; Lee, "Subjects, Clients, Allies, or Mercenaries?" Webb, in a variation of this argument, asserts that Andros deserves the credit for New England's victory over the hostile coalition because he mobilized the victorious Iroquois. *1676*, 366.
31. "Active Defense" normally refers to an element of U.S. military doctrine of the 1970s, but I use the phrase here to highlight that Connecticut's defenses were not only of a passive nature.
32. Grenier, "Recent Trends in the Historiography on Warfare in the Colonial Period," 358–67.
33. Leach, *Flintlock and Tomahawk*, 93.
34. In addition to Leach, see Malone, *Skulking Way of War*, 128; Grenier, *First Way of War*, 33; Hirsch, "Collision of Military Cultures," 1204; Ellis and Morris, *King Philip's War*, 55–56; J. Drake, *King Philip's War*, 2; Starkey, *European and Native American Warfare*, 32–39; Dederer, *War in America to 1775*, 19; Schultz and Tougias, *King Philip's War*, 16; Mandell, *King Philip's War*, 116, 122; Zelner, *Rabble in Arms*, 214–16; Romero, *Making War and Minting Christians*, 191; and Melvoin, *New England Outpost*, 113. Melvoin argues that the colonists adopted the Indians' tactics as the war progressed, but this transition did not ultimately defeat Philip because the Mohawks did first.
35. Malone, *Skulking Way of War*, 128. Conversely, Guy Chet argues that conventional European tactical skills remained effective in the New World, except for King Philip's War, where the second generation of colonists lacked military experience. *Conquering the American Wilderness*, 3. I challenge this contention below.
36. The following recognize Connecticut's military success but do not examine it in detail: Malone, *Skulking Way of War*, 109; Oberg, *Uncas*, 180; J. Drake, *King Philip's War*, 80; Ellis and Morris, *King Philip's War*, 9; Steele, *Warpaths*, 103; Starkey, *European and Native American Warfare*, 71; Philbrick, *Mayflower*, 319; R. Black, *Younger John Winthrop*, 350; Bodge, *Soldiers in King Philip's War*, 136; Johnson, "Search for a Usable Indian," 627; Shultz and Tougias, *King Philip's War*, 4; and Radune, *Pequot Plantation*, 189–233.

37. Wayne Lee expands in *Empires and Indigenes* the idea that local relations were critical to successful colonization in North America to a worldwide focus for the early modern era, highlighting as well the significance of Military Revolution techniques. Jeremy Black cites the Spanish use of indigenous confederates against the Aztecs and the Russians use of local allies to subdue Siberia. *Fighting for America*, 26, 37.

1. Forging an Alliance

1. As quoted in Oberg, *Uncas*, 18, 66.
2. McBride, "War and Trade in Eastern New Netherland," 84–85. Wayne Lee states in "Fortify, Fight, or Flee" that he has also found similar evidence for additional examples of total war conducted by Indians. He takes up the issue again in *Barbarians & Brothers*, 139. There were numerous instances of unrestrained Indian warfare postcontact, as was the case with the "Beaver Wars," in which the Iroquois confederacy decimated Native populations from eastern Ohio to the Mississippi River. These findings call into question the traditional historical view that European trade caused economic competition, in turn generating violent warfare among Native Americans for the first time. See, for example, Neal Salisbury's commentary on Mohawk warfare, *Manitou and Providence*, 79. In Connecticut the arrival of Delaware peoples into the western–southwestern regions west of the Housatonic watershed probably led to increased warfare during this period. Lucianne Lavin argues that this migration was peaceful. She later discloses, however, that there were excavations in this area that revealed warfare from the Late Woodland Period (1000–1500 A.D.), which corresponds to McBride's findings. *Connecticut's Indigenous Peoples*, 246–49, 253. This evidence of violence could have been from Delaware peoples coming into contact with existing Connecticut groups and fighting them. Steven A. LeBlanc's study *Constant Battles* further demonstrates weaknesses in the standard historical view of precontact American Indian warfare.
3. Summarized in Salisbury, *Manitou and Providence*, 22–30. Salisbury himself argues that the population between the Saco and Quinnipiac Rivers ranged from 126,000 to 144,000 people. Ibid., 26–27.
4. Lavin, *Connecticut's Indigenous Peoples*, 286.
5. Demeritt, "Agriculture, Climate, and Cultural Adaptation in the Prehistoric Northeast," 183–202. As primary documents make clear, the Indians of New England's coast also grew corn, though in less quantity than those inland, in part by having ocean food sources nearby and also other conditions that Demeritt discusses in his article.
6. Schroeder, "Maize Productivity," 499–516. Schroeder relies on primary sources such as the contemporary writings of Roger Williams and Daniel Gookin. He defends his calculations in a follow-up article, "Understanding Variation in Prehistoric Agricultural Productivity," 517–25.
7. See chapter 2 for the logistical requirements of warriors.

8. Romero defines the gender roles of New England Indians in *Making War and Minting Christians*.
9. Kevin McBride, phone interview by author, April 2013.
10. Salisbury bases his ratio off an observation of multiple Indian families living in longhouses as well as a comment of an early explorer. *Manitou and Providence*, 26. McBride and Schroeder estimate a 5–1 adult male ratio to other members of an Indian nuclear family, as does Jennings (see below). Kevin McBride, interview with author, Foxwoods, Conn., Mar. 2011; Schroeder, "Maize Productivity," 510.
11. For other summaries of the historical arguments about disease, stretching back to observers of the seventeenth century, see Jennings, *Invasion of America*, 16–31; and Vaughan, *New England Frontier*, 21–22n40. Patricia Seed explains that the loss of military leadership due to disease was a significant obstacle for Indian military systems. "Conquest of the Americas," 144. Although this was true to an extent, as discussed in chapter 6 below, the leadership of Connecticut's Indian allies appeared unaffected by disease, given the allies' battlefield dominance during the Great Narragansett War.
12. Testimony of James Quannapohit, Massachusetts Colony Miscellaneous Records, Massachusetts Historical Society, Boston (hereafter cited as Testimony of James Quannapohit, MHS). Quannapohit was a highly reliable Praying Indian spy for Massachusetts Bay and barely escaped with his life from this reconnaissance mission. He reported to Boston authorities that 700 Narragansett warriors encamped with the coalition in the immediate aftermath of the Great Swamp Fight in December 1675. The colonial army killed some warriors in the battle, and it is also likely that at least another 200–250 of them joined up with the Indian coalition after Quannapohit's report or remained in the general vicinity of their traditional Rhode Island territory, thus bringing the total number of available warriors for the Narragansetts to approximately 1,000 at the time of the 1675 war.
13. Though he discounts the evidence, Salisbury recounts that the initial New England inhabitants encountered "some hundreds" of the Massachusetts tribe that apparently escaped the initial wave of European diseases. *Manitou and Providence*, 176. There is no reason to believe this report to be inaccurate, especially given Salisbury's reliance on similar primary evidence.
14. Anthropologist Kevin McBride and Connecticut State Archaeologist Nicholas Bellantoni have stated that excavations have not uncovered burials in southern New England that indicate historians have adequately accounted for losses from disease. Both caution that this data is difficult to obtain from excavations, however, and that disease generally took a considerable toll on Native peoples. McBride, interview with author, Foxwoods, Conn., July 2011; Bellantoni, discussion with author, June 2011, Avery Family Memorial Conference, Groton, Conn.
15. Salisbury depends on Daniel Gookin as a basis for his estimates, but Gookin counted the Indians of Long Island and various Nipmuck

groups of the Blackstone Valley in his estimate of 5,000 Narragansett warriors in the precontact era. *Manitou and Providence*, 29. I arrived at my number by stripping away the non-Narragansett groups.
16. Gookin contends that there were 4,000 Pequot warriors prior to English settlement, but he includes all of Connecticut's Indians along the coast to the Quinnipiac River and somewhat inland, hence overestimating the people's size. Salisbury, *Manitou and Providence*, 30.
17. Kevin McBride, phone interview by author, July 2013.
18. See chapter 6 for the number of Pequot warriors campaigning for Connecticut during the years 1675–76.
19. Salisbury points out that Gookin could not estimate the Indian population of the "virtually inaccessible inland areas" and even the portions of rivers far beyond the seaboard. *Manitou and Providence*, 27.
20. As Salisbury indicates, Gookin included non-Massachusetts groups in his figure of 3,000 warriors for the tribe, which I account for here. Gookin's approximation of the nearby Wampanoag groups was more accurate than for the Massachusetts, whose territory ranged farther into the unexplored west at the time that he wrote. Ibid., 28.
21. With the focus on Connecticut, my estimate includes the area of the upper Connecticut River valley and Connecticut Native groups west of the Quinnipiac River to the current border with eastern New York, for which previous historians did not fully account. I did omit from my estimate, which Gookin and Salisbury included in theirs, the population of the Pawtuckets, a native group that inhabited the area of the Merrimac River of Massachusetts. They are not included because as Salisbury contends, northern New England Indians also lived within their territory. Ibid., 27.
22. Alfred A. Cave's *The Pequot War* remains the authoritative account of that conflict. Cave places the majority of the blame for the war on Massachusetts Bay Colony. Ibid., 121. Tensions had been building in Connecticut for some time, with conflict over the fur and wampum trade in the early 1630s, leading to war between the Pequots and both the Dutch and the Narragansetts. The "murders" of merchantmen John Stone and John Oldham further aggravated the situation, with both killings involving cases of mistaken identity. The Pequots killed Stone because they thought that he was Dutch, and the English blamed the confederacy for Oldham's death even though Narragansett tributaries had killed him. For these issues, see ibid., 49–121. Kate Grandjean argues that climate and weather conditions in the 1630s created food shortages, which in turn sparked violence over scarce foodstuffs. "New World Tempests," 75–100. Kevin McBride rejects this claim on the basis that there is no anthropological or archaeological evidence to sustain the food-shortage argument and that primary records do not persuasively indicate that climate and weather factored into the causes of the war. McBride, interview with the author, Apr. 2013.
23. Report, Battle of Mystic Archaeological Project, Mashantucket Pequot Museum and Research Center, Mashantucket Pequot Reservation,

Conn.; interviews by the author with museum and research staff. Kevin McBride's interdisciplinary team since 2008 has excavated and analyzed part of Mystic Fort, providing new insight into the battle. A summary of a portion of the center's analysis can be found in "The Mystic Fort Campaign," updated July 2013, Battlefields of the Pequot War Project, Mashantucket Pequot Museum and Research Center, http://pequotwar.org/.

24. Karr, "Why Should You Be So Furious?" 876–909. Russell Bourne maintains that the Pequot War was the beginning of the undoing of the Indian-English biracial community in southern New England. See *Red King's Rebellion*, xii–xiii, and chap. 2.

25. Romero examines how English and Indian cultural beliefs and practices influenced the conduct of warfare in early colonial New England in *Making War and Minting Christians*, 137–91.

26. Cave, *Pequot War*, 68.

27. Tensions over the fur and wampum trade precipitated the obscure Dutch-Pequot War, when the Pequots murdered other Indians at the Dutch trading post of Hartford. In a botched attempt to intimidate the Pequots, the Dutch then killed one of their sachems, Tatobem. Cave, *Pequot War*, 58–60. McBride maintains that the Pequots learned to respect European firepower during this conflict. "War and Trade in Eastern New Netherland," 68–95.

28. Cave, *Pequot War*, 70–72, 109–21, 128–33.

29. Ibid., 135.

30. Ibid., 142.

31. Historians originally contended that the Pequots and Mohegans were one tribe and that Uncas had changed the name back to the old tribal moniker "Mohegan" when he broke with Sassacus. Ceramic pottery, hunting disputes, and a Dutch map from 1614 are among the evidence demonstrating that the peoples, although closely related, were separate entities. See Oberg, *Uncas*, 18; Cave, *Pequot War*, 66; Dutch map, 1614, Mashantucket Pequot Museum and Research Center. Salisbury also discusses Dutch accounts portraying two distinct tribes. *Manitou and Providence*, 82–83. In addition, the Pequots and Mohegans maintained different creation narratives. Kevin McBride, interview with author, June 2009.

32. Oberg, *Uncas*, 18, 48.

33. Cave, *Pequot War*, 137; Oberg, *Uncas*, 50–51; Selesky, *War and Society in Colonial Connecticut*, 7.

34. Oberg, *Uncas*, 52. Vaughan makes the important point that Uncas "chose" Connecticut. *New England Frontier*, 141.

35. Cave, *Pequot War*, 145–48.

36. Walking the terrain of this position, one easily observes how suitable it was as a rallying point for the operation against Mystic Fort.

37. Battle of Mystic Archaeological Project, Mashantucket Pequot Museum and Research Center; author interviews with participants of the dig team; and various artifacts at Foxwoods Museum, March 2011. It appears

that the allied Indians and a portion of the colonists established blocking positions on avenues of egress from the fort and that both Mason and Underhill encountered heavy resistance inside the palisades.
38. Lee, *Barbarians & Brothers*.
39. Karr, "Why Should You Be So Furious?" 876–909; Ó Siochrú, "Atrocity, Codes of Conduct, and the Irish in the British Civil Wars," 55–86.
40. Romero, *Making War and Minting Christians*, 162–64.
41. Battle of Mystic Archaeological Project, Mashantucket Pequot Museum and Research Center.
42. Ibid.
43. Cave argues that it was the devastation at Mystic that caused disillusionment among the Indian allies. *Pequot War*, 151–52. But Lee suggests in "Subjects, Clients, Allies, or Mercenaries" that when the remaining Narragansetts protested the slaughter of the Pequots, they were actually protesting the destruction of the spoils of war. For the same argument, see Lee, *Barbarians & Brothers*, 154–55.
44. Oberg describes Mohegan assistance during the Pequot War in *Uncas*, 72. Johnson briefly describes the Mohegans and Connecticut Colony relationship as "balanced and mutually profitable interdependence." "Search for a Usable Indian," 646.
45. As quoted in Starkey, *European and Native American Warfare*, 19.
46. Some historians repeat the colonists' misunderstanding of Indian "cutting off" tactics. Leach derides Indian fighting ability as "not very far advanced in the science of organized warfare. . . . Apparently little attention was given to formal tactics except for ambush." *Arms for Empire*, 2–3. That the Indians usually would not stand and fight—although during the Great Narragansett War the Native coalition fought pitched battles at the Great Swamp Fight, Sudbury, and Pierce's Fight—did not render their form of warfare any less effective than European tactics.
47. Chet singles out the Indians' inability to attack fortified positions, which is somewhat true given their lack of artillery but completely in accordance with their "cutting off way of war" described herein. *Conquering the American Wilderness*, 43.
48. Lee, "Fortify, Fight, or Flee," 719–20.
49. Lee, "Using the Natives against the Natives," 89.
50. Lee, *Barbarians & Brothers*, 138–39.
51. The sanguine battles of the contemporaneous Thirty Years' War offer ample evidence of this mentality. For a description of the colonists' cultural-military prerogatives, see Romero, *Making War and Minting Christians*, 137–92.
52. Chase, *Firearms*, 22.
53. Winthrop Papers, vol. 16, as transcribed in the Eva Butler Collection, Connecticut State Library, Hartford (hereafter EBC-CSL), 65. There are two versions of the Eva Butler Collection, one at the library and the other at the Indian and Colonial Research Center, Old Mystic,

Conn. (hereafter EBC-ICRC). There are also copies of the research center's documents at the Foxwoods Museum. Although useful for primary-source information that does not seem to appear in any of the various published series of Winthrop papers, these two variations of the Eva Butler Collection are randomly assembled and difficult to follow.
54. Battle of Mystic Archaeological Project, Mashantucket Pequot Museum and Research Center.
55. Cave, *Pequot War*, 160–61; "Mystic Fort Campaign."
56. "Mystic Fort Campaign."
57. Harris, *Rhode Islander Reports on King Philip's War*, 53; Muehlbauer, "'They . . . Shall No More Be Called Peaquots but Narragansetts and Mohegans,'" 167–76.
58. Oberg, *Uncas*, 103.
59. Salisbury, *Manitou and Providence*, 234–35.
60. For the Pequot War through the death of Miantonomi and Pessicus's siege of Fort Shantok, see Oberg, *Uncas*, 72–114.
61. Thomas Peters to John Winthrop, Sr., [?] May 1645, *Winthrop Papers*, 5:19.
62. Oberg, *Uncas*, 116.
63. Winthrop's influence on Connecticut Colony's policy of moderation is detailed in chapter 3. For a recent account of this episode, see Radune, *Pequot Plantation*.
64. John Winthrop, Jr., to Dutch New Amsterdam governor Peter Stuyvesant, *Winthrop Papers*, ser. 5, 5:49. In this letter he refers to a mandate of the Connecticut General Court to change the name of Pequot Plantation to New London.
65. Winthrop, Jr., to Thomas Peters, 3 Sept. 1646, ibid., 100.
66. Samuel Symonds to Winthrop, Jr., [?] Sept. 1646, ibid.
67. Pynchon advised Governor Winthrop about this intelligence from the Mohegans. William Pynchon at Springfield to John Winthrop, Sr., at Boston, 27 Sept. 1646, ibid., 114–15, 115n1.
68. Ibid., 124.
69. Treaty, 24 Feb., 1647, ibid., 131.
70. Oberg, *Uncas*, 155; Johnson, "Search for a Usable Indian," 649. The Masons represented the Mohegans during a major land controversy with Connecticut that stretched over decades, eventually reaching the British king in the mid-eighteenth century. Forest, *History of the Indians of Connecticut*, chap. 8.
71. Mason and Winthrop, Jr., were not always at odds, the former advising that Wequash's Pequots at Pawcatuck were "very desireous of frindship with the English." Mason at Saybrook to Winthrop, Jr., at Nameag, 9 Sept. 1648, *Winthrop Papers*, ser. 5, 5:250.
72. Winthrop, Jr., to John Mason, 19 Sept. 1648, ibid., 355.
73. Winthrop, Jr., to Commissioners of United Colonies, [?] July 1649, ibid., 354.
74. Winthrop, Jr., to John Haynes, 28 Aug. 1649, ibid., 360.
75. Ibid., 360n.

76. *Winthrop Papers*, ser. 5, 8:42.
77. The English did not always understand the complexities of Indian-European relations, as Winthrop explained in a letter to his son-in-law about Dutch and Wappinger overtures to Uncas in 1658. See *Winthrop Papers*, ser. 5, 8:53. The Wappingers were an Algonquian people of the Lenni Lenape or Delaware cultural group inhabiting the Hudson River north of Manhattan toward Mahican territory and northwestward toward Mohawk territory.
78. Roger Williams of the Providence Plantations was the most vocal supporter of the Narragansetts, but because of Puritan distaste for his religious beliefs, his diplomatic efforts never held much sway with the United Colonies.
79. McBride, "Legacy of Robin Cassacinamon," 74–92. Uncas's compelling story has overshadowed Cassacinamon's important role in supporting the colonists.
80. Oberg, *Uncas*, 130–35.
81. Both Niantic groups, although of Algonquian lineage, shared more linguistic similarities with the Narragansetts (Eastern Niantics) and Pequots (Western Niantics) than with each other. The American Indian exhibit at Yale's Peabody Museum depicts differing cultural wares and languages for both groups.
82. The Dutch eventually gave way to the English at Hartford in the early 1650s, but there were continual tensions between the Dutch traders and English colonists.
83. Oberg, *Uncas*, 132–50. The Western Niantics had become tributaries of the Mohegans after the Pequot War, and intermarriage bolstered filial ties between the peoples. Uncas's son Attawanhood, Joshua to the English, was sachem of the Western Niantics during the Great Narragansett War.
84. IS, 1:1:1. I cite items from the Indian Series and the Colonial Wars Series numerically, series : volume : document. I viewed these documents on microfilm at the Connecticut State Library unless noted as "Original Manuscript." I viewed original manuscripts from these series in the reading room of the Connecticut State Archives, Connecticut State Library.
85. McBride, "Legacy of Robin Cassacinamon," 82–83.
86. See, for example, Warren, "Beyond Emotion," 181–94.
87. Vaughan, *New England Frontier*, 60.
88. Although there are many histories that cover the prologue to King Philip's War, among the best are Starkey, *European and Native American Warfare*, 59–67; and Steele, *Warpaths*, 80–99.
89. This is a major theme in James Drake's *King Philip's War*, though it is more accurate to argue that as Indians and English approached a more joint society, the war erupted because of the tensions this generated. Adam Hirsch argues for a process of military acculturation that was occurring between the Indians and the English as a part and not a product of the overall acculturation process. He concludes that there was

no significant change in New England's military affairs between the Pequot War and Great Narragansett War because of the general absence of combat. Like other historians, he omits the effectiveness of certain English military methods. "Collision of Military Cultures," 1187.

90. The Mohegans, Narragansetts, and Wampanoags all appealed directly to the English throne at various times during land disputes with the colonists. For the Mohegan case, see De Forest, *History of the Indians of Connecticut*, 323. After the Miantonomi episode described below, "the Narragansetts tried to free themselves from the [New England Confederation or United Colonies] domination by submitting themselves directly to King Charles I." Richard C. Goode, "Narragansett," in Gallay, *Colonial Wars of North America*, 469. Pulsipher describes how Philip appealed to King Charles II. *Subjects unto the Same King*, 104–105. Mandell details the Narragansetts' submission to the English throne during the interwar years. *King Philip's War*, 21.

91. This theme runs throughout Pulsipher, *Subjects unto the Same King*.

92. Oberg, *Uncas*, 87.

93. Starkey, *European and Native American Warfare*, 64; Bourne, *Red King's Rebellion*, 89–90.

94. Salisbury asserts that women only occasionally assumed political leadership in the early seventeenth century. One was "the 'Squaw Sachem' of the Mystic River Pawtucket." *Manitou and Providence*, 41, 121.

95. These women sachems were Quaiapen, alias "the Old Queen" of the Narragansetts; Awashonks and Weetamoo of the Wampanoags; and Shaumpishuh of the Quinnipiacs. For the little-known Shaumpishuh, see Lavin, *Connecticut's Indigenous Peoples*, 322.

96. Salisbury, *Manitou and Providence*, 41.

97. Lavin, *Connecticut's Indigenous Peoples*, 216–17.

98. Kevin McBride has concurred with the plausibility of this argument but noted that there is little anthropological or archaeological evidence to support it. McBride, interview with the author, New Haven, Conn., Feb. 2012. For the debate on sunksquaws, including the argument that death from disease disrupted "royal" lines, ultimately leading to their political rise, see Romero, *Making War and Minting Christians*, 207n4.

99. Ellis and Morris, *King Philip's War*, 48.

100. S. Drake, *Old Indian Chronicle*, 229.

101. Pulsipher also concludes that the issue of Philip's sovereignty over Indians was the primary factor in the onset of hostilities, but she characterizes it as a battle over rights instead of the sachem's more practical concern that he would not maintain authority without countering a major challenge to his power. *Subjects unto the Same King*, 102–106. Mandell also discusses the issues of sovereignty leading up to the

Great Narragnsett War, though he focuses on land as the major issue. *King Philip's War*, 2, 11–12, 31. Schultz and Tougias provide an example of one of Philip's warriors turning on him when he concluded that the sachem had failed to counter a colonial challenge to his authority. *King Philip's War*, 25.
102. Salisbury makes a similar point about Massasoit's position earlier in the seventeenth century. *Manitou and Providence*, 119.
103. Vaughan, *New England Frontier*, 314.
104. Ellis and Morris also argue that the Indian coalition numbered 2,500 once the Narragansetts joined the war, not including the Abenaki. *King Philip's War*, 17–18.
105. Simmons argues that the white New England population was 46,188 in 1670, with a black population of fewer than 400. *American Colonies*, 100. A very conservative estimate, then, is that the white English population by 1675 counted 50,000 inhabitants, as Ellis and Morris also argue. *King Philip's War*, 10. Statisticians have calculated that the militia to total population ratio was 5:1. See "Note on Methods of Calculation" in Greene and Harrington, *American Population before the Federal Census*.
106. Mandell, *King Philip's War*, 78–81, 115. Leach and Ellis and Morris also discuss the northern portion of the conflict. Only the conclusion of the French and Indian War in 1763 completely settled frontier fighting in northern New England.
107. Vaughan accurately approximates that the colonies had the support of 5,000 Indians during the war, which would correspond to 1,000 warriors. Half of this number were Connecticut Indians, mainly the Mohegans, Pequots, and Western Niantics, and the other half the Massachusetts and Plymouth Praying Indians. *New England Frontier*, 314. In fact, Greene and Harrington relate that in 1680, Connecticut reported 500 Indians capable of bearing arms in the colony. *American Population before the Federal Census*, 48.
108. Rhode Island governor William Coddington complained of Connecticut aggression before and during the conflict: "And further Those of Conecticutt have also formerly threatened by force that wee should not use the Kings authority there, and not to maintain it for the Kings Province as confirmed to us, It intimates their force was as much therefore as their pretence against our Indyans." Coddington to New York governor Edmund Andros, 21 July 1675, *Andros Papers*, 193.
109. A typical example is captured in Massachusetts Bay to Connecticut, 5 Apr. 1676, CWS, 1:1:59a–b. The Bay Colony admonished Connecticut for allegedly allowing its surplus corn to waste in storehouses, while Massachusetts had to send to the "Sumer Islands" for wheat to make bread. It threatened to end supplying the colony with ammunition if Connecticut refused to provide it with corn. Geoffrey Parker in *Global Crisis* addresses the damaging effect of climate change on agriculture in the early modern era and the corresponding impact on warfare.
110. Vaughan reaches the same conclusion. *New England Frontier*, 309.

2. "Endangering Also the Neighbor Colony of Connecticut"

1. Hezekiah Spencer Sheldon, "Committee for Suffield meeting notes, 20 December 1676, Present John Pynchon, George Colton, Benjamin Cooley, Rowland Thomas," in *Documentary History of Suffield.*
2. Hubbard notes the hostile Indians who moved toward Windsor. *History of the Indian Wars in New England,* 132. Ellis and Morris identify hostile forces near the other two towns. *King Philip's War,* 122–23.
3. Hubbard, *History of the Indian Wars in New England,* 88–89.
4. Hubbard, *Narrative of the Troubles with the Indians,* 28.
5. Letter from Major Pynchon, the initial commander of Massachusetts's western forces, [5 July 1648], in Temple and Adams, *History of the Town of North Brookfield,* 35–38. See also ibid., 42–46.
6. Avenues of approach are more than mere trails or pathways. These corridors are marked by traversable terrain that allows for rapid movement. Valleys and large, flat meadows are good examples of terrain that corresponds with avenues of approach. Also of note, the terrain surrounding a trail is sometimes more important than the trail itself. If forces can occupy ground that allows them to cover with weapon fire the trail, then they effectively control any movement along that route.
7. Connecticut, Google Maps, http://maps.google.com.
8. Jesse Russell and Ronald Cohn, *The Metacomet Ridge* (N.p.: Books on Demand, 2012).
9. "Perform 12-Mile Tactical Foot March," U.S. Army Expert Infantrymen Badge Standards, ArmyStudyGuide.com, http://www.armystudyguide.com/content/EIB/Task_Summary/perform-12mile-tactical-f.shtml. Although not an exact comparison given the disparity in equipment and the improved trails on today's military bases compared to the primordial New England forest paths, this juxtaposition at least creates a baseline for understanding the capabilities of Indian warriors.
10. Malone, *Skulking Way of War,* 27.
11. Ibid., 128.
12. Steven C. Eames also argues that in the later French and Indian wars, "no defense could totally stop the small Indian raiding parties." "Forts, Provincial," in Gallay, *Colonial Wars of North America,* 217. The same applies to Connecticut's defenses during the Great Narragansett War, though they proved excellent at preventing large-scale attacks.
13. Malone, *Skulking Way of War,* 13.
14. Foxhall and Forbes, "Sitometria," 51.
15. Engels, *Alexander the Great and the Logistics of the Macedonian Army,* 123. The 200-calorie difference between the two studies is negligible for our purposes, although Foxhall and Forbes completed the more reliable study. They show errors in Engels's additional calculations, such as his contention that calories were lost during the processing of wheat flour into bread. Foxhall ground the wheat in his experiment, and no calories were lost during the process of baking the ground flour

into bread. Foxhall further argues that the Macedonians would have carried whole grain instead of ground wheat flour because it kept better and was easier to transport. Foxhall and Forbes, "Sitometria," 80–81. Whole grain also packs more calories, with over 3,900 calories/kg compared to 3,400 calories/kg for flour. See "Wheat Flour, Whole-Grain," National Nutrient Database, SR26, USDA, accessed 30 Dec. 2013, http://ndb.nal.usda.gov/ndb/foods/show/6421?fg=&man=&lfacet=&count=&max=25&qlookup=Wheat%2C+whole+grain&offset=&sort=&format=Abridged&reportfmt=other&rptfrm=&ndbno=&nutrient1=&nutrient2=&nutrient3=&subset=&totCount=&measureby=&_action_show=Apply+Changes&Qv=10&Q12230=1.0.

16. Schroeder cites studies of 3,600 calories/kg for maize, which appears on the low end for the crop. "Maize Productivity," 511. The caloric output could be as high as 4,000 calories/kg. Langworthy and Hunt, *Corn Meal as a Food*, 7.
17. My calculation in deriving this is 3,500 calories (needed by soldiers in field operations) divided by 4,000 calories/kg (of ground maize) multiplied by 2.2 (to convert to pounds) equals 1.93 pounds of ground-maize rations carried by each warrior. I base this figure on the high end of maize caloric output to calculate for the maximum weight of the ration.
18. One intercolony letter describes the use of wagons in Bay Colony military formations. Massachusetts Bay to Connecticut, [?] July 1675, CWS, 1:1:5a. Also mentioning the provisioning of dragoons and accompanying wagons is United Colonies to Connecticut, 16 Sept. 1675, CWS, 1:1:19a.
19. Lee discusses these issues in "Fortify, Fight, or Flee."
20. Peterson, "Military Equipment," 198.
21. Ibid.
22. Hirsch, "Collision of Military Cultures," 1204.
23. Peterson, "Military Equipment," 199. John F. Guilmartin, Jr., describes the effectiveness of Spanish steel against the Incas. "Cutting Edge," 40–64. The New England Indians by the mid-seventeenth century had largely adopted flintlock muskets, however, allowing them to engage the colonists at a distance, unlike the Incas, who had to move within striking distance with their handheld war clubs.
24. There is no evidence of plug bayonets from excavated battle sites for the Great Narragansett War or in the inventories of colonial armories.
25. War Journal, PRCC, 385. By "War Journal," I refer to the Connecticut War Council's journal, volume 2 of which is included in Trumbull, *Public Records of the Colony of Connecticut*, volume 2 (PRCC). Other records of the General Court, Connecticut Colony, are also included in this volume (which are cited as General Court Records, PRCC). Many of the CWS documents also appear in the PRCC.
26. I describe seventeenth-century tactics, including Turner's Falls, in chapter 6. In hand-to-hand combat, one could make the argument that

swords were more effective against handheld tomahawks and knives in open terrain because of their greater reach.
27. Selesky, *War and Society in Colonial Connecticut*, 20-32.
28. For the difference between dragoons and cavalry in the colonial era, see Ward, *War of the Revolution*, 1:27.
29. General Court Records, PRCC, 270.
30. Eames, *Rustic Warriors*, 119.
31. Maj. Edward Palmes to Mr. Wharton, 3 Apr. 1676, CWS, 1:1:56. Palmes, military leader of New London, was expecting supplies from Wharton, who was one of the major weapons suppliers during "ye Dutch war," and had sent to France for muskets. Eames also discusses the issue of weapons production and procurement during the colonial era. *Rustic Warriors*, 122.
32. General Court Records, PRCC, 270, 293. The field forces were distinguished, in part, by how they were armed.
33. War Journal, PRCC, 386. Selesky in *War and Society in Colonial Connecticut* attributes this instance to a lack of feed during the winter.
34. Guilmartin, "Cutting Edge," 40-64.
35. War Journal, PRCC, 238. Faith Davison of the Mohegan Tribe alerted me to this reference and sent a compilation of references to Joshua in a document entitled "Joshua Trust/Joshua Tract, Attawanhood's Legacy," Mohegan Reservation, Montville, Conn.
36. Letter containing Thomas Warner's captivity narrative, forwarded to Governor Andros, 25 Feb. 1676, *Andros Papers*, 330-31.
37. Leach, *Flintlock and Tomahawk*, 99.
38. Mandell, *King Philip's War*, 48-53.
39. Ibid., 57, 70.
40. Naumec, "National Park Service Battlefield Protection Program Technical Report: Military History Analysis of the Battles at Nipsachuck."
41. Leach, *Flintlock and Tomahawk*, 76.
42. Mandell, *King Philip's War*, 62.
43. War Journal, PRCC, 333, 336. These Narragansetts might have been related through kinship to the Podunk Indians or on a longer-term diplomatic mission. Podunk now encompasses portions of South Windsor and East Hartford. Winthrop described this area as "a place between ys towne & Windsor," meaning Hartford and Windsor. *Winthrop Papers*, ser. 5, 8:100. Both towns extended over the Connecticut River at the time, accounting for Podunk's location on the east side. Hoccanum is now part of East Hartford.
44. Mandell, *King Philip's War*, 64-65; Leach, *Flintlock and Tomahawk*, 81-84.
45. War Journal, PRCC, 353.
46. Letter to Connecticut governor, 31 Aug. 1676, in "Minutes Relative to the Indian War in 1675 and 1676 from Letters in the Secretary's Office," Trumbull Manuscript Collections, vol. 2, Beinecke Library, Yale University, attached to p. 112. The letter's date is likely in error and should read "1675" because the colonists abandoned Derby during the fall of 1675 and had not resettled it by August 1676.

47. Mandell, *King Philip's War*, 73; Leach, *Flintlock and Tomahawk*, 87. Chapter 6 discusses Bloody Brook in more detail.
48. War Journal, PRCC, 358.
49. Ibid., 359.
50. Winthrop Papers, vol. 10, EBC-CSL, 22.
51. Letter, 10 Sept. 1675, Winthrop Papers, EBC-ICRC.
52. Mandell, *King Philip's War*, 73, 75; Leach, *Flintlock and Tomahawk*, 87–88.
53. War Journal, PRCC, 372–73; Hubbard, *History of the Indian Wars in New England*, 119–23.
54. The council received the report on 9 October 1675. War Journal, PRCC, 374. It wrote the Massachusetts council a few days later stating that its inhabitants had observed hostile scouts and tracks near Hartford. It is unclear if this letter was related to the report of 9 October. Connecticut War Council to Massachusetts War Council, 12 Oct. 1675, Massachusetts MSS, vol. 67, doc. 298, trans. William Farley, Mashantucket Pequot Museum and Research Center, Mashantucket Pequot Reservation, Conn. For the Springfield attack, see Mandell, *King Philip's War*, 75–77; and Leach, *Flintlock and Tomahawk*, 89–91.
55. Chapter 6 discusses the Connecticut-Massachusetts rift over strategy.
56. Samuel Appleton to the Connecticut War Council, 15 Oct. 1675, in Jewett, *Memorial of Samuel Appleton*, app., 113–14.
57. Christoph and Christoph, *New York Historical Manuscripts (English)*, 81.
58. "Minutes Relative to the Settlement and History of the Town of Milford," signed 1813, Trumbull Manuscript Collection, vol. 1, Beinecke Library, Yale University, 106.
59. Ellis and Morris, *King Philip's War*, 127.
60. Leach, *Flintlock and Tomahawk*, 98–99.
61. Appleton to Gov. John Leverett, 10 Nov. 1675, in Jewett, *Memorial of Samuel Appleton*, 130.
62. Appleton to Gov. John Leverett, 19 Nov. 1675, ibid., 132–33.
63. John Richards to [?] Winthrop of Connecticut, 8 Nov. 1675, Winthrop Papers, vol. 17, EBC-CSL, 175.
64. Chapter 3 further discusses Winthrop's dissent.
65. Mandell, *King Philip's War*, 87.
66. Ellis and Morris, *King Philip's War*, 149–53, 157.
67. Testimony of James Quannapohit, MHS.
68. Ibid.
69. Mandell, *King Philip's War*, 89.
70. Pulsipher, *Subjects unto the Same King*, 202.
71. Harris, *Rhode Islander Reports on King Philip's War*, 59.
72. Hubbard, *Narrative of the Troubles with the Indians*, 29.
73. Harris, *Rhode Islander Reports on King Philip's War*, 27.
74. Winthrop Papers, vol. 10, EBC-CSL, 199.
75. Temple and Adams, *History of the Town of North Brookfield*, 128. The authors also claim that the loss of Canonchet sounded the death knell of the hostile coalition.

76. Hubbard, *History of the Indian Wars in New England*, 39–40.
77. Harris, *Rhode Islander Reports on King Philip's War*, 57.
78. Pessicus to Connecticut, 29 Apr. 1676, Wyllys Papers, vol. 21, Published Manuscript Collections, Connecticut Historical Society, Hartford, 241–42. The elderly Narragansett sachem blamed the colony's allied Indians for the deaths of his men and not the English.
79. Testimony of James Quannapohit, MHS.
80. Ellis and Morris imply the Narragansetts' refusal of peace with Connecticut. *King Philip's War*, 219–20. The Wabbaquassets, a subtribe of the Nipmucks, placed themselves under Uncas's protection during the war, and various Wampanoag groups went over to Benjamin Church. War Journal, PRCC, 474; Hubbard, *History of the Indian Wars in New England*, 251. Other Nipmuck groups surrendered to Massachusetts Bay. Vaughan, *New England Frontier*, 315.
81. Jennings, *Invasion of America*, 320–21. Also see chapter 6 below.
82. These efforts are discussed below.
83. Testimony of James Quannapohit, MHS.
84. Connecticut obtained this intelligence from Governor Andros, which was a summation of a letter that he in turn had received, containing the testimony of Thomas Warner's captivity. Hostile Indians had captured Warner when he was scouting along the upper Connecticut River, and he survived an ordeal that included torture. The Indians apparently released him to carry a warning to the English, and he made it to the Massachusetts territory of Maine, where another colonist recorded his report and then relayed the information to New York. The motive for sending the letter to New York is unclear—perhaps the colonist in Maine was a royalist agent in the employ of Andros. Warner's captivity narrative, *Andros Papers*, 330–31.
85. Wyllys, *Papers*, 241–42.
86. CWS, 1:1:44a–c.
87. Grenier, *First Way of War*, 34.
88. War Journal, PRCC, 406–407.
89. Harris, *Rhode Islander Reports on King Philip's War*, 63. The Mohawks only killed a small number of Philip's warriors, though in June 1676 they may have scored larger successes. CWS, 1:1:44a–c, 1:1:98.
90. War Journal, PRCC, 402–403.
91. War Journal, PRCC, 397, 406, 461–62. For another warning from Andros, see S. Drake, *Old Indian Chronicle*, 226–27.
92. War Journal, PRCC, 407.
93. War Journal, PRCC, 334–35. Connecticut militia commanded by Captain Thomas Bull and flying the king's colors received Andros at Fort Saybrook. If New York forces had fired on them, such action would have arguably constituted an act of treason, not to mention probably the governor's defeat. But without firing a shot, Andros's men reembarked and continued eastward to supply royalist strongholds along coastal New England and at Martha's Vineyard.

94. Christoph and Christoph, *New York Historical Manuscripts (English)*, 57–58.
95. Brodhead, "London Documents," in Brodhead, Fernow, and O'Callaghan, *Documents Relative to the Colonial History of the State of New York*, 3:230–31.
96. CWS, 1:1:98.
97. War Journal, PRCC, 395–96.
98. Ibid., 403; Radune, *Pequot Plantation*, 218; Davis, *History of Wallingford Connecticut*, 351n2. Davis names the two men killed as Josiah Rockwell and John Reynolds, apparently not father and son as reported elsewhere. The teenage captive was the son of one of the men.
99. James Noyes to Gov. John Winthrop, 21 Feb. 1676, Winthrop Papers, vol. 16, EBC-CSL, 65.
100. John Stanton to Governor Andros, 9 Feb. 1676, *Andros Papers*, 326–27.
101. Mandell, *King Philip's War*, 90; Leach, *Flintlock and Tomahawk*, 157–58, 159–60, 163.
102. Noyes to Winthrop, 21 Feb. 1676, 65.
103. CWS, 1:1:145a.
104. Ray Johnson, former teacher at Hockanum School, e-mail correspondence with author.
105. War Journal, PRCC, 409–11.
106. Mandell, *King Philip's War*, 57, 96–97, 100, 101; Leach, *Flintlock and Tomahawk*, 157, 168.
107. "Minutes Relative to the Settlement and History of the Town of Milford," signed 1813, Trumbull Manuscript Collection, vol. 1, Beinecke Library, Yale University, 108.
108. Connecticut Colony to Governor Andros, 8 Mar. 1676, Wyllys, *Papers*, 240.
109. War Journal, PRCC, 423.
110. Ibid., 472.
111. Menta, "Quinnipiac," 138. "Goodman," the title equivalent of "Mr." today, was a standard designation for a male church member at the time.
112. CWS, 1:1:55. Menta asserts that a number of soldiers and colonists had seen "Rum" Tom's band proceed from Wethersfield, helping verify the group's whereabouts. "Quinnipiac," 138. George Munson Curtis and C. Bancroft Gillespie cite a land transfer to Henry Cole in 1673 from the original owner of the farmstead, Edward Higbey, probably the first Meriden resident. *Century of Meriden*, 18. The author had identified the farm's location as south of the intersection of present-day Kensington Avenue and Colony Street. The Old Colony Path from New Haven to Hartford, and later the New Colony Path from New York to Boston, ran through this portion of Meriden, and Cole's farm was not far from this throughway. The current Connecticut Routes 5 and 15 roughly traces the route from Hartford to New York.

113. Davis, *History of Wallingford Connecticut*, 126n2. Davis also places Cole's farm in what is now Meriden, although Curtis and Gillespie might have relied on his account in *A Century of Meriden.*
114. Jacobus, "Reunion of Descendants of Nathaniel Merriman," 75–76, 80. This account confirms the location of the farmstead. A serendipitous find in my family papers days before the submission of the final manuscript corroborates that Cole died in the attack probably along with his wife, though their children survived, having reached an age to move out of the family home or having been removed to the safety of other dwellings. Unpublished genealogy of William Plumb Bacon (listing his 385 early New England ancestors, including Henry Cole), courtesy of William Bacon, Jr., copy in author's possession.
115. Davis, *History of Wallingford Connecticut*, 126n2; Curtis, *A Century of Meriden*, 18; Jacobus, "Reunion of Descendants of Nathaniel Merriman," 75–76.
116. Curtis, *A Century of Meriden*, 13–25.
117. CWS, 1:1:55.
118. Mandell, *King Philip's War*, 100.
119. Ibid.; Leach, *Flintlock and Tomahawk*, 167; Ellis and Morris, *King Philip's War*, 190–92.
120. Ellis and Morris, *King Philip's War*, 202.
121. See chapter 6 for a more detailed description of these raids and an account of Canonchet's capture.
122. Reverend Russell of Hadley to unknown recipient [likely Connecticut's War Council], 15 May 1676, in Temple and Adams, *History of the Town of North Brookfield*, 129.
123. CWS, 1:1:56.
124. Ibid., 1:1:60.
125. War Journal, PRCC, 472.
126. "Minutes Relative to the Indian War in 1675 and 1676 from Letters in the Secretary's Office," Trumbull Manuscript Collections, vol. 2, Beinecke Library, Yale University, 112.
127. Menta spells Anthony's name as "Howd." "Quinnipiac," 138–39.
128. War Journal, PRCC, 472, 479–80.
129. Mandell, *King Philip's War*, 107–108; Leach, *Flintlock and Tomahawk*, 172–75; Ellis and Morris, *King Philip's War*, 210–13.
130. Mandell, *King Philip's War*, 114–15; Leach, *Flintlock and Tomahawk*, 201–204; Ellis and Morris, *King Philip's War*, 232–40.
131. Mandell, *King Philip's War*, 115; Leach, *Flintlock and Tomahawk*, 206; Ellis and Morris, *King Philip's War*, 242–43.
132. Shultz and Tougias correct Ellis and Morris's erroneous placement of the massacre at Nachek. Shultz and Tougias, *King Philip's War*, 254; Ellis and Morris, *King Philip's War*, 249–50. Mandell, unfortunately, repeats the Nachek misnomer. *King Philip's War*, 120. Shultz and Tougias are supported by Naumec, "National Park Service Battlefield Protection Program Technical Report: Military History Analysis of the Battles at Nipsachuck."

133. Leach, *Flintlock and Tomahawk*, 233–36.
134. E. Hoyt, "Indian Wars," in Lockwood, *Westfield and Its Historic Influences*, 249–50.
135. Hubbard briefly mentions Menowalett. *History of the Indian Wars in New England*, 281–82.
136. CWS, 1:1:108, 214, 217; War Journal, PRCC, 471–72.
137. CWS, 1:1:108, 217; War Journal, PRCC, 479–80. Hubbard recounts some of the Cohas episode but focuses on the retreat of hostile groups to the Hudson River. *History of the Indians Wars in New England*, 281–82.
138. Harris, *Rhode Islander Reports on King Philip's War*, 23.
139. Salisbury, *Manitou and Providence*, 41–42.
140. Lepore makes the case in *Name of War* that violence in war alters individual identity.

3. Puritan Outlier

1. CWS, 1:1:60.
2. War Journal, PRCC, 272.
3. Hubbard relates that the colonists felt betrayed by the Nipmucks, especially after sending several expeditions to secure their neutrality. *History of the Indian Wars in New England*, 104–105. Also see Schultz and Tougias, *King Philip's War*, 149.
4. Temple and Adams, *History of the Town of North Brookfield*, 46, 47, 74, 75; Jennings, *Invasion of America*, 293. Temple argues that Massasoit, the famous Wampanoag sachem who greeted the Pilgrims, might have been the leader of the Brookfield Nipmucks in the early 1660s before his death. Regardless of Massasoit's whereabouts, Temple's assertion about the close relationship between the Wampanoags and Nipmucks holds true.
5. Connecticut General Court secretary John Allyn to James Richards of Boston, 10 Sept. 16/5, Winthrop Papers, EBC-JCRC. Governor Leete refers to the disarmament and other incidents in this chapter's epigraph.
6. Schultz and Tougias, *King Philip's War*, 163.
7. Mandell, *King Philip's War*, 75–77; Leach, *Flintlock and Tomahawk*, 89–91; Schultz and Tougias, *King Philip's War*, 178–79.
8. War Journal, PRCC, 372–73. Hubbard describes the events at Springfield and the colonists' strong feelings of betrayal. *History of the Indian Wars in New England*, 119–23.
9. *Winthrop Papers*, ser. 5, 8:170.
10. Hubbard, *History of the Indian Wars in New England*, 74; Malone, *Skulking Way of War*, 45, 87.
11. Hubbard, *History of the Indian Wars in New England*, 260.
12. New England colonists had feared French and Dutch support for this conspiracy.
13. IS, 1:1:1.
14. CWS, 1:1:13.

15. War Journal, PRCC, 369. For the agreement with the Middletown Indians (Wangunks), see CWS, Original Manuscript, doc. 176.
16. CWS, 1:1:89.
17. Capt. George Denison to the War Council, early July 1676, CWS, 1:1:96b.
18. War Journal, PRCC, 379. Lavin views this as a negative situation for the Wangunks. *Connecticut's Indigenous Peoples*, 332–33.
19. War Journal, PRCC, 419.
20. CWS, 1:1:60.
21. John Allyn to Wait Winthrop, 8 July 1675, Wyllys Papers, vol. 21, doc. 71, Published Manuscript Collections, Connecticut Historical Society, Hartford.
22. One official reported that he perceived Uncas to be ungrateful for English supplies. Thomas Stanton to John Allyn, 10 May 1676, CWS 1:1:69. Lt. Thomas Minor noted in his diary that he retrieved "bread and ammunition" for the Indians at New London. This was probably for the Mohegans and Pequots, though possibly other friendly groups as well. Minor, *Diary*, 2–4 May 1676, 130–37.
23. War Journal, PRCC, 272.
24. CWS, 1:1:12; War Journal, PRCC, 349.
25. War Journal, PRCC, 400.
26. CWS, Original Manuscripts, docs. 178–79; War Journal, PRCC, 374–76.
27. Norwich inhabitants to the War Council, 7 Oct. 1676, CWS, 1:1:114.
28. For the driving off of friendly tribes, see Ellis and Morris, *King Philip's War*, 98. For the Deer Island captivity, see Schultz and Tougias, *King Philip's War*, 107; and Vaughan, *New England Frontier*, 318–19. The Massachusetts War Council banned Indians from Boston, though it urged other towns in the colony not to harass friendly groups. Massachusetts War Council to town administrators, [?] July 1675, Massachusetts MSS, vol. 67, doc. 210a, Mashantucket Pequot Museum and Research Center, Mashantucket Pequot Reservation, Conn. This attitude hardened as the war progressed and Massachusetts suffered heavy losses.
29. Bodge, *Soldiers in King Philip's War*, 67.
30. Moseley to Massachusetts Bay governor John Leverett, 16 Oct. 1675, in ibid., 69.
31. James Quannapohit, "Relation," in Temple and Adams, *History of the Town of North Brookfield*, 113. Note that the account Temple and Adams used is slightly different than my transcription of Testimony of James Quannapohit, MHS.
32. CWS, 1:59a–b.
33. O'Brien, *Dispossession by Degrees*, 61–62.
34. Original Manuscript Collection, Plymouth Colony Records, Plymouth County Courthouse, Plymouth, Mass., vol. 5, doc. 130. Philbrick briefly mentions the atrocity. *Mayflower*, 297.

35. Philbrick, *Mayflower*, 74–75.
36. For an example of one such celebration, see GateHouse News Service, "Rural and Historical Society to Host Clark's Island Picnic, July 26," 21 July 2009, WickedLocal Duxbury, accessed 17 Dec. 2010, http://www.wickedlocal.com/duxbury/homepage/x737373883/Rural-and-Historical-Society-to-host-Clark-s-Island-Picnic-July-26.
37. Original Manuscript Collection, Plymouth Colony Records, doc. 130.
38. See chapter 6.
39. Original Manuscript Collection, Plymouth Colony Records, doc. 127.
40. S. Drake, *Old Indian Chronicle*, 229.
41. Governor Coddington to Governor Andros, 21 July 1675, *Andros Papers*, 193.
42. Bartlett, *Records of the Colony of Rhode Island and Providence Plantations*, 534–35.
43. Massachusetts Governor and Council to Governor Winthrop, late June or early July 1675, Massachusetts MSS, vol. 67, doc. 209 3/4. Among other things, this letter explains that Rhode Island inhabitants were fortifying houses or fleeing to Aquidneck Island.
44. Bartlett, *Records of the Colony of Rhode Island and Providence Plantations*, 535–36.
45. Salisbury also makes the point that earlier in the seventeenth century, the Narragansetts lacked the English support enjoyed by the Mohegans and Wampanoags. *Manitou and Providence*, 229.
46. Christoph and Christoph, *New York Historical Manuscripts (English)*, 70.
47. Fernow, *New York (Colony) Council . . . Minutes*, 23.
48. Ibid., 24.
49. Christoph and Christoph, *New York Historical Manuscripts (English)*, 75.
50. Ibid., 80.
51. Ibid., 85.
52. Fernow, *New York (Colony) Council . . . Minutes*, 24.
53. Christoph and Christoph, *New York Historical Manuscripts (English)*, 102.
54. Ibid., 113.
55. Fernow, *New York (Colony) Council . . . Minutes*, 25.
56. Minutes of Andros's meeting with Indians from Westchester, Stamford, and the head of the Stratford River, 27 Apr. 1676, *Andros Papers*, 358.
57. Ibid., 354, 355.
58. Hostile groups fleeing New England tended toward the mid-Hudson River valley, described in a letter from Connecticut to the royal colony warning of their approach in late May 1676. Fernow, *New York (Colony) Council . . . Minutes*, 26. New York offered a potential safe haven for Indians under the authority of the Mohawks, as negotiated by

Andros, though New England groups feared these "Man Eaters." Webb views Andros in especially favorable light, maintaining that his policy was lenient compared to that of Connecticut and the other Puritan colonies. Webb believes that New England colonists were intent on wiping out the Indians of southern regions. See *1676*, 370–74. He cites one example from the New York Council's minutes claiming that "elements" of three southern Connecticut Indian tribes sought refuge in lower New York (Council minutes, 30 May 1676, in *A Narrative of the Causes which Led to Philip's Indian Wars*, ed. Franklin Hough [Albany, 1858], 167). The actual entry, however, makes no such reference. Fernow, *New York (Colony) Council... Minutes*, 26. Andros did negotiate with Indians in the Stamford and Stratford areas of Connecticut, however, and possibly convinced them to remain neutral, at least to further New York's interests.

59. Lee, "Fortify, Fight, or Flee," 46. Lee further develops the cultural norms for warfare and diplomacy in "Peace Chiefs and Blood Revenge" and *Barbarians & Brothers*.
60. Vaughan, *New England Frontier*, 317–18.
61. Vaughan reaches the same conclusion, pointing out American behavior toward German and Japanese Americans respectively in 1917 and 1941. Ibid., 316.
62. B. Trumbull, *Complete History of Connecticut*, 333.
63. Stiles, *History of Ancient Windsor*.
64. War Journal, PRCC, 425.
65. For a description of the attack on Simsbury, see Schultz and Tougias, *King Philip's War*, 274–75.
66. War Journal, PRCC, 435, 439. The hostile Indians offered a counterproposal for the several English captives in their possession. Temple, Sheldon, and Stratton, *History of the Town of Northfield*, 89. The colonists, probably correctly, considered it a ruse to buy time to regroup.
67. War Journal, PRCC, 458–59; Ellis and Morris, *King Philip's War*, 249–50.
68. R. Taylor, *Colonial Connecticut*, 84. Margaret Newell argues that indentured servitude in New England sometimes became slavery, including in Connecticut after 1676. "Indian Slavery in Colonial New England," 33–66.
69. Bartlett, *Records of the Colony of Rhode Island and Providence Plantations*, 549–51.
70. Unknown author to unknown recipient, 3 July 1676, Winthrop Papers, vol. 16, EBC-CSL, 65. Ralph Parker is listed in Minor, *Diary*. Sam Rogers is noted in James S. Rogers, *James Rogers and His Descendants of New London, Conn.* (Boston, 1902). See also J. H. Trumbull, *Public Records of the Colony of Connecticut*, vols. 1–2; and John Rogeres Bolles and Anna Bolles Williams, *The Rogerenes: Some Hitherto Unpublished Annals Belonging to the Colonial History of Connecticut* (Springfield, Mass., 1904). Thanks to Ashley Bissonnette, Mashantucket Pequot Museum and Research Center, for directing me to these last four sources.

71. "Appendix—Indian Captives," in *Mather Papers*, ser. 4, vol. 8, Collections of the Massachusetts Historical Society (Boston: Wiggin and Lunt for the Society, 1868), docs. 2–4.
72. Schultz and Tougias, *King Philip's War*, 128.
73. Harris, *Rhode Islander Reports on King Philip's War*, 77.
74. War Journal, PRCC, 376.
75. New Haven town meeting, 6 Mar. 1676, New Haven Colony Historical Society, *Ancient Town Records*, 2:349–51.
76. War Journal, PRCC, 359.
77. Lepore details some of the torture. *Name of War*, 3–18.
78. War Journal, PRCC, 344–45, 378.
79. Ibid., 455. Catharine North identifies Turramuggus as the sachem who in the late 1660s sold the land that became the town of Berlin. *History of Berlin*, 23. The popular notion of hostages bound and gagged by their captors did not apply in seventeenth-century New England, as trusted English families essentially took the hostages into their homes for the duration of the conflict. There were some escapees, indicating the loose "internment" of such captives.
80. CWS, 1:1:149–50.
81. War Journal, PRCC, 403.
82. John Stanton to Governor Andros, 9 Feb. 1676, *Andros Papers*, 326–27.
83. War Journal, PRCC, 472–74.
84. War Journal, PRCC, 499–500.
85. Jennings, *Invasion of America*, 217.
86. I detail this point below.
87. John Winthrop, Sr., to John Winthrop, Jr., 6 June 1627, *Winthrop Papers*, 1:352.
88. R. Black, *Younger John Winthrop*, 32.
89. Ibid., 33.
90. John Winthrop, Jr., to John Winthrop, Sr., [?] Sept. 1627, *Winthrop Papers*, 1:359; Richard Dunn does not specify how the La Rochelle expedition shaped Winthrop Jr.'s feelings about war. *Puritans and Yankees*, 62. Neil Kamil claims that his experience there developed an aggressive mindset that sprung from militant international Protestantism of the era. *Fortress of the Soul*, 630–31, 863. Jennings argues that Winthrop was an expansionist, a term corresponding to his characterization of the Europeans as "invaders." *Invasion of America*, 308. He elsewhere asserts that Winthrop attended a meeting of English and Pequot leaders, where colonial demands were delivered to the tribe prior to the Pequot War. *Warpaths*, 204–206. Steele, agreeing with Jennings, implies that Winthrop was heavy handed in his negotiations with the Pequots as chief negotiator for Massachusetts Bay during the Pequot War. *Warpaths*, 91. Vaughan asserts, however, that the beginning of the conflict preempted Winthrop's delivery of the colony's terms. *New England Frontier*, 126. Cave does not indicate that Winthrop met with the Pequots, though this might be the implication of his claim that

their allies, the Western Niantics, offered the negotiator land. *Pequot War*, 102. All accounts refer to Lion Gardiner's (commander of Fort Saybrook) relation of the event, which lacks detail and thus cannot be relied upon to form a judgment. *History of the Pequot War*, 11. The evidence is sparse concerning the younger Winthrop's involvement in the Pequot War, thus it is difficult to ascertain if he had always been sympathetic to Connecticut's Indians or if he was more heavy handed against the Pequots just prior to the earlier conflict, only to change his attitude thereafter.
91. Sir Henry Vane to John Winthrop, Jr., 5 Aug. 1636, *Winthrop Papers*, 3:282.
92. Dunn, *Puritans and Yankees*, 185.
93. Two of Winthrop's letters of resignation still exist, one to the Connecticut General Court and another sent a month later "To the Deputy-Governor and Assistants of Connecticut"; both were written prior to the onset of major hostilities. *Winthrop Papers*, ser. 5, 8:168–70. See also Dunn, *Puritans and Yankees*, 185. Robert Black notes that the second resignation attempt was on 1 July 1675. *Younger John Winthrop*, 346.
94. Dunn, *Puritans and Yankees*, 185. The crisis in early July was not only due to the hostile Indian threat but also to Governor Andros's appearance at Fort Saybrook.
95. *Winthrop Papers*, ser. 5, 8:171.
96. Ibid., 173.
97. Ibid.
98. R. Black, *Younger John Winthrop*, 350.
99. *Winthrop Papers*, ser. 5, 8:279–80; Dunn, *Puritans and Yankees*, 208; War Journal, PRCC, 408.
100. R. Black, *Younger John Winthrop*, 348.
101. Dunn, *Puritans and Yankees*, 185.
102. R. Black, *Younger John Winthrop*, 351–52.
103. As quoted in ibid., 353.
104. *Winthrop Papers*, ser. 5, 8:177.
105. R. Black, *Younger John Winthrop*, 355.
106. Ibid., 354.

4. Influences of the European Military Revolution on the New England Frontier

1. Parker, "Artillery Fortress as an Engine of European Overseas Expansion."
2. The gunpowder revolution was the spark of a broader military revolution that, according to Geoffrey Parker, included advances in addition to artillery and artillery fortresses, such as linear tactics and ships of the line equipped with the new artillery. *Military Revolution*, 6–44.
3. Quotes in Parker, "Artillery Fortress as an Engine of European Overseas Expansion."
4. Ellis and Morris claim that the Narragansetts at Great Swamp fired a volley that killed Captain Davenport and decimated his company of

Massachusetts Bay soldiers. *King Philip's War*, 151. At Bloody Brook, Hubbard recounts that Captain Moseley used European tactics for a charge through the Indians, who were pillaging the dead from Captain Lathrop's command, as part of a larger discussion criticizing the colonists' adoption of the "skulking way of war." Pierce's Fight witnessed the Indians advance en masse in a way that resembled ranks (see chapter 6 for further discussion of this battle). S. Drake, *Old Indian Chronicle*, 221, 307; Ellis and Morris, *King Philip's War*, 191; Hubbard in ibid., 113.
5. Starkey, *European and Native American Warfare*, 81. Also refer back to the introduction for historians in agreement with Starkey.
6. Philip's forces successfully assaulted at least four garrison houses: at Lancaster; one of Groton's garrison houses, though most of its inhabitants escaped; William Clark's garrison house outside of Plymouth; and Bulls's Garrison near the shore of Narragansett Bay, the appointed rendezvous for colonial forces for the attack on Great Swamp. Hubbard in Ellis and Morris, *King Philip's War*, 113; S. Drake, *Old Indian Chronicle*, 252; Ellis and Morris, *King Philip's War*, 147–48, 187.
7. Hubbard, *History of the Indian Wars in New England*, 260–61.
8. General Court Records, PRCC, 268–69. The court ordered each town to provide for its own protection, and at this stage of the war, it was almost always garrison defense. The records have instances of the War Council approving or requiring garrison houses in certain towns.
9. Steven C. Eames, "Garrison Houses," in Gallay, *Colonial Wars of North America*, 259.
10. As quoted in Townshend, "Quinnipiack Indians and Their Reservation," 184.
11. War Journal, PRCC, 375. Eames relates that "flankers . . . built at opposite corners of the palisade that could . . . cover the outer walls in case of attack" only occurred "as the French and Indian wars progressed." "Garrison Houses," 260. In fact, the New England colonies utilized garrison flankers in 1675–76.
12. Malone, *Skulking Way of War*, 32.
13. Eames, "Garrison Houses," 260.
14. Lee, "Fortify, Fight, or Flee," 745n100.
15. Vaughan, *New England Frontier*, 130.
16. Larry E. Ivers, "Rangers," in Gallay, *Colonial Wars of North America*, 620–21.
17. Cave, *Pequot War*, 91–92. Vaughan also discusses Gardiner's European military engineering pedigree. *New England Frontier*, 117.
18. Cave, *Pequot War*, 92.
19. Ten Raaa and de Bas, *Het Staatsche Leger*. This source is the official Dutch military history that details the English regiments in Dutch service, which John Stapleton, West Point, translated for me.
20. Benjamin Trumbull relates that Mason had served under Sir Thomas Fairfax, who was in college until joining Vere's Brigade in Dutch service in 1628–29. *Complete History of Connecticut*, 322; Ian J. Gentles, "Fairfax, Thomas, Third Lord Fairfax of Cameron (1612–1671)," *Oxford*

Dictionary of National Biography, online ed. 2008 (Oxford: Oxford University Press, 2004). And if Stiles is correct in his assertion that Mason arrived in the New World in 1630, then 1629, the year that the great siege took place, was the only overlapping year of their service. *History of Ancient Windsor*, 124. Hergatobosch was known for the novel tactics employed, with the chief Dutch engineer rerouting two streams and thus deswamping the area, allowing for a formal siege. As a participant of the operation, Mason may have learned unusual approaches to assaulting fortresses, informing his later actions at Mystic. Underhill, who was probably in the same unit as Mason, employed a similar technique for the Dutch during Kieft's War against Indians in what is now Westchester County, New York.

21. Battle of Mystic Archaeological Project. Historians consider Mason's actions immoral and against the rules of war even by the standards of the early modern era.
22. Chet, *Conquering the American Wilderness*, 39, 67.
23. Selesky, *War and Society in Colonial Connecticut*, 16n23.
24. Trumbull, *Public Records of the Colony of Connecticut*, 3:15; Robert Chapman [at Saybrook] to War Council at Hartford, 28 July 1676, Box 12, Chapman, Saybrook Families, Frank Stevenson Archives, Old Saybrook Historical Society, Old Saybrook, Conn., 1; "William Pratt," The Founders of Hartford, Society Descendants of the Founder of Hartford, video genealogy, 2006, http://www.foundersofhartford.org/founders/pratt_william.htm; undated document, Box 12 DB 12.43, Pratt, Saybrook Families, Stevenson Archives, Old Saybrook Historical Society; Society of the Colonial Wars in the State of Ohio, *Register of the Society of Colonial Wars in the State of Ohio* (Cleveland, 1916), 72; D. Tracy, *Lieutenant Thomas Tracy and 'The Widow Mason' of Wethersfield, Connecticut* (Boston, 1907). These sources were located in Bissonnette, File of Pequot War–King Philip's War Veterans, Mashantucket Pequot Museum and Research Center, Mashantucket Pequot Reservation, Conn.
25. Trumbull, *Public Records of the Colony of Connecticut*, 3:22n.
26. Trumbull Papers, ser. 5, vol. 9, Massachusetts Historical Society Collections, Boston; William R. Cutter and William F. Adams, *Genealogical and Personal Memoirs: Relating to the Families of the State of Massachusetts*, vol. 4 (New York: Lewis Historical Publishing, 1910), 2225; MSS, RG 150, Society of Colonial Wars of Connecticut, Original Applications, Connecticut State Library, Hartford; Trumbull, *Public Records of the Colony of Connecticut*, 4:276; D. H. Hurd, ed., *History of Essex County, Massachusetts*, vol. 2 (Boston: J. W. Lewis, 1888), 1179; Thomas P. Hughes and Frank Munsell, *American Ancestry: Given the Name and Descent, in the Male Line of Americans Whose Ancestors Settled in the United States Previous to the Declaration of Independence, A.D., 1776*, vol. 12 (Albany, N.Y.: Joel Munsell's Sons, 1899), 22; Hartford County Court Records, iv. 25, 399; Caulkins, *History of New London*, 295, in "Ye Ancientest Book," Winthrop Papers, EBC-ICRC.

These sources were located in Bissonnette, File of Pequot War–King Philip's War Veterans.
27. *Burke's Landed Gentry of Great Britain*, quoted in Hill, *Modern History of New Haven*, 240; Stearns, Whitcher, and Parker, *Genealogical and Family History of the State of New Hampshire*, 310.
28. S. Gardiner, *History of the Great Civil War*, 442–47.
29. Gentles, *New Model Army*, 55–60.
30. *Winthrop Papers*, ser. 5, 8:43n; PRCC, app. 14, 566–67; Schenck, *History of Fairfield*, 170–71.
31. I interviewed a number of combat veterans in the History Department at West Point, and they unanimously agreed that training can only approximate battlefield conditions to an extent, that no peacetime activity can truly replicate direct combat. This is also what I observed from my experience with 3rd Infantry Division in Afghanistan during 2012–13.
32. Clausewitz, *On War*, 122. Also see ibid., 119–21.
33. Compare the representations of trainband flags in K. Roberts, *Cromwell's War Machine*, diagram 179; and Chartrand, *Colonial American Troops*, 32.
34. K. Roberts, *Cromwell's War Machine*, 92. See chapter 6 for Connecticut's employment of dragoons.
35. Gentles, *New Model Army*, 384.
36. Ibid., 382–84.
37. Dunn, *Puritans and Yankees*, 62.
38. *Winthrop Papers*, ser. 5, 8:23.
39. "Landguard Fort," Fortified Places, accessed Aug. 2012, http://www.fortified-places.com/landguard/.
40. *Winthrop Papers*, ser. 5, 8:30.
41. Reverend Russell to Connecticut War Council, 15 May 1676, CWS, 1:1:71a.
42. The New York State Library maintains Winthrop, Jr.'s surviving library collection of 270 books and pamphlets. "Catalogue of the Books Belonging to the New-York Society Library." Ward's book is the one specific military text in the remaining collection. There has been some debate over the authenticity of the library, however. Some of the texts were originally and probably correctly attributed to Winthrop, Sr. Also, as Herbert Greenberg argues, at least 20 volumes were printed after the date of Winthrop, Jr.'s death (April 1676), proving these tracts were added to the collection at a later time. "Authenticity of the Library of John Winthrop the Younger," 448–52. See also Winthrop, Starkey, and Browne, "Notes from the Books and Letters of John Winthrop, Jr.," 325–42. Ward's book was published in 1639, and the copy in the collection was assuredly in New England during the Great Narragansett War.
43. Complete title found at Newton Library Online Catalog, University of Cambridge, U.K.
44. Nathaniel Merriman's will and final testament from the original of 1692, in Jacobus, "Reunion of Descendants of Nathaniel Merriman."

45. Parker, "Artillery Fortress as an Engine of European Overseas Expansion"; Lee, "Using the Natives against the Natives."
46. General Court Records, PRCC, 334–35; Cave, *Pequot War*, 92.
47. Governor Winthrop recorded the threat of the Dutch fleet to Connecticut's coastline in 1665 and 1667. *Winthrop Papers*, ser. 5, 8:97, 118. During the English-Dutch war of 1673–74, he sent intelligence to his son Fitz-John on Long Island when the Dutch fleet sailed from New York. Ibid., 152. The fleet's destination was unknown, but it easily could have raided the Connecticut coast.
48. Ibid., 158.
49. War Journal, PRCC, 556–57; Schenk, *History of Fairfield*, 170–71.
50. Testimony of James Quannapohit, MHS.
51. Selesky mentions this temporary French-Dutch alliance. *War and Society in Colonial Connecticut*, 14.
52. *Winthrop Papers*, ser. 5, 8:98, 100, 102, 118.
53. Ibid., 100.
54. Ibid., 102. Bodge notes that Major Mason "organized a troop of horse of thirty-seven members" in 1658 and that it had increased in size to sixty members by 1672. *Soldiers in King Philip's War*, app., 466–67. This unit of regular cavalry (not dragoons) was known as the First Connecticut Cavalry and was probably the one sent by Governor Winthrop to reconnoiter the route to Canada.
55. *Winthrop Papers*, ser. 5, 8:104.
56. Cohen, *Conquered into Liberty*, 11.
57. *Winthrop Papers*, ser. 5, 8:103, 119.
58. As described in an earlier chapter, Connecticut leadership rarely demanded the surrendering of firearms. That Mason, the patron of the Mohegans, made some members surrender weapons testifies to the colonists' perception of the seriousness of the threat. Other leaders believed strongly in the plot, such as veteran Indian agent Thomas Stanton and Secretary Allyn. IS, 1:1:1, 4, 10, 12–22.
59. McBride, "Pequot in King Philip's War."
60. Hubbard ultimately concludes that the French were not actively aiding Philip. *History of the Indian Wars in New England*, 266. For the French at Pocumtuck, see ibid., 203. Certainly Hubbard did not have at his disposal much evidence in 1677 to make this claim. Although the French failed to send an army to aid the coalition, they did provide material assistance such as ammunition. Testimony of James Quannapohit, MHS.
61. Testimony of James Quannapohit, MHS.
62. CWS, 1:1:17.
63. Deputy Governor Leete to Governor Andros, 6 Oct. 1675, Wyllys Papers, vol. 21, Published Manuscript Collections, Connecticut Historical Society, Hartford, 226–27.
64. A letter dated 8 August 1676 references French movements from Canada. New York officials held a conference with Mohawk sachems

on 10 August about French encroachments in this area. Fernow, *New York (Colony) Council . . . Minutes*, 26.
65. Parker, "Artillery Fortress as an Engine of European Overseas Expansion."
66. The War Council's journal has at least two notations for "flankers" and one for "forelorns," defenses in front of the main works. See War Journal, PRCC, 375, 413, 444. Forelorns served the same purpose as the forelorn body of musketeers in front of the main line of infantry, serving as an alert to the main defenses and a disruption of enemy formation. Due to the exposure to the enemy and the chance that they would fail in their mission, such units on the march or manning defenses were thus often referred to as a "forelorn hope."
67. R. Roberts, *Encyclopedia of Historic Forts*, 122, 125.
68. I have walked the terrain at Saybrook Point on a number of occasions and believe that the original fort was on the ten-meter-high hillock approximately seventy-five meters to the northeast of the current (as of 2013) park display for the fort. The National Park Service established a grant for Foxwoods Museum staff to locate the original site, and Kevin McBride's initial archaeological survey and finds from a June 2013 dig indicate that the fort very likely was at this alternate location.
69. Deputy Governor Leete and Secretary Allyn [letter written in two scripts] to seaside towns, 19 July 1675, Wyllys Papers, 215–16.
70. John Talcott Record Book, Connecticut Historical Society, Hartford, 43.
71. "New Haven Colony Laws," in Hoadly, *Records of the Colony or Jurisdiction of New Haven*, 569.
72. Ibid., 577.
73. New Haven General Court meeting, 14 July 1654, New Haven Colony Historical Society, *Ancient Town Records*, 1:217; Town meeting, 4 Aug. 1673, ibid., 2:312.
74. *Winthrop Papers*, ser. 5, 8:149.
75. Massachusetts War Council journal, Oct. 1675, in Shurtleff, *Records of the Governor and Company of the Massachusetts Bay*.
76. Town meeting, 24 Sept. 1675, New Haven Colony Historical Society, *Ancient Town Records*, 2:340–41.
77. Town meeting, 12 Oct. 1675, ibid., 341–42.
78. Town meeting, 30 Oct. 1675, ibid., 343–45.
79. Town meeting, 11 Mar. 1676, ibid., 351–52.
80. Town meeting, 30 Oct. 1675, 343–45; town meeting, 7 Feb. 1676, 348–49; and town meeting, 25 Apr.1676, ibid. 352–53. Townshend claims that an "outline" from the Colonial Records of New Haven Colony described New Haven's defensive works: "The fortifications consisted of a palisade line of wooden posts of timber that would square twelve (12) inches set close together five (5) feet in the ground and several thicknesses and ten (10) feet above and at the top pointed; which

were properly braced and filled in between with earth and clay excavated from the ditch dug on the outside ten (10) feet deep and fifty (50) feet wide which was flooded with water from the harbor, and perhaps from the Beaver Ponds. This Palisade was built wide enough for a soldier to march on top and may have had also a platform on the inside low enough for a sentinel to walk, with body protected by the works, with loopholes for observation. On the sea side in full view were the king's arms cut in wood and great guns mounted, also at the meeting house in the Market Place, which was protected by flankers and palisades (with a 'watch tower' on top)." "Quinnipiack Indians and Their Reservation," 189. Although I have not found any such reference in the New Haven Colony records or the *Ancient Town Records*, aspects of Townshend's description correspond with available records concerning the town's defenses.

81. Orcutt, *History of the Old Town of Stratford*, 143–44.
82. Plymouth rebuilt its original fortification at least four times along the original trace in 1632, 1635, 1642, and 1675, while Massachusetts Bay rebuilt its "castle" a number of times as well. Arthur, "Coast Forts of Colonial Massachusetts," 106, 108–21.
83. Barner, *Connecticut Historical Collections*, 49.
84. John F. Guilmartin, conversation with author concerning ranges for trained gun crews of the early modern era, Spring 2011. For the limitations of black-powder technology, see Guilmartin, *Gunpowder & Galleys*, apps.
85. Stiles, *History of Ancient Windsor*, 155, 162.
86. Meeting notes, Committee for Suffield, 20 Dec. 1676, in Sheldon, *Documentary History of Suffield*. The committee consisted of John Pynchon, George Colton, Benjamin Cooley, and Rowland Thomas.
87. Orcutt, *History of Stratford*, 139, 169.
88. The author completed a terrain analysis of the site of the Denison fortress and interviewed the Denison Homestead staff, who provided this information. Kevin McBride's Foxwoods archaeological team completed an initial survey (mentioned in note 69 above) and found no convincing evidence of military occupation of this terrain, though all members agreed that this was the most likely site of the Denison fort. Also see Wheeler, *History of Stonington*, 22.
89. Selesky, *War and Society in Colonial Connecticut*, 18.
90. Thomas Topping to Connecticut War Council, 4 Mar. 1676, Wyllys, *Papers*, 232–33.
91. For palisades at Wethersfield. see R. Roberts, *Encyclopedia of Historic Forts*, 125. Wethersfield voted to construct a palisade, but it remains unclear if the project was completed. A town historian from the Wethersfield Historical Society, with whom I discussed the issue in June 2008, doubts that the colonists completed it.
92. Schenck, *History of Fairfield*, 170, 192.
93. Merriman's barn was chosen for flankers as noted on 5 October in a Town Record entry, Wallingford. Jacobus, "Reunion of Descendants

of Nathaniel Merriman," 72; War Journal, PRCC, 425 (Haddam). For the Rye garrison house, see "Old Rye Fort, 1675," Historical Marker Database, accessed Fall 2010, http://www.hmdb.org/marker.asp?marker=34485.
94. Caulkins, *History of New London*, 183; and *History of Norwich*, 106.
95. General Court Records, PRCC, 266, 269; General Court to New Haven and other towns, 1 July 1675, in Orcutt and Beardsley, *History of the Old Town of Derby*, 53.
96. Orcutt, *History of the Old Town of Stratford*, 196; Orcutt and Beardsley, *History of the Old Town of Derby*, 55–56; Prichard, *Town and City of Waterbury*, 137. A letter in the fall of 1676 from John Bower of Derby and Zachariah Walker of Woodbury, representing the settlers, who had deserted their plantations, requested garrisons funded by the colony as a precondition for returning. CWS 1:1:115.
97. For a description of the flankers, see Captain Henchman to Governor Leverett, 31 July 1675, Massachusetts Manuscript Collections, vol. 67, doc. 232, University of Massachusetts, Dorchester. Ellis and Morris elaborate on the fort's purpose. *King Philip's War*, 80.
98. Massachusetts leaders informed Governor Winthrop that Rhode Islanders had fled to Aquidneck Island (Newport and other towns there) or were fortifying their houses on the mainland and requested that Connecticut engage the hostiles. Massachusetts War Council to John Winthrop, Jr., 10 July 1675, Massachusetts MSS, vol. 67, doc. 209 3/4, Mashantucket Pequot Museum and Research Center, Mashantucket Pequot Reservation, Conn.
99. Rhode Island authorities advised residents to abandon their towns and move to Aquidneck Island. Rhode Island General Assembly to Warwick and Providence, 13 Mar. 1675, in Bartlett, *Records of the Colony of Rhode Island and Providence Plantations*, 533.

5. The Defense of Connecticut

1. General Court Records, PRCC, 331. Connecticut had relied on committees similar to the War Council during the Pequot War and Third Anglo-Dutch War. Selesky, *War and Society in Colonial Connecticut*, 10, 17.
2. General Court Records, PRCC, 261. The "assistants" were advisors to the governor and deputy governor rather than clerical staff.
3. Romero, *Making War and Minting Christians*, 36–37.
4. Shurtleff, *Records of the Colony of Plymouth*, 197.
5. Fernow, *New York (Colony) Council . . . Minutes*, introduction.
6. Chapter 6 discusses this episode.
7. Fernow, *New York (Colony) Council . . . Minutes*, introduction.
8. Wayne Lee describes organizational subcultures that also apply to the war councils of the Great Narragansett War. *Barbarians & Brothers*, 6–7.
9. Shurtleff, *Records of the Colony of Plymouth*, 176.

10. Ibid., 173–210.
11. Ibid., 197.
12. War Journal, PRCC, 362.
13. CWS, 1:83. Leete was concerned that Talcott had failed to complete this mission as ordered and was worried about the prospect of the campaign failing. CWS, 1:87.
14. See chapter 6 for numbers deployed in offensive operations.
15. "Necessitated to Meet Daily in Councill," Massachusetts Council journal, 28–29 June 1676, Massachusetts MSS, vol. 67, doc. 210, Mashantucket Pequot Museum and Research Center, Mashantucket Pequot Reservation, Conn.
16. General Court Records, PRCC, 331.
17. Ibid., 331, 333. This might have been in part a response to a report from Uncas that suspicious Indians were lurking in the woods. *Winthrop Papers*, ser. 5, 8:402.
18. War Journal, PRCC, 336.
19. Ibid., 337.
20. S. Drake, *Old Indian Chronicle*, 229.
21. Stephen C. Eames, "Scout," in Gallay, *Colonial Wars of North America*, 679.
22. War Journal, PRCC, 345. Robert Black also concludes that it was an emergency meeting because of the unusual time of the session. *Younger John Winthrop*, 350.
23. General Court Records, PRCC, 333, 336.
24. War Journal, PRCC, 353.
25. Ibid., 358–59.
26. Ibid., 359–60.
27. A feint is a military maneuver that involves combat and distracts the enemy from the friendly forces' main objective. A demonstration is a maneuver without engaging in combat for the same purposes as a feint. Coalition forces employed both techniques in Connecticut, killing lone colonists at times or making their presence known without actual combat in other instances.
28. War Journal, PRCC, 361.
29. Ibid., 362.
30. Ibid., 372–73.
31. Ibid., 374.
32. Ibid., 375.
33. General Court Records, PRCC, 290. I estimate Connecticut's total population at 11,000 colonists in 1675 based on the total population of 12,535 in 1679. Greene and Harrington, *American Population before the Federal Census*, 48. An estimate of 11,000 colonists also is largely consistent with the accepted 5–1 ratio of militia to total population.
34. Lee, "Fortify, Fight, or Flee," 43.
35. War Journal, PRCC, 382.
36. S. Drake, *Old Indian Chronicle*, 226–27.
37. War Journal, PRCC, 389.

38. Orcutt, *History of the Old Town of Stratford*, 139; Caulkins, *History of New London*, 183.
39. North, *History of Berlin*, 9.
40. War Journal, PRCC, 403.
41. Ibid., 408.
42. Ibid., 409–10.
43. Ibid., 411.
44. Ibid., 413.
45. Ibid., 417.
46. Ibid., 423, 426.
47. Ibid., 423.
48. Ibid., 451–52.
49. Fischer, *Washington's Crossing*.
50. War Journal, PRCC, 469.
51. Ibid., 420.
52. Parker, "Artillery Fortress as an Engine of European Overseas Expansion."
53. Hubbard, *History of the Indian Wars in New England*, 146.
54. S. Drake, *Old Indian Chronicle*, 181.
55. Hubbard states that the Narragansetts killed more than eighty colonists. *History of the Indian Wars in New England*, 152. Ellis and Morris report that eighty-two officers and soldiers died at the Great Swamp and immediately following the battle. *King Philip's War*, 154. Considering those soldiers who died months later of wounds, the final tally was nearer to one hundred killed in action and mortally wounded.
56. Hubbard, *History of the Indian Wars in New England*, 152.
57. S. Drake, *Old Indian Chronicle*, 181; Hubbard, *History of the Indian Wars in New England*, 153.
58. Hubbard, *History of the Indian Wars in New England*, 146, 153.
59. For a recent account of the debate, see Marilyn Bellemore, Townnews.com 1995–2008, Zwire.com, *NKStandardTimes.com*, accessed 5 May 2008, http://www.zwire.com/site/news.cfm?newsid=13684198&BRD=1715&PAG=461&dept_id=73974&rfi=6 (content discontinued).
60. Ellis and Morris, *King Philip's War*, 145–46n2; quote from Sidney S. Rider, *The Lands of Rhode Island*, 236, cited in ibid.
61. Ellis and Morris, *King Philip's War*, 147n1.
62. S. Drake, *Old Indian Chronicle*, 194, 197.
63. City Distance Tool, Geobytes, http://www.geobytes.com/CityDistanceTool.htm?loadpage. I calculated the distance from Exeter to Kingston, Rhode Island, using this website, though the two forts were at a slightly greater distance as Queen's Fort was north of Exeter and Great Swamp west of South Kingston.
64. Ibid. Here I used the calculated distance between Kingston and Charlestown, Rhode Island.
65. For part of the popular debate surrounding the idea that the Dutch, Portuguese, or English built this European-style fort, see Michael Luciano da Silva, "Ninigret—A Portuguese Fort," *Portuguese Pilgrims and*

Dighton Rock, accessed 2 May 2008, http://www.dightonrock.com/pilgrim_chapter_10.htm. Jeremy Black alludes to the Portuguese influence on New England maritime traditions, lending academic weight to this discussion. *Fighting for America*, 24.
66. C. C. Taylor, "Fort Ninigret," 277–86.
67. Ibid., 280–81.
68. R. Roberts, *Encyclopedia of Historic Forts*, 704.
69. S. Drake, *Old Indian Chronicle*, 193.
70. Lee, "Fortify, Fight, or Flee," 728–30. Steele reports that the Susquehannocks also built upon an earlier Indian construction. They used the site of a European-style fortification with an "earthen fort, complete with cannon, bastions, and ditch, to which they added a strong exterior stockade." *Warpaths*, 53. Subsequent research has shown that colonists actually manned the Indian cannons. Starkey discusses how the Indians "undermined the wall by tunneling" at Fort Presu'Isle in 1763. *European and Native American Warfare*, 24.
71. Lee, "Fortify, Fight, or Flee," 734.
72. Ibid. The colonists in New England and the Southeast similarly blamed English fugitives for assisting the various Indians in building their fortresses, a further parallel between the two examples. In the Narragansett case, there was the additional anecdote of "Stonewall John," an English-trained mason who purportedly designed the Indian forts. Ellis and Morris, *King Philip's War*, 146n1.
73. S. Drake, *Old Indian Chronicle*, 193.
74. Ibid., 300. Samuel Drake agrees with Benjamin Church's assertion that the reinforcements were from "Pumham's town," the village of another Narragansett sachem. Ibid., 300n367. This was poor military intelligence since Pumham's village was on Warwick Neck, even further removed than the Queen's Fort from Great Swamp. Thus, there was possibly a supporting fortification adjoining Great Swamp.
75. Eames, "Scout," 679.

6. "To Prosecute the Enemie Wth All Vigor"

1. Ellis and Morris, *King Philip's War*, 202.
2. The one exception was that Connecticut sustained heavy casualties at the Great Swamp Fight; the Narragansetts killed or mortally wounded more than forty soldiers. B. Trumbull, *Complete History of Connecticut*, 286n. The heavy casualties had less to do with incompetence than with the unique situation of the battle.
3. Hubbard, *History of the Indian Wars in New England*, 173n275, 175–78; S. Drake, *Old Indian Chronicle*, 307–308. Toward the end of the war, Philip's men ambushed one of Church's expeditions in another case of Plymouth's allied Indians not discovering the hostile Indians, although they only killed one colonist. Ellis and Morris, *King Philip's War*, 264. Starkey indicates that the Narragansetts ambushed Pierce even with friendly Indian support but does not compare this with the Mohegan-Pequot success. *European and Native American Warfare*, 77.

Perhaps the Praying Indians' "cutting off way of war" military skills had degenerated from living among the English.
4. Ellis and Morris, *King Philip's War*, 105–108, 111–14, 190–92, 210–11, 232–34.
5. Grenier claims that Church inaugurated a new form of warfare with raids into Nipmuck country in early 1676. *First Way of War*, 33. There were a number of expeditions prior to this with Connecticut forces, however, as well as the joint English and Indian expeditions of the Pequot War. Grenier creates the prequel to Russell Weigley's *American Way of War*. Weigley contends that an "American Way of War" emerged once the United States developed the power to wage wars of annihilation. According to this theory, before this time, Americans relied on Grenier's proposed "First Way of War" and returned to it sporadically afterward. The targeting of noncombatants did serve as a major facet of American warfare, yet it was neither novel nor the only kind of warfare practiced. John Lynn's *Battle*, Patrick Porter's *Military Orientalism*, and Wayne Lee's *Warfare and Culture in World History* each challenge the "ways of wars" methodology. Porter argues for an experience of a universal soldier in place of a ways-of-war concept, while Lynn argues against both the universal soldier and a ways-of-war methodology. Lee implies that the ways-of-war argument is limited, a critique seemingly at odds with the "cutting off way of war" concept.
6. Chet, *Conquering the American Wilderness* 40, 46, 47, 52. Chet argues that the colonists won the war through the disruption of the Indians' supply base alone. Ibid., 63. This disruption was a decisive factor in the coalition's defeat, but it was *offensive* operations that created this situation. Such operations also led to the killing and capturing of key coalition leaders, throwing the hostile Indian groups into disarray and rendering their supply base vulnerable.
7. S. Drake, *Old Indian Chronicle*, 221, 307; Ellis and Morris, *King Philip's War*, 191.
8. Chet, *Conquering the American Wilderness*, 52. Starkey also argues that the Great Swamp Fight was "a failure." *European and Native American Warfare*, 77.
9. Howard, "Use and Abuse of Military History," 4–5.
10. The "metrics" to quantify competence include the number of successful engagements that the allied Indians assisted in facilitating as well as the fact that Connecticut forces were never ambushed. The latter is a negative way to measure success but a significant metric in light of the failures of the other colonies.
11. Clayton, *Warfare in Woods and Forests*, 21–29.
12. Steven C. Eames, "Scout," in Gallay, *Colonial Wars of North America*, 679. Eames here is discussing the French and Indian wars, but the same held true during the Great Narragansett War.
13. Selesky, *War and Society in Colonial Connecticut*, 20.
14. Major Talcott's forces killed and captured 238 Narragansetts during this campaign, mostly noncombatants. CWS, 1:1:97. It appears

that Connecticut soldiers served in the defense of Hatfield, where hostile Indians killed a handful in action, though they might have been responding from Hadley. CWS, 1:1:84a.
15. Romero views the training of European skills as reinforcing Puritan hierarchy and masculinity, though he goes on to argue that there was no practical purpose for it, ignoring the European threat to New England. *Making War and Minting Christians*, 151–54, 159.
16. The inhabitants of Fairfield County, Connecticut's nearest county to New Amsterdam, feared a Dutch invasion by land and sea. Schenck, *History of Fairfield*, 171.
17. Childs, *Warfare in the Seventeenth Century*, 152.
18. Appleton to Leverett, 10, 19 Nov. 1675, in Jewett, *Memorial of Samuel Appleton*, 130, 132. Highlighting the importance of fodder for operations, Appleton mentioned the lack of it above other missing necessities.
19. Colonists and Indians both appealed to arbitration and usually accepted the outcome. European affairs often precipitated other crises in the New World, such as the English wars with the Dutch, French, and Spanish.
20. "STRATEGIC CONSUMPTION: A term not used by Clausewitz, but derived from his observation that attacking forces diminish in strength as they advance into enemy territory due to the diversions of manpower imposed by the expansion of one's area of operations. The many causes of strategic consumption include the need to defend lines of communications, disease, desertion, and battle casualties." "Course Notebook for the History of the Military Art," 15.
21. Anderson, *War That Made America*, 114.
22. Fitz-John Winthrop attempted to invade Canada via the Lake Champlain corridor during King William's War, as did Colonel Nicholson during Queen Anne's War and Abercromby during the French and Indian War. Carleton and Burgoyne failed on the same route in reverse. Braddock miscarried against Fort Duquesne; Howe failed to gain the colonial capital of Philadelphia during 1776, forcing him to enter winter quarters; and the French and colonists trapped Cornwallis at Yorktown after failed operations in the Carolinas and Virginia. All of these campaigns were limited by weather, terrain, disease, and a lack of logistical capability. For the failures along Lake Champlain, see McCully, "Catastrophe in the Wilderness," 441–56. For descriptions of various campaigns along the Richelieu-Champlain-Hudson Rivers invasion route and the author's claims for the resulting effect on the American way of war, see Cohen, *Conquered into Liberty*.
23. Anderson, *War That Made America*, 195.
24. As often happened in colonial operations around the world with slow transmission of messages, this campaign occurred after the English and Dutch had already agreed upon a peace accord.
25. Maj. Fitz-John Winthrop to Connecticut Court or War Council, n.d., PRCC, app. 14, 566–67; Schenk, *History of Fairfield*, 170–71.

26. Gallay, *Indian Slave Trade*, 181.
27. Published testimony of George Memicho, an allied Indian, in Temple and Adams, *History of the Town of North Brookfield*, 100.
28. Orcutt, *History of the Old Town of Stratford*, 197.
29. Temple, Sheldon, and Stratton, *History of the Town of Northfield*, 92; War Journal, PRCC, 385.
30. Sir Edward Walker, as quoted in K. Roberts, *Cromwell's War Machine*, 90.
31. As quoted in Gallay, *Indian Slave Trade*, 167.
32. John Talcott Record Book, Connecticut Historical Society, Hartford, 43.
33. "Necessitated to Meet Daily in Councill," Massachusetts Council journal, 28 or 29 June 1676, Massachusetts MSS, vol. 67, doc. 210, Mashantucket Pequot Museum and Research Center, Mashantucket Pequot Reservation, Conn.
34. War Journal, PRCC, 270.
35. Zelner, *Rabble in Arms*, 214.
36. For an example of a press order for dragoons, see War Journal, PRCC, 346. Also see Minor, *Diary*, 16 Feb. 1676, 134.
37. Radune, *Pequot Plantation*, 221.
38. Minor, *Diary*, 24 June 1676, 136. Minor's entry refers to his son coming home from the army. Merriman's son was killed in combat during the war. Jacobus, "Reunion of Descendants of Nathaniel Merriman." Also Surgeon Simon Cooper of Newport issued a bill for services rendered for, among others, Mason, Jr., who was mortally wounded: "Capt: Mason of Norrodg his scull brocke I did for him & tooke out many peeses not Cured & accomidated him." CWS, 1:1:72a.
39. War Journal, PRCC, 437.
40. Ibid., 420.
41. Zelner, *Rabble in Arms*, 214.
42. The British armies of the American Revolution and the Napoleonic Wars exemplified soldiers of the lower classes performing well in battle. Frederick the Great's vaunted Prussian infantry were usually healthy farm boys recruited from the regimental cantons. Showalter, "Wars of Frederick the Great," 31–38.
43. Pynchon to Connecticut leaders, 6 Aug. 1675, Wyllys Papers, 1590–1746, vol. 21, Connecticut Historical Society Published Manuscript Collections, Hartford, 215–16.
44. Harris, *Rhode Islander Reports on King Philip's War*, 61.
45. Hutchinson quoted in Avery and Avery, *Groton Avery Clan*, 61.
46. The "Appleton affair" described in this section is from Jewett, *Memorial of Samuel Appleton*, 87–143; and War Journal, PRCC, 378, 379, 381, 382. Leach briefly describes the episode in *Flintlock and Tomahawk*, 96–100.
47. *Winthrop Papers*, ser. 5, 8:280.
48. Fitz-John to Wait Winthrop, 8 July 1675, ibid., 279. This was written before the expedition into Narragansett territory.

49. T. Church, *History of King Philip's War*, 30–35.
50. Harris, *Rhode Islander Reports on King Philip's War*, 63, 67.
51. Romero, *Making War and Minting Christians*, 56.
52. On the temporary resurgence of combined tribes in northwestern Connecticut in the eighteenth century, see De Forest, *History of the Indians of Connecticut*, chap. 10.
53. Ibid., 65.
54. Anderson, *War That Made America*, 7.
55. New Haven deed, 14 Nov. 1638, quoted in Orcutt, *Indians of the Housatonic and Naugatuck Valleys*, 8.
56. Temple, Sheldon, and Stratton, *History of the Town of Northfield*, 28–29.
57. LeBlanc, *Constant Battles*, 140.
58. Ibid., 210.
59. De Forest, *History of the Indians of Connecticut*, 66.
60. Gallay, *Indian Slave Trade*, 174.
61. The Pequots and Mohegans did not emerge victorious from every engagement in the greater northeastern region, for the Rahway Indians of Long Island delivered a Pequot scalp to Governor Andros at Manhattan on 29 February 1676. *Andros Papers*, 332. The circumstances of that event and the true identity of the scalp in question, however, remain unclear. This might have been a group of Pequots that had fled Connecticut during the earlier Pequot War and remained hostile to the English. The Mohawks also captured Uncas's son Owaneco after the Great Narragansett War.
62. Wait Winthrop to John Winthrop, Jr., 8 July 1675, Wyllys, *Papers*, 209–11.
63. Ellis and Morris, *King Philip's War*, 79–81.
64. Allyn reported the total as 80 Pequots and 100 Mohegans upriver. Allyn to Pynchon, 8 Aug. 1675, CWS, 1:111d. The War Council's journal indicates that it was a combined total of 80–100 allied Indians, but Allyn's letter is the more accurate source. War Journal, PRCC, 348.
65. War Journal, PRCC, 348, 363.
66. Ellis and Morris, *King Philip's War*, 113.
67. War Journal, PRCC, 369, 371; Connecticut War Council to United Colony Commissioners, 7 Oct. 1675, Wyllys, *Papers*, 227–28.
68. Ellis and Morris, *King Philip's War*, 148.
69. War Journal, PRCC, 400, 450, 458–60.
70. Hubbard, *History of the Indian Wars in New England*, 173.
71. Temple and Adams, *History of the Town of North Brookfield*, 89–90.
72. Massachusetts Council journal, 13 July 1675, Massachusetts MSS, vol. 67, doc. 213.
73. John Stanton to Governor Andros, 9 Feb. 1676, *Andros Papers*, 326–27. Stanton refers to both the Pequots and Mohegans as "Pequets" or "Pecaits."
74. Oberg, *Uncas*, 183.

75. Lee, "Fortify, Fight, or Flee," 722. Starkey describes this tactic as envelopment with a "horseshoe formation." *European and Native American Warfare*, 22.
76. The term "skirmishing" had not entered the lexicon of European warfare in the seventeenth century. Military history, however, is replete with instances of formations employing skirmishing techniques before this time. Both sides utilized such tactics during the Great Narragansett War.
77. Ellis and Morris, *King Philip's War*, 249–50. As a platoon leader, I conducted a "hammer and anvil" style operation during training with two relatively proficient platoons of the Tenth Mountain Division. It was not an easy tactical maneuver to carry out, even with modern communications equipment, suggesting that the English and Indians were either well drilled or at least fortunate on this occasion.
78. Oberg, *Uncas*, 180.
79. Kenneth Chase discusses the influence of low birth and high mortality rates on tactics in *Firearms*, 22.
80. Ellis and Morris, *King Philip's War*, 184, 243.
81. Lee, "Using the Natives against the Natives," 92.
82. Order, Connecticut War Council to Talcott, 15 July 1676, Wyllys, *Papers*, 247.
83. Naumec, "National Park Service Battlefield Protection Program Technical Report: Military History Analysis of the Battles at Nipsachuck."
84. Ellis and Morris, *King Philip's War*, 111–13.
85. Ibid., 100.
86. Melvoin, *New England Outpost*, 100–101.
87. With only a few English survivors from Lathrop's column, a lack of sources precludes an accurate consideration of his men's fate, while the chroniclers' narrative of carelessness has become the standard explanation for Bloody Brook.
88. A modern example of the difficulties of river-crossing operations is the U.S. Army's difficulty in crossing the Sava River during the Bosnia campaign in the mid-1990s. The army since has dedicated an entire field manual (FM 90-13) to river-crossing operations. It also published FM 3-90.12 on "combined arms gap crossings," which includes rivers.
89. For the battle between Mason's force and the Pequots, see Battle of Mystic Archaeological Project.
90. Hubbard, *History of the Indian Wars in New England*, 110.
91. Allyn to Wait Winthrop, 22 Sept. 1675, Winthrop Papers, vol. 10, EBC-CSL, 24.
92. For an example of how the militia would deploy in parade-ground fashion, see John Underhill's account of a battle during the Pequot War in Romero, *Making War and Minting Christians*, 160.
93. Temple, Sheldon, and Stratton, *History of the Town of Northfield*, 78.
94. The technical description of tactics in this paragraph relies on K. Roberts, *Cromwell's War Machine*, 88–91.

95. Hubbard, *History of the Indian Wars in New England*, 146, 152, 153; S. Drake, *Old Indian Chronicle*, 181.
96. Hubbard, *History of the Indian Wars in New England*, 146.
97. Someone, probably Major Treat, informed Governor Winthrop that more than forty Connecticut soldiers had been killed. Letter to Gov. John Winthrop, 13 Jan. 1676, Winthrop Papers, vol. 17, EBC-CSL, 77. More would die of wounds, eventually bringing the number closer to fifty.
98. Ellis and Morris, *King Philip's War*, 149–53.
99. Testimony of James Quannapohit, MHS.
100. Leach, *Flintlock and Tomahawk*, 139; testimony of James Quannapohit, MHS.
101. Testimony of James Quannapohit.
102. Malone, *Skulking Way of War*, 74.
103. Harris, *Rhode Islander Reports on King Philip's War*, 77.
104. E. Hoyt, "Indian Wars," in Lockwood, *Westfield and Its Historic Influences*, 249–50.
105. S. Drake, *Old Indian Chronicle*, 310; Hubbard, *History of the Indian Wars in New England*, 182; Ellis and Morris, *King Philip's War*, 222–23; Starkey, *European and Native American Warfare*, 32, 79; Chet, *Conquering the American Wilderness*, 53, 63. Church went on to lead successful raids in similar fashion during the early French and Indian wars. See Eames, *Rustic Warriors*.
106. CWS, 1:1:96a.
107. Hutchinson quoted in Avery and Avery, *Groton Avery Clan*, 61.
108. McBride, "Pequot in King Philip's War," 322–32.
109. Ellis and Morris, *King Philip's War*, 201.
110. Harris, *Rhode Islander Reports on King Philip's War*, 49.
111. 7 Apr 1676 letter from Secretary Allyn to Major Palmes, CWS, 1:1:58b.
112. Minor, *Diary*, 29 Apr. 1676, 130–37; Ellis and Morris, *King Philip's War*, 223.
113. Minor, *Diary*, 25 Mar.–9 Aug. 1676, 130–37.
114. Harris, *Rhode Islander Reports on King Philip's War*, 65.
115. Scully, *Robert Treat*, 177.
116. New Haven Colony Records as quoted in Treat, *Treat Family*, 132.
117. Ibid., 136.
118. Ibid., 152; Ford, *Robert Treat*, 171.
119. Connecticut War Council to the Massachusetts Governor and Council, 12 Oct. 1675, Massachusetts MSS, vol. 67, doc. 298, trans. William Farley.
120. Minor, *Diary*, 27–28 June 1676, 130–37.
121. Wait to John Winthrop, Jr., 8 July 1675, Wyllys, *Papers*, 209–11.
122. Connecticut War Council to United Colonies, 7 Oct. 1675, ibid., 228.

Bibliography

Archival Sources and Manuscript Collections

Battle of Mystic Archaeological Project, 2010–11. Mashantucket Pequot Museum and Research Center, Mashantucket Pequot Reservation, Conn.

Bissonnette, Ashley, comp. File of Pequot War–King Philip's War Veterans. Mashantucket Pequot Museum and Research Center, Mashantucket Pequot Reservation, Conn.

The Connecticut Colonial Records. Colonial Wars Series. Ser. 1, vol. 1. Connecticut State Library, Hartford. Microfilm.

———. Indian Series. Vol. 1. Connecticut State Library, Hartford. Microfilm

Connecticut Records. Colonial War Series, Manuscripts Collection. Vol. 1. Connecticut State Library, Hartford.

Davison, Faith, ed. "Joshua Trust/Joshua Tract, Attawanhood's Legacy." Mohegan Archives, Mohegan Reservation, Oxoboxo River, Conn.

Eva Butler Collection, Documents Related to King Philip's War. The Indian and Colonial Research Center, Old Mystic, Conn. Courtesy of Mashantucket Pequot Museum and Research Center, Mashantucket Pequot Reservation, Conn.

Eva Butler Collection. Connecticut State Library, Hartford.

John Talcott Record Book. Connecticut Historical Society, Hartford.

Mashantucket Pequot Museum and Research Center, Mashantucket Pequot Reservation, Conn.

Massachusetts Colony Records. Vol. 67. Massachusetts State Archives, University of Massachusetts, Dorchester.

Massachusetts Miscellaneous Records, Massachusetts Historical Society, Boston.

Plymouth Colony Records. Vol. 5. Plymouth County Courthouse, Plymouth, Mass.

Trumbull Manuscript Collections. Beinecke Library, Yale University, New Haven, Conn.

Wyllys, George. *The Wyllys Papers: Correspondence and Documents Chiefly of Descendants of Gov. George Wyllys of Connecticut, 1590–1796*. Collections of the Connecticut Historical Society, vol. 21. Hartford: Connecticut Historical Society, 1924.

Published Primary Sources

Andros, Edmund. *The Andros Papers: Files of the Provincial Secretary of New York during the Administration of Governor Sir Edmund Andros, 1674–1680*. Edited by Peter R. Christoph and Florence Christoph. Translated by Charles T. Gehring. Syracuse, N.Y.: Syracuse University Press, 1989.

Bartlett, John Russell, ed. *Records of the Colony of Rhode Island and Providence Plantations in New England, Proceedings of the General Assembly of the Colony of Rhode Island and Providence Plantations, Held at Newport, the 13th of March, 1675–6.* Vol. 2, 1664 to 1677. Elibron Classics Series. New York: Adamant Media, 2005.

Brodhead, John; Berthold Fernow; and E. B. O'Callaghan, eds. and trans. *Documents Relative to the Colonial History of the State of New York.* 15 vols. Albany: Weed and Parsons, 1886.

Christoph, Peter R., and Florence A. Christoph, eds. *New York Historical Manuscripts (English): Books of General Entries of the Colony of New York, 1674–1688: Orders, Warrants, Letters, Commissions, Passes, and Licenses Issued by Governors Sir Edmund Andros and Thomas Dongan and Deputy Governor Anthony Brockholls.* Baltimore: Genealogical Publishing, 1982.

Church, Benjamin. *The Diary of Benjamin Church.* Reprint, Guilford, Conn.: Pequot, 1975.

Drake, Samuel G., ed. *The Old Indian Chronicle; Being a Collection of Exceeding Rare Tracts, Written and Published in the Time of King Philip's War, by Persons Residing in the Country.* 1867. Reprint, New York: AMS, 1976.

Fernow Berthold, ed. *New York (Colony) Council, Calendar of Council Minutes, 1668–1783.* Harrison, N.Y.: Harbor Hill Books, 1987.

Gardiner, Lion. *A History of the Pequot War: Or a Relation of the War between the Powerful Nation of Pequot Indians, Once Inhabiting the Coast of New England, Westerly from near Narraganset Bay, and the English Inhabitants, in the Year 1638.* Cincinnati: J. Harpel, 1860.

Harris, William. *A Rhode Islander Reports on King Philip's War: The Second William Harris Letter of August, 1676.* Edited and transcribed by Douglas Edward Leach. Providence: Rhode Island Historical Society, 1963.

Hoadly, Charles, J., ed. *Records of the Colony or Jurisdiction of New Haven from May 1653 to the Union, Together with the New Haven Code of 1656. Transcribed and Edited in Accordance with a Resolution of the General Assembly of Connecticut.* Hartford, Conn.: Case, Lockwood, 1858.

Hubbard, William. *The History of the Indian Wars in New England.* Boston: John Foster, 1677. Reprint, edited by Samuel G. Drake, New York: Kraus, 1969.

———. *A Narrative of the Troubles with the Indians . . . to This Present Year 1677.* Boston: John Foster, 1677.

Jewett, Isaac Appleton, ed. *Memorial of Samuel Appleton of Ipswich, Massachusetts.* Cambridge, Mass.: Bolles and Houghton, 1850.

Mather, Increase. *A Brief History of the Warr with the Indians in New England.* Boston, 1676.

Mather Papers. Ser. 4, vol. 8. Collections of the Massachusetts Historical Society. Boston: Wiggin and Lunt for the Massachusetts Historical Society, 1868.

Minor, Thomas. *The Diary of Thomas Minor, Stonington, Connecticut, 1653–1684.* Edited by Sidney H. Minor and George D. Stanton. [New London, Conn.: Press of the Day], 1899. Reprinted as *The Minor Diaries*, Ann Arbor, Mich.: Edwards Brother, 1993.
New Haven Colony Historical Society. *Ancient Town Records: New Haven Town Records, 1650–1684.* Edited by Franklin B. Dexter. 2 vols. New Haven, Conn.: Printed for the society by Tuttle, Morehouse, & Taylor, 1917, 1919.
Shurtleff, Nathaniel B., ed. *Records of the Colony of Plymouth in New England, Proceedings of the General Court of the Colony of Plymouth, Held at Plymouth, 1668–1678.* Vol. 5, *Court Orders, 1668–1678.* Boston: William White, 1856.
———, ed. *Records of the Governor and Company of the Massachusetts Bay in New England, Printed by Order of the Legislature.* Boston: William White, 1853–54.
Trumbull, J. H., ed. *The Public Records of the Colony of Connecticut, from April 1636 to October 1776 . . . Transcribed and Published (in Accordance with a Resolution of the General Assembly).* 15 vols. Hartford, Conn.: Brown & Parsons, 1850–90. Available online at http://www.colonialct.uconn.edu.
The Winthrop Papers. Vol. 1, 1498–1628, edited by Worthington C. Ford. Boston: Plimpton Press for the Massachusetts Historical Society, 1929.
The Winthrop Papers. Vol. 3, 1631–1637, edited by Allyn B. Forbes. Boston: Merrymount Press for the Massachusetts Historical Society, 1943.
The Winthrop Papers. Vol. 5, 1645–1649, edited by Allyn B. Forbes. Boston: Merrymount Press for the Massachusetts Historical Society, 1947.
The Winthrop Papers. Ser. 5, vols. 5, 8. Cambridge, Mass.: University Press, John Wilson and Son, 1882.
Wyllys Papers. Vol. 21. Published Manuscript Collections. Connecticut Historical Society, Hartford.

Books, Articles, Theses, and Papers

Anderson, Fred. *The War That Made America: A Short History of the French and Indian War.* New York: Penguin, 2006.
Arthur, Robert. "Coast Forts of Colonial Massachusetts." *Coastal Artillery Journal* 58, no. 2 (23 February 1923).
Avery, Elroy McKendree, and Catharine Hitchcock (Tilden) Avery. *The Groton Avery Clan.* Vol. 1, no. 3112. Cleveland, 1912.
Baker, Emerson W., and John G. Reid. "Amerindian Power in the Early Modern Northeast: A Reappraisal." *William and Mary Quarterly* 61, no. 1 (August 2004).
Barner, John W. *Connecticut Historical Collections.* New Haven, Conn.: Durrie & Peck and J. W. Barber, 1836.
Black, Jeremy. *Fighting for America: The Struggle for Mastery in North America, 1519–1871.* Indianapolis: Indiana University Press, 2011.
Black, Robert C., III. *The Younger John Winthrop.* New York: Columbia University Press, 1966.

Bodge, George M. *Soldiers in King Philip's War: Being a Critical Account of that War with a Concise History of the Indian Wars of New England from 1620–1677.* Boston, 1906. Reprint, 3rd ed., Baltimore: Genealogical Publishing, 1967.

Bourne, Russell. *The Red King's Rebellion: Racial Politics in New England, 1675–1676.* New York: Atheneum, 1990.

Caulkins, Frances M. *History of New London, Connecticut: From the First Survey of the Coast in 1612 to 1860.* Hartford, Conn.: Case, Tiffany, 1852.

———. *History of Norwich, Connecticut: From Its Possession by the Indian to the Year 1866.* Hartford, Conn.: Case, Lockwood, 1866.

Cave, Alfred A. *The Pequot War.* Amherst: University of Massachusetts Press, 1996.

Chartrand, Rene. *Colonial American Troops, 1610–1774.* Vol. 3, Men-at-Arms Series. Oxford: Osprey, 2003.

Chase, Kenneth. *Firearms: A Global History to 1700.* Cambridge: Cambridge University Press, 2003.

Chet, Guy. *Conquering the American Wilderness: The Triumph of European Warfare in the Colonial Northeast.* Amherst: University of Massachusetts Press, 2003.

Childs, John. *Warfare in the Seventeenth Century.* Smithsonian History of Warfare Series. Washington, D.C.: Smithsonian Books, 2001.

Church, Thomas. *The History of King Philip's War.* Edited by Samuel G. Drake. Boston: Howe & Norton, 1825.

Clausewitz, Carl V. *On War.* Edited and translated by Michael Howard and Peter Paret. Princeton, N.J.: Princeton University Press, 1989.

Clayton, Anthony. *Warfare in Woods and Forests.* Indianapolis: Indiana University Press, 2012.

Cohen, Eliot A. *Conquered into Liberty: Two Centuries of Battles along the Great Warpath That Made the American Way of War.* New York: Free Press, 2011.

Cooper, J. P., ed. "The Decline of Spain and the Thirty Years War, 1609–48/59." In *The New Cambridge Modern History.* 4th ed. Cambridge: Cambridge University Press, 1970.

"Course Notebook for the History of the Military Art." West Point, N.Y.: U.S. Military Academy, 2010.

Curtis, George Munson, and C. Bancroft Gillespie. *A Century of Meriden: An Historic Record and Pictorial Description of the Town of Meriden, Connecticut.* Meriden, Conn.: Journal Publishing, 1906.

da Silva, Michael Luciano. *Portuguese Pilgrims and Dighton Rock.* http://www.dightonrock.com/opening_page_for_pilgrims.htm.

Davis, Charles H. S. *History of Wallingford Connecticut: From Its Settlement in 1670 to the Present Time, including Meriden, which Was One of Its Parishes until 1806, and Cheshire, which Was Incorporated in 1780.* Meriden, Conn.: Published by the author, 1870.

Dederer, John M. *War in America to 1775: Before Yankee Doodle.* New York: New York University Press, 1990.

De Forest, John W. *History of the Indians of Connecticut from the Earliest Known Period to 1850*. Hartford, Conn.: Wm. Jas. Hamersley, 1851.

Demeritt, David. "Agriculture, Climate, and Cultural Adaptation in the Prehistoric Northeast." *Archaeology of Eastern North America* 19 (1991).

Drake, James D. *King Philip's War: Civil War in New England, 1675–1676*. Amherst, Mass.: University of Massachusetts Press, 1999.

Dunn, Richard S. *Puritans and Yankees: The Winthrop Dynasty of New England, 1630–1717*. Princeton, N.J.: Princeton University Press, 1962.

Eames, Steven C. *Rustic Warriors: Warfare and the Provincial Soldiers on the New England Frontier, 1689–1748*. New York: New York University Press, 2011.

Ellis, George W., and John E. Morris. *King Philip's War*. Edited by Henry R. Stiles. New York: Grafton, 1906.

Engels, Donald W. *Alexander the Great and the Logistics of the Macedonian Army*. Berkeley: University of California Press, 1978.

Fischer, David H. *Washington's Crossing*. New York: Oxford University Press, 2004.

Ford, George Hare. *Robert Treat, Founder, Farmer, Soldier, Statesman, Governor*. New Haven, Conn.: Tuttle, Morehouse, & Taylor, 1914.

Foxhall, L., and H. A. Forbes. "Sitometria: The Role of Grain as a Staple Food in Classical Antiquity." *Chiron* 12 (1982).

Gallay, Alan, ed. *Colonial Wars of North America, 1512–1763: An Encyclopedia*. New York: Garland, 1996.

———. *The Indian Slave Trade: The Rise of the English Empire in the American South*. New Haven, Conn.: Yale University Press, 2002.

Gardiner, Samuel R. *History of the Great Civil War, 1642–1649*. Vol. 1. London: Longmans, Green, 1886.

Gentles, Ian. *The New Model Army: In England, Ireland, and Scotland, 1645–1653*. Cambridge: Blackwell, 1992.

Grandjean, Kate A. "New World Tempests: Environment, Scarcity, and the Coming of the Pequot War." *William and Mary Quarterly* 68, no. 1 (January 2011).

Greenberg, Herbert. "The Authenticity of the Library of John Winthrop the Younger." *American Literature* 8, no. 4 (January 1937).

Greene, Evarts B., and Virginia D. Harrington. *American Population before the Federal Census of 1790*. New York: Columbia University Press, 1932. Reprint, Gloucester, Mass.: Peter Smith, 1966.

Grenier, John. *The First Way of War: American War Making on the Frontier, 1607–1814*. Cambridge: Cambridge University Press, 2005.

———. "Recent Trends in the Historiography on Warfare in the Colonial Period (1607–1765)." *History Compass* 8, no. 4 (2010).

Guilmartin, John F., Jr. "The Cutting Edge: An Analysis of the Spanish Invasion and Overthrow of the Inka Empire, 1532–39." In *Transatlantic Encounters: Europeans and Andeans in the Sixteenth Century*, edited by Kenneth Andrien and Rolena Adorno, 40–64. Berkeley: University of California Press, 1991.

———. *Gunpowder & Galleys: Changing Technology & Mediterranean Warfare at Sea in the 16th Century.* 2nd ed. London: Conway Maritime, 2003.
Hall, John W. *Uncommon Defense: Indian Allies in the Black Hawk War.* Cambridge, Mass.: Harvard University Press, 2009.
Hill, Everett Gleason. *A Modern History of New Haven and Eastern New Haven County.* Vol. 2. New York: S. J. Clarke, 1918.
Hirsch, Adam J. "The Collision of Military Cultures in 17th Century New England." *Journal of American History* 74, no. 4 (March 1988).
Howard, Michael. "The Use and Abuse of Military History." In *Selected Readings History of the Military Art, 1648–1914,* edited and compiled by Eugenia C. Kiesling. New York: Pearson Learning Solutions, 2010.
Jacobus, Donald L. "Reunion of Descendants of Nathaniel Merriman at Wallingford, Conn., June 4, 1913; with a Merriman Genealogy for Five Generations." Internet Archive. Accessed 1 January 2011. www.archive.org/stream/reunionofdescendoomerriala/reunionofdescendoomerriala_djvu.txt. Hardcopy in author's possession.
Jennings, Francis. *The Invasion of America: Indians, Colonialism, and the Cant of Conquest.* Chapel Hill: University of North Carolina Press, 1975.
Johnson, Richard R. "The Search for a Usable Indian: An Aspect of the Defense of Colonial New England." *Journal of American History* 64, no. 3 (December 1977).
Kamil, Neil. *Fortress of the Soul: Violence, Metaphysics, and Material Life in the Huguenots' New World, 1517–1751.* Baltimore: John Hopkins University Press, 2005.
Karr, Ronald D. "Why Should You Be So Furious?" *Journal of American History* 85, no. 3 (December 1998).
"Landguard Fort." Dominic Goode, Fortified Places. http://www.fortified-places.com/landguard/.
Langworthy, C. F., and Caroline L. Hunt. *Corn Meal as a Food and Ways of Using It.* Farmers' Bulletin 565. Washington, D.C.: USDA, 1914, rev. 1917.
Lavin, Lucianne. *Connecticut's Indigenous Peoples: What Archaeology, History, and Oral Traditions Teach Us about Their Communities and Cultures.* New Haven, Conn.: Yale University Press, 2013.
Leach, Douglas E. *Arms for Empire: A Military History of the British Colonies in North America, 1607–1763.* New York: Macmillan, 1973.
———. *Flintlock and Tomahawk: New England in King Philip's War.* New York: Macmillan, 1958.
LeBlanc, Steven A., with Katherine E. Register. *Constant Battles: The Myth of the Peaceful, Noble Savage.* New York: St. Martin's, 2003.
Lee, Wayne E. *Barbarians & Brothers: Anglo-American Warfare, 1500–1865.* Oxford: Oxford University Press, 2011.
———. *Empires and Indigenes: Intercultural Alliance, Imperial Expansion, and Warfare in the Early Modern World.* New York: New York University Press, 2011.

———. "Fortify, Fight, or Flee: Tuscorora and Cherokee Defensive Warfare and Military Culture Adaptation." *Journal of Military History* 68, no 3 (July 2004).
———. "Peace Chiefs and Blood Revenge: Patterns of Restraint in Native American Warfare, 1500–1800." *Journal of Military History* 71, no. 3 (July 2007).
———. "Subjects, Clients, Allies, or Mercenaries? The British Use of Irish and Amerindian Military Power, 1500–1815." In *Britain's Oceanic Empire: Atlantic and Indian Ocean Worlds, 1550–1850*. Edited by H. V. Bowen, Elizabeth Mancke, and John G. Reid, 179–217. Cambridge: Cambridge University Press, 2011.
———. "Using the Natives against the Natives: Indigenes as 'Counterinsurgents' in the British Atlantic, 1500–1800." *Defence Studies* 10, no. 1 (2010).
———. *Warfare and Culture in World History*. New York: New York University Press, 2011.
Lepore, Jill. *The Name of War: King Philip's War and the Origins of American Identity*. New York: Alfred A. Knopf, 1998.
Lockwood, John H., ed. *Westfield and Its Historic Influences, 1669–1919: The Life of an Early Town*. Published by author, 1922.
Lynn, John. *Battle: A History of Combat and Culture*. Colorado: Boulder, 2003.
Malone, Patrick M. *The Skulking Way of War: Technology and Tactics among the New England Indians*. Baltimore: Johns Hopkins University Press, 1991.
Mandell, Daniel R. *King Philip's War: Colonial Expansion, Native Resistance, and the End of Indian Sovereignty*. Baltimore: John Hopkins University Press, 2010.
McBride, Kevin. "Fort Island: Conflict and Trade in Long Island Sound." In *Native Forts of the Long Island Sound Area*, edited by Gaynell Stone, 254–66. Readings in Long Island Archaeology and Ethnohistory, vol. 8. New York: Sheridan, 2006.
———. "Fort Mohantic, Connecticut: The Pequot in King Philip's War." In *Native Forts of the Long Island Sound Area*, edited by Gaynell Stone, 323–36. Readings in Long Island Archaeology and Ethnohistory, vol. 8. New York: Sheridan, 2006.
———. "The Legacy of Robin Cassacinamon: Mashantucket Pequot Leadership in the Historic Period." In *Northeastern Indian Lives, 1632–1816*, edited by Robert S. Grumet, 74–92. Amherst: University of Massachusetts Press, 1999.
———. "War and Trade in Eastern New Netherland." Presented at the Thirtieth Rensselaerswijck Seminar: The Truce, 1609–1621. New Netherland Institute, Albany, N.Y., 15 September 2007. Also in *A Beautiful and Fruitful Place: Selected Rensselaerswijck Papers*, vol. 3, edited by Margriet Lacy, 272–83. Albany: New Netherland Institute, 2013.

———, ed. "The Mystic Fort Campaign." Battlefields of the Pequot War Project. Mashantucket Pequot Museum and Research Center. http://www.pequotwar.org.

McCully, Bruce T. "Catastrophe in the Wilderness: New Light on the Canada Expedition of 1709." *William and Mary Quarterly* 11, no. 3 (1954).

Melvoin, Richard I. *New England Outpost: War and Society in Colonial Deerfield.* New York: W. W. Norton, 1989.

Menta, John. "The Quinnipiac: Cultural Conflict in Southern New England." *Yale University Publications in Anthropology.* Issue 86. New Haven, Conn.: Yale University Press, 2003.

Muehlbauer, Matthew S. "'They . . . Shall No More Be Called Peaquots but Narragansetts and Mohegans': Refugees, Rivalry, and the Consequences of the Pequot War." *War & Society* 30, no. 3 (October 2011).

Naumec, David J. "National Park Service Battlefield Protection Program Technical Report: Military History Analysis of the Battles at Nipsachuck." Prepared for the Rhode Island Historical Preservation & Heritage Commission, the Blackstone Valley Historical Society, and the Narragansett Indian Tribal Historical Preservation Office, 2010.

Newell, Margaret E. "Indian Slavery in Colonial New England." In *Indian Slavery in Colonial America,* edited by Alan Gallay, 33–66. Lincoln: University of Nebraska Press, 2010.

New York State Library. "A Catalogue of the Books Belonging to the New-York Society Library." New York: C. S Van Winkle, 1813.

North, Catharine M. *History of Berlin, Connecticut.* Edited by Adolph B. Benson. New Haven, Conn.: Tuttle, Morehouse, & Taylor, 1916.

Oberg, Michael L. *Uncas First of the Mohegans.* Ithaca, N.Y.: Cornell University Press, 2003.

O'Brien, Jean M. *Dispossession by Degrees: Indian Land and Identity in Natick, Massachusetts, 1650–1790.* Cambridge: Cambridge University Press, 1997.

———. *Firsting and Lasting: Writing Indians Out of Existence in New England.* Minneapolis: University of Minnesota Press, 2010.

Orcutt, Samuel. *History of the Old Town of Stratford and the City of Bridgeport, Connecticut.* New Haven, Conn.: Tuttle, Morehouse, & Taylor, 1886.

———. *The Indians of the Housatonic and Naugatuck Valleys.* Hartford, Conn.: Case, Lockwood, & Brainard, 1882.

Orcutt, Samuel, and Ambrose Beardsley. *The History of the Old Town of Derby, Connecticut, 1642–1880.* Springfield, Mass.: Springfield Printing, 1880.

Ó Siochrú, Micheál. "Atrocity, Codes of Conduct, and the Irish in the British Civil Wars, 1641–1653." *Past and Present* 195 (May 2007).

Parker, Geoffrey. "The Artillery Fortress as an Engine of European Overseas Expansion, 1480–1750." Chap. 8 in *Empire, War, & Faith in Early Modern Europe.* London: Allen Lane/Penguin, 2002.

———. *Global Crisis: War, Climate Change, and Catastrophe in the Seventeenth* Century. New Haven, Conn.: Yale University Press, 2013.
———. *The Military Revolution: Military Innovation and the Rise of the West, 1500–1800.* Cambridge: Cambridge University Press, 1996.
Peterson, Harold L. "The Military Equipment of the Plymouth and Bay Colonies, 1620–1690." *New England Quarterly* 20, no. 2 (June 1947).
Philbrick, Nathaniel. *Mayflower: A Story of Courage, Community, and War.* New York: Viking Penguin, 2006.
Porter, Patrick. *Military Orientalism: Eastern War through Western Eyes.* London: Hearst, 2009.
Prichard, Sarah J. *The Town and City of Waterbury, Connecticut, from the Aboriginal Period to the Year Eighteen Hundred and Ninety-Five.* Edited by Joseph Anderson. New Haven, Conn.: Price & Lee, 1896.
Pulsipher, Jenny H. *Subjects unto the Same King: Indians, English, and the Contest for Authority in Colonial New England.* Philadelphia: University of Pennsylvania Press, 2005.
Radune, Richard A. *Pequot Plantation: The Story of an Early Colonial Settlement.* Branford, Conn.: Research in Time Publications, 2005.
Richter, Daniel K. *The Ordeal of the Longhouse: The Peoples of the Iroquois League in the Era of European Colonization.* Chapel Hill: University of North Carolina Press, 1992.
Roberts, Keith. *Cromwell's War Machine: The New Model Army, 1645–1660.* Barnsley, U.K.: Pen & Sword Military, 2005.
Roberts, Robert B. *Encyclopedia of Historic Forts: The Military, Pioneer, and Trading Posts of the United States.* New York: Macmillan, 1988.
Romero, R. Todd. *Making War and Minting Christians: Masculinity, Religion, and Colonialism in Early New England.* Boston: University of Massachusetts Press, 2011.
Russell, Jesse, and Ronald Cohn. *The Metacomet Ridge.* N.p.: Books on Demand, 2012.
Salisbury, Neal. *Manitou and Providence: Indians, Europeans, and the Making of New England, 1500–1643.* Oxford: Oxford University Press, 1982.
Schenck, Elizabeth H. *The History of Fairfield, Fairfield County, Connecticut: From the Settlement of the Town in 1639–1818.* Vol. 1. New York: J. J. Little, 1889.
Schultz, Eric B., and Michael J. Tougias. *King Philip's War: The History and Legacy of America's Forgotten Conflict.* Woodstock, Vt.: Countryman, 1999.
Schroeder, Sissel. "Maize Productivity in the Eastern Woodlands and Great Plains of North America." *American Antiquity* 64, no. 3 (July 1999).
———. "Understanding Variation in Prehistoric Agricultural Productivity: The Importance of Distinguishing among Potential, Available, and Consumptive Yields." *American Antiquity* 66, no. 3 (July 2001).
Scully, Charles Alison. *Robert Treat, 1622–1710.* Philadelphia: n.p., 1959.

Seed, Patricia. "The Conquest of the Americas, 1500–1650." In *The Cambridge History of Warfare*, edited by Geoffrey Parker, 131–47. Cambridge: Cambridge University Press, 2005.
Selesky, Harold E. *War and Society in Colonial Connecticut*. New Haven, Conn.: Yale University Press, 1990.
Sheldon, Hezekiah, S. *Documentary History of Suffield: In the Colony and Province of the Massachusetts Bay in New England, 1660 to 1749*. Springfield, Mass.: Clark W. Bryan, 1879.
Showalter, Dennis E. "The Wars of Frederick the Great." In *Selected Readings History of the Military Art, 1648–1914*, edited and compiled by Eugenia C. Kiesling, 31–38. New York: Pearson Learning Solutions, 2010.
Simmons, R. C. *The American Colonies: From Settlement to Independence*. New York: W. W. Norton, 1976.
Starkey, Armstrong. *European and Native America Warfare, 1675–1815*. Norman: University of Oklahoma Press, 1998.
Stearns, Ezra S.; William F. Whitcher; and Edward E. Parker. *Genealogical and Family History of the State of New Hampshire: A Record of the Achievements of Her People in the Making of a Commonwealth and the Founding of a Nation*. Vol. 1. New York: Lewis, 1908.
Steele, Ian K. *Warpaths: Invasions of North America*. New York: Oxford University Press, 1994.
Stevens, Sherrill H., comp. "The Early History of Suffolk County, Long Island, New York." Rootsweb, an Ancestry.com Community. Last modified 14 September 2000. Accessed 9 July 2008. http://www.rootsweb.ancestry.com/~nysuffol/history5.html.
Stiles, Henry R. *The History of Ancient Windsor, Connecticut*. New York: Charles B. Norton, 1859.
Taylor, Charles. "Harwich Redoubt." Castles and Fortifications of England and Wales. 1997–2008. Accessed May 2008. http://www.ecastles.co.uk/harwich.html.
Taylor, Charlotte C. "Fort Ninigret, Rhode Island: The History and Archaeology of Fort Ninigret, a 17th-Century Eastern Niantic Site in Charlestown, R.I." In *Native Forts of the Long Island Sound Area*, edited by Gaynell Stone, 277–86. Readings in Long Island Archaeology and Ethnohistory, vol. 8. New York: Sheridan Books, 2006.
Taylor, Robert J. *Colonial Connecticut—A History*. A History of the American Colonies Series. Millwood, N.Y.: KTO, 1979.
Temple, Josiah H., and Charles Adams. *A History of the Town of North Brookfield, Massachusetts*. Boston: Rand Avery, 1887.
Temple, Josiah H.; George Sheldon; and Mary T. Stratton. *A History of the Town of Northfield Massachusetts*. Albany, N.Y.: J. Munsell, 1875.
Ten Raa, F. J. G., and F. De Bas. *Het Staatsche Leger, 1568–1795: Van den dood van Mauritus, prins van Oranje, graaf van Nassau, tot het sluiten van den vrede te Munster (1625–1648)*. Deel 4. Breda, Netherlands: De Koninklijke Militaire Academie, 1918.
Tiro, Karim. "The Dilemmas of Alliance: The Oneida Nation in the American Revolution." In *War and Society in the American*

Revolution: Mobilization and Home Fronts, edited by John Resch and Walter Sargent, 215–34. DeKalb: Northern Illinois University Press, 2007.

Townshend, Charles Hervey. "The Quinnipiack Indians and Their Reservation." In *Papers of the New Haven Colony Historical Society*, vol. 6, 180–256. New Haven, Conn.: Tuttle, Morehouse, & Taylor, 1900.

Treat, John Harvey A. M. *The Treat Family: A Genealogy of Trott, Tratt, and Treat*. Salem, Mass.: Salem, 1893.

Trumbull, Benjamin. *A Complete History of Connecticut Civil and Ecclesiastical: From the Emigration of the First Planters, from England, in the Year 1630 to the Year 1764; and to the Close of the Indian Wars*. Vol. 1. New London, Conn.: U. D. Hutley, 1898.

U.S. Army Expert Infantrymen Badge Standards. ArmyStudyGuide.com. Accessed Spring 2008. http://www.armystudyguide.com/content/EIB/Task_Summary/perform-12mile-tactical-f.shtml.

Van Zandt, Cynthia J. "Nations Intertwined: Getting Beyond Regional Boundaries in Seventeenth-Century American History" Paper presented at Boston Area Early American History Seminar, Massachusetts Historical Society, 8 November 2001.

Vaughan, Alden T. *New England Frontier: Puritans and Indians, 1620–1675*. 3rd ed. Norman: University of Oklahoma Press, 1995.

Ward, Christopher. *The War of the Revolution*. Edited by John R. Alden. 2 vols. New York: Macmillan, 1952.

Warren, Jason. "Beyond Emotion: The Epidamnian Affair and Corinthian Policy, 480–421 B.C." *Ancient History Bulletin* 17, nos. 1–4 (2003).

Webb, Stephen Saunders. *1676: The End of American Independence*. Syracuse, N.Y.: Syracuse University Press, 1995.

Weigley, Russell F. *The American Way of War: A History of United States Military Strategy and Policy*. New York: Macmillan, 1973.

Wheeler, Richard A. *History of Stonington, County of New London, Connecticut, from Its First Settlement in 1649 to 1900*. New London, Conn.: Press of the Day, 1900.

Winthrop, John; George Starkey; and C. A. Browne. "Notes from the Books and Letters of John Winthrop, Jr. (1606–1676)." *Isis* 11, no. 2 (December 1928).

Zawodniak, Brian. "Connecticut in King Philip's War." Master's thesis, Trinity College, 1993.

Zelner, Kyle F. *A Rabble in Arms: Massachusetts Towns and Militiamen during King Philip's War*. War and Culture Series. New York: New York University Press, 2009.

Index

Abenaki (tribal group), 39, 40, 55, 195n104
Abercromby, James, 146, 220n22
African American(s), population estimate, 195n105
Agawam (tribal group), 16, 56, 74, 79–80
Alexander (aka Wamsutta, Wampanoag sachem), 36
Algonquin (tribal group), 40, 45, 65, 76, 86, 95, 106, 154, 193n77, 193n81
Allyn, John, 163, 171, 212n58, 222n64
American Indian(s): adaptation to English culture, 87; agricultural production, 16–18, 187n5; confiscation of firearms, 32, 79–80, 86–87, 91, 95; family structure, 18, 19, 188n10; identity and tribal loyalty, 15, 75–77, 87–88, 124, 160, 180–81; intermarriage and kinship, 21, 36, 37, 39, 60, 193n83, 198n43; intertribal conflict, 6–8; losses to European diseases, 36–37, 188nn13–14; marginalization in colonial society, 185n24; population estimate, 188–89nn15–21; sachem authority and power, 37–39; success in battle, 162; tactics and fighting ability, 154, 191nn46–47. *See also entries for individual tribal groups*; Land/landholdings; New England; Women
American Revolutionary War, 128, 133, 146, 221n42
American Way of War (Weigley), 219n5

Amherst, Jeffrey, 146, 221n42
Andros, Edmund: appointment as United Colonies head, 41; directing war effort, 123–24; Indian policies, 11, 87, 205n58; role in Great Narragansett War, 67; threats to Connecticut Colony, 122
Anglo-Dutch Wars (1652–74), 11, 32, 147, 170, 178
Animadversions of Warre . . . (Ward), 104
Appleton, Samuel, 57, 60, 145, 151–52, 220n18
Aquidneck Island, 85, 121, 205n43, 215nn98–99
Atherton, Humphrey, 31
Avery, James: adopting Indian tactics, 12–13, 140; battlefield tactics, 169; role in Great Swamp Fight, 61; search-and-destroy operations, 72–73, 167; use of Indian allies, 171
Awashonks (Wampanoag sachem), 194n95

Battle of Bloody Brook, 6, 55, 140, 143, 157, 159, 161–64, 209n4, 223n87
Battle of Hopewell Swamp, 162
Battle of Marston Moor, 101
Battle of Naseby, 101–102, 148
Battle of Nipsachuck, 44, 53–54, 62, 137, 147, 156, 161
"Battle of the Northeast," 26
Battle of Turner's Falls, 52, 72–73, 140, 148, 197n26
Bay Colony. *See* Massachusetts Bay Colony
Beaver Wars (Iroquois Wars), 124, 187n2

237

Beckley Homestead, 69–71
Beers, Richard, 55–56, 125, 140, 153, 156, 162, 163
Behr, Johann, 97
Belcher farm, 70–71, 131–32
Berlin, Conn., 207n79
Black, Robert, 92
Bloody Brook, Battle of, 6, 55, 140, 143, 157, 159, 161–64, 209n4, 223n87
Braddock, Edward, 146, 220n22
Brookfield, Mass., 54, 79, 82, 153, 157, 181, 203n4
Bull, Thomas, 100–101, 110, 127, 200n93, 209n6
Burgoyne, John, 146, 220n22
Burnham, John and Thomas, 101

Canada, 10, 42, 146, 212n54, 220n22. *See also* France
Canonchet (son of Miantonomi): capture and execution, 64–65, 72, 133–34, 139, 161, 167, 169, 177; rise as war leader, 45–46, 62–63; victory over colonial forces, 71–72, 84, 141
Cassacinamon (Pequot sachem), 8, 11, 26, 30–33, 92, 95
Castle Fort (Boston), 112, 121, 180
Cave, Alfred A., 20, 189n22, 191n43, 207n90
Chapman, Robert, 101
Charles II (king of England), 102
Charlestown (fort), 134–36
Cherokee (tribal group), 130, 135, 160
Chet, Guy, 100, 140–41, 148, 186n35, 191n47, 219n6
Children: in Indian family units, 18; noncombatant deaths, 16, 166; in system of matrilineal kinship, 37–38
Choctaw (tribal group), 147
Church, Benjamin: adopting Indian tactics, 12–13, 140–42, 219n5; attacked by hostile forces, 153, 218n3; exaggerating role in conflict, 6; killing of King Philip, 3–4, 167; search-and-destroy operations, 72; use of Indian allies, 74
Church, Thomas, 4, 6
Clarke's Island, 83, 94, 178
Clausewitz, Carl Von, 102, 220n20
Clayton, Anthony, 142
Coddington, William (governor), 84, 195n108
Cohas (renegade leader), 75, 77, 132, 203n137
Cole (Goodman), 70
Cole, Henry, 70–71, 201n112, 202n114
Colonial America. *See* New England; United Colonies
Colony. *See entries for individual colonies*
Concord, N.H., 82
Connecticut Colony: about the Narragansett War narrative, 6–9; avoidance of coalition hostilities, 43–44; battlefield victories, 141–44, 173; coalition raids and hostilities, 54–60; costs and casualties, 4–5, 139; Dutch as a threat, 10, 11–12, 19–20, 102, 105–106, 113–17, 144–45, 153, 175–76, 180; fortress defenses, 11–12, 105, 107–17; garrison defenses, 117–21, 129–32; Indian policies, 9–12, 88–92; Indians as "resident aliens," 87; lessons from Pequot War, 91–93; maps, 34–35, 48–49, 58–59, 118–19, 137; military obstacles and "avenues of approach," 46–50; militia forces, 12, 21–22, 52–53, 102, 106, 126–27, 143–49, 216n33; Mohegan alliance, 15–16, 25–32, 127; population estimates, 125, 130; post-war treatment of Indians, 93–95; relations with local Indians, 21, 80–82; role in Great Swamp

Fight, 60–62; support to adjoining colonies, 44–45
Connecticut General Court: compensation for wounds, 68; creation of the War Council, 122; directing the war effort, 52–53, 93, 127; Indian policies, 79, 82, 174
Connecticut Historical Society, 183n5
Connecticut War Council: comparison to other colonies, 151–52, 173–74, 180–81; creation and authority, 122–27; directing the war effort, 12–13, 56–57, 68, 96–97, 127–30, 138, 167–71; disarming local Indians, 80; fortification construction and repair, 99, 110–17, 130–32; Indian policies, 88–93, 174; organizing and arming troops, 52, 149; responding to French involvement, 107; treatment of local Indians, 81–83; use of Indian allies, 143–44, 156–57, 182
Cooper, Thomas, 56, 79
Cornwallis, Charles, 146, 220n22
Council. *See* War Council(s), formation and authority
Cromwell, Oliver, 101, 103, 144, 148
Crow, Christover, 55, 129
Cruso, John, 97
Culver, Edward, 101
Custer, George A., 162

Davenport (Captain), 208n4
De Forest, John, 155
Deer Island, 82–84, 87, 94, 178
Deerfield, Mass. (formerly Pocumtuck), 55, 107, 155, 161–62, 181
Delaware (tribal group), 19, 65, 86, 95, 105, 113, 156, 187n2, 193n77

Denison, George: adopting Indian tactics, 12–13, 140; battlefield experience, 101–102, 164, 178; battlefield tactics, 169; capture of Canonchet, 167; military experience, 174; search-and-destroy operations, 72–74; use of Indian allies, 81, 171
Denison Fort, 116–17, 214n88
Denslow, Henry, 69
Derby, Conn. (formerly Paugasset), 54, 120, 198n46
Disease: devastation of Indian populations, 8, 16, 18–19, 188nn13–14; factor in strategic consumption, 146, 220n20; loss of Indian leadership, 188n11, 194n98
Drake, James, 9, 10, 193n89
Dutch New Amsterdam, 144–45, 147, 220n16
Dutch New Netherlands, 40, 105
Dutch Republic: as colonial threat, 10, 11–12, 105–106, 175–76; European military conflict, 99–100, 104, 121; military training and tactics, 164, 210n20; support of Indian war effort, 40, 106; suspected Indian conspiracies, 32, 86. *See also* Anglo-Dutch Wars (1652–74)
Dutch-Pequot War, 19, 20, 189n22, 190n27

Eames, Stephen, 143
Eastern Niantic (tribal group): construction of Charlestown fort, 134–35; cooperation with the English, 11, 22, 31–32; intertribal war after Pequot collapse, 26–27, 32; lineage and linguistics, 193n81; neutrality in King Philip's War, 40; role in Dutch conspiracies, 86, 105; role in Great Swamp Fight, 165; treaty with colonies, 29

240 INDEX

Eighty Years' War (1568–1648), 100, 102
Elmer, Edward, 101
Elmore, G., 73
Engels, Donald, 50
English Civil Wars (1638–52), 11, 101–103, 121, 148, 164, 178
English-Dutch War of 1673–74, 102–106, 212n47
Equipment and rations: calorie requirements, 50; combat gear and mobility, 47, 50, 51; helmets and body armor, 51. See also Weapons/weaponry
Extirpative war, 140, 185n25

Fairfax, Sir Thomas, 102, 209n20
Fairfield, Conn., 81, 117
Farmington, Conn., 74, 90, 114, 117
First Anglo-Dutch War (1652–54), 32
First Connecticut Cavalry, 212n54
Fitch, James (Rev.), 53, 57, 90, 132
Forbes, H. A., 50
Fort Duquesne, 220n22
Fort Harwich (England), 103
"Fort Hill," 100
Fort Ninigret, 93–94, 135
Fort Saybrook, 24, 99, 100–102, 105, 110–12, 176
Fort Shantok, 28–29, 32
Fort Ticonderoga (formerly Carillon), 162
Fort William Henry, 146
Fort/fortresses: design and construction, 11–12, 108–17, 121, 132, 144; European defensive practices, 96–97; European-style "castle" defenses, 112, 114, 116, 121, 180, 214n82; flankers and forelorns, defined, 213n66; fortress defenses, 107–17; garrison defenses, 45, 52, 54, 56, 71, 115, 117–21, 129–32; garrison houses, 98–99; gunpowder revolution and impact on, 208n2; Indian construction and use, 116, 134–37, 155, 167–69, 218n70, 218n72; maps, 34–35, 108–109, 118–19, 137; palisade defensive works, 114–16, 213n80; siege and assault tactics, 209n20; tactics and strategy, 97–98; as trading posts, 105. See also Tactics and fighting ability
Foxhall, L., 50
France: aid to Philip and Indian coalition, 40, 107, 212n60; colonial diplomatic efforts with, 92–93; role in King Philip's War, 9; as threat to the colonies, 105–7; as weapons supplier, 198n31. See also Canada
French and Indian Wars: Abercromby invasion of Canada, 220n22; continuation of English-Indian conflict, 74, 107; end of frontier fighting, 195n106; Indians as colonial scouts, 127–28; success of Indian attacks, 162, 196n12
French and Iroquois Wars. See Beaver Wars (Iroquois Wars)
French Canada, 105
Fur and wampum trade, 18, 27–31, 37, 135, 145, 154, 189n22, 190n27

Gallop, John, Jr., 101
Garrison house defense. See Fort/fortresses
General Court (the court). See Connecticut General Court; Massachusetts General Court
Genocide, 103, 185n25, 206n58
Gilbert, Marshal, 82
Gilbert farm, 70–71
Glorious Revolution of 1688, 41
Great Migration, Puritan, 16, 37
Great Narragansett War: about King Philip's War

INDEX   241

as component of, 4–7;
annihilation of Beer's
command, 55; annihilation
of Lathrop's command, 161–
62; annihilation of Pierce's
command, 71–72; annihilation
of Wadsworth's command,
73; annihilation of Wheeler's
command, 54; beginning of
hostilities, 44; causes, 26, 38;
coalition counteroffensive,
65–67; coalition spring
offensive, 68–74; coalition
summer operations, 74–77;
colonial war effort and Indian
relations, 7–12; cost and
casualties, 4–5, 53–54, 139–40,
183n4, 217n55; Indian loyalty
to colonists, 54, 71, 79–80,
82–84, 95; Indian removal and
internment, 10, 64–65, 83–84,
87–89, 91, 94, 177, 207n79;
leadership role of Canonchet,
62–63; military leadership,
100–102; naming of, 7; peace
negotiations, 40, 63–64, 81,
88, 94, 177, 200n80; Pequot
role in, 33, 36. *See also* King
Philip's War
Great Swamp Fight (1675): as
preemptive attack, 9–10,
60–62; casualties, 188n12,
217n55, 218n1, 219n14;
fortifications, 133–34; map,
137; tactics and strategy, 97–98,
164–66; utilization of allied
Indian forces, 157. *See also*
Narragansett (tribal group)
Grenier, John, 66, 140, 185n25,
219n5
Groton, Conn., 68

Hadley, Conn., 14, 63, 73, 88, 143,
151, 160, 170
Harris, William, 75–76, 151, 153
Hartford, Conn., 28, 43, 54–57,
60, 69, 72, 81–82, 90, 99, 110,
113–14, 117, 124, 131–33, 175–
76, 180, 190n27, 193n82
Haynes, John (governor), 31
Henchman, Daniel, 121, 156
Higbey, Edward, 201n112
Hill, William, 68, 77, 132
Hirsch, Adam, 51, 193n89
*The History of Ancient Windsor,
Connecticut* (Stiles), 183n5
Hoccanum, Conn., 54, 68, 72, 77,
81, 132, 198n43
Holland. *See* Dutch Republic
Hopewell Swamp, Battle of, 162
Horses. *See* Tactics and fighting
ability
Hostages, 20, 60, 93, 178, 207n79.
See also Prisoners and captives
Howe, Anthony, 72–73
Howe, William, 146, 220n22
Hubbard, William (Rev.), 5–6, 63,
98, 133, 209n5, 212n60
Hutchinson, Thomas (governor),
151, 167

Indentured servitude. *See* Slavery
and indentured servitude
Iroquois confederacy: expansion
during Beaver Wars, 124,
187n2; King Philip overtures
to, 39–40; role in colonial
victory, 11; support of English
war effort, 45, 65–66, 86, 124;
threat to Connecticut Colony,
105–106, 113

Jennings, Francis, 10, 18, 19, 103,
185n25, 207n90
Joshua (aka Attawanhood, Western
Niantic sachem), 53, 54, 76,
129–30, 156, 193n83

Keith, James, 89
Kieft's War (1643–45, aka
Wappinger War), 210n20
King Philip (aka Metacomet,
Wampanoag sachem): accounts
of the killing, 3–4, 74, 167;

King Philip (aka Metacomet, Wampanoag sachem) (*continued*)
  becoming sachem, 36; coalition leadership, 5–6, 39–40, 62–64, 77, 173, 176; peace negotiations, 94; rejection of Christianity, 37
King Philip's War: about tensions leading to, 36, 193n89; as part of "Great Narragansett War," 4–7, 173; beginning of hostilities, 9, 36; Connecticut Colony influence on, 13–14; experience of colonial commanders, 100–101; Indian tactics and operations, 156–60. *See also* Great Narragansett War
King Philip's War (Mandell), 4, 5–6
King William's War, 220n22

Lancaster, Mass., 67
Land/landholdings: colonial disputes, 33, 41, 145, 186n27; concept in Indian culture, 155; English-Indian disputes, 37, 79, 181, 194n90; Indian dispossession of, 21, 185n24; upholding Indian rights, 30, 192n70
Lathrop, Thomas, 6, 55, 79, 125, 153, 157, 161–62, 209n4
Leach, Douglas, 5, 6, 12, 184n19, 191n46
LeBlanc, Steven, 155
Lee, Wayne, 23, 25, 50, 87, 130, 160, 187n2, 187n37, 219n5
Leete, William (governor), 67, 72, 78–79, 82, 90–91, 94, 126, 216n13
Lepore, Jill, 6
Leverett, John (governor), 94, 121
Long Island: Dutch as military threat, 102, 105, 113, 147, 212n47; Indian population, 86–87, 154–55, 189n15; Indians during Pequot War, 25–27, 222n61; wartime defense, 124

Longmeadow, Mass., 43
Lords, Richard, 122

Mahican (tribal group), 19, 40, 65, 156, 193n77
Malone, Patrick, 13, 47–48, 99, 140, 148
Mandell, Daniel, 4, 6, 62, 184n18, 185n22, 194n101
Maricopa (tribal group), 155
Marlborough, Conn., 68
Marston Moor, Battle of, 101
Martha's Vineyard, 11, 19, 40, 67, 123, 200n93
Masecap (son of Miantonomi), 60
Mashuntuckett, Conn., 167–69
Mason, John, Jr., 135, 157, 162, 171, 174, 177, 191n37
Mason, John, Sr., 15, 21–24, 26–27, 30–32, 80, 92, 99–100, 106, 177, 209n20
Massachusetts (tribal group): colonial defense against, 44–45; losses to disease, 18, 36, 188n13; losses to hostilities, 204n28; population estimate, 19, 189nn19–21; support of King Philip, 39–40; violence and attitude toward, 82–83. *See also* Natick Praying Indian(s)
Massachusetts Bay Colony: about the war effort and Indian policy, 9–12; banning Indians from Boston, 204n28; Boston Castle Fort, 112, 121, 180; coalition military objectives, 44–46; coalition raids and hostilities, 54–55; defense costs and casualties, 4–5; fortifications, 113; Indian policies, 42, 88–89; maps, 34–35; militia forces, 22, 52, 157, 161–62; population estimates, 125; Praying Indians' treatment by, 82–83, 87–88, 177–78; role in Great Swamp Fight, 60–61; role in Pequot War, 20–21, 26–27, 91–93, 147;

support from Connecticut
  Colony, 44–45; utilization of
  allied Indian forces, 157–58
Massachusetts General Court, 178
Massachusetts War Council, 122–
  26, 151–52
Massasoit (Wampanoag sachem), 8,
  36, 203n4
Mather, Increase, 6, 89
Medfield, Mass., 67
Menowalett (renegade leader),
  74–77
Merriman, Caleb, 104–105
Merriman, Nathaniel, 70–71, 101,
  104–105, 149–50, 202n114,
  221n38
Metacomet (Wampanoag
  sachem). See King Philip (aka
  Metacomet, Wampanoag
  sachem)
Miantonomi (Narragansett
  sachem), 22, 28, 33–34, 63, 154
Milford, Conn., 54, 57, 69, 75, 81,
  116–17
Militiamen (trainbands): culture
  and leadership, 126; dragoons
  and cavalry forces, 52–53,
  102, 127–29, 142, 148–50,
  179, 212n54; equipment and
  weapons, 51–52, 147–49; flags
  and heritage, 102, 163, 200n93;
  "hourmen" forces, 128;
  infantry forces, 47–49, 106,
  112, 150, 164, 179, 213n66;
  population estimates, 130,
  195n105; recruits and draftees,
  145, 149–51; training and
  missions, 133, 143–51, 164,
  179; volunteers, 13, 74, 81–82,
  142, 162
Minutemen, Revolutionary War,
  128
Mohantic Fort (Pequot), 116, 136,
  167–69
Mohawk (tribal group): alliance
  with the English, 25–27;
  battling coalition forces, 65–67,
  73, 177; fighting reputation,
  22, 154–56, 178; intertribal
  hostilities, 32; King Philip
  overtures to, 39–40, 62–63;
  population estimates, 19;
  resisting French encroachment,
  106–107; role in Great
  Narragansett War, 9, 154–56;
  role in Pequot War, 13
Mohegan (tribal group): alliance
  with the English, 25–33;
  relationship with Pilgrim
  settlers, 205n45; tribal
  relationship to Pequots,
  190n31; use as Indian allies,
  152–59. See also Uncas
  (Mohegan sachem)
Montcalm, Louis-Joseph de, 146
Moseley, Samuel, 82–83, 94, 140,
  143, 157, 161–63, 170–72, 177–
  78, 209n4
Mosse, John, Sr., 70
Mount Hope, 53, 74
Muddy Brook. See Bloody Brook,
  Battle of
Munson, Thomas, 101
Mystic Fort: archaeological
  excavation, 190n23; attack
  and capture, 20–26; burning/
  massacre, 13, 61, 100, 159, 165,
  191n43

Name of War, The (Lepore), 6
Nantucket Island, 11, 19, 40, 123
Napoleonic Wars, 221n42
Narragansett (tribal group): about
  the role in the war, 6–9;
  alliance with the Dutch, 32,
  86; alliance with the English,
  15–16, 27–28; alliance with the
  French, 106–107; "Battle of the
  Northeast," 26; defeat in battle,
  143, 159; female sachems, 37;
  fortifications and defenses,
  135–37; intertribal conflict and
  warfare, 31–33, 156; joining the
  coalition, 43–46, 61–66, 75, 99,
  127–31; Mystic fort attack, 22;
  neutrality during the early

Narragansett (tribal group) (*continued*)
   conflict, 84–85, 96; population estimate, 18–19, 39–40, 118n15; relationship with Connecticut Colony, 27–29, 76–77, 90–91; relationship with Pilgrim settlers, 205n45; revenge on Connecticut Colony, 67–73; role in Pequot War, 93; tactics and fighting ability, 140–41, 154; treaty of 1645, 29. *See also* Great Swamp Fight (1675)
Naseby, Battle of, 101–102, 148
Natick Praying Indian(s): defined, 38; favored colonial status, 9; integration into colonial society, 185n24; murder of John Sassamon, 38–39; support of war effort, 40–41, 188n12, 195n107; violence and attitude toward, 82–83, 87–88, 177–78
Native. *See* American Indian(s)
New England: colonial administration, 41; Dutch as a threat, 144–47; Indian policies, 42; Indian removal and internment, 10, 64–65, 83–84, 87–89, 94, 207n79; population estimates, 16–19, 39, 188n10, 188–89nn13–21, 195n105; Puritan Great Migration, 16, 37; slavery and indentured servitude, 3, 26, 42, 89–91, 94, 130, 177, 206n68; war objectives and land disputes, 40–41. *See also* American Indian(s); *entries for individual colonies*; United Colonies
New France, 106, 146
New Haven, Conn., 54, 78, 90, 110–13, 116–17, 132, 170, 176, 180, 213n80
New London, Conn. (formerly Pequot Plantation), 29–31, 91, 117, 120, 192n64
New Model Army, 101–103, 144, 148

New York. *See* Royal Colony of New York
Newbery, Benjamin, 122
Newport, R.I., 121, 176, 215n98
Nicholson, Francis, 146, 220n22
Ninigret (Eastern Niantic sachem), 11, 32, 37, 40, 135
Ninigret (fort), 93–94, 135
Nipmuck (tribal group), 13, 19, 36, 39, 44, 54, 64, 76–77, 79, 91, 161–62, 200n80
Nipsachuck, Battle of, 44, 53–54, 62, 137, 147, 156, 161
Northampton, Mass., 55, 67–68, 74, 79, 80, 143, 151, 160, 170, 181
Northfield, N.Y. (formerly Squakeag), 55, 65, 79, 143, 163, 181, 203n4
Norwich, Conn., 43, 54, 57, 67, 72, 82, 85, 90–91, 117, 120, 127, 129, 131–32, 152, 169, 175
Norwottock (tribal group), 55, 74, 80

O'Brien, Jean M., 10–11, 184n11, 185n24
Oldham, John, 189n22
"Old Queen, the" (Narragansett sachem). *See* Sunk Squaw (Narragansett sachem, aka Quaiapen)
Olmstead, Nicolas & Richard, 101
Opechancanough's Rebellion (1622), 154, 183n4
Owaneco (Mohegan), 53–54, 60, 76, 80–81, 91, 106, 161, 222n61

Palmes, Edward, 66, 77, 91, 132, 198n31
Parker, Geoffrey, 105
Paugussett (tribal group), 154
Pequot Plantation (aka Nameag, renamed New London), 29–31
Pequot War (1636–37): attack on Mystic Fort, 23–26; "Battle of the Northeast," 26; causes, 20–21; fatalities, 16; military leadership, 100–101, 127;

Mohegan-colonial alliance,
15–16, 26–28; use of Indian
allies, 78–79
Pequot War, The (Cave), 189n22,
191n43
Pequot (tribal group): coalition
formation and fighting ability,
20; collapse following Pequot
War, 26–32; Mohantic Fort,
116, 136, 167–69; population
estimate, 18–19, 189n16; role
in Great Narragansett War, 33,
36, 127–28; tribal relationship
to Mohegans, 190n31; use as
Indian allies, 152–59
Pessicus (Narragansett sachem), 28,
63, 72, 200n78
Peters, Thomas, 29
Peterson, Harold, 51
Pierce, Michael, 71, 84, 141, 218n3
Pierce's Fight, 97–98, 137, 140–41,
157, 162, 191n46, 209n4
Plymouth Colony: about the war
effort and Indian policy, 9–12;
as coalition military objective,
44–46; defense costs and
casualties, 4–5; fortifications,
113–15, 121; Indian policies,
83–84, 88–89; role in Great
Narragansett War, 36, 38; role
in Pequot War, 147; support
from Connecticut Colony,
44–45; use of Indian allies,
157–58
Plymouth Colony War Council,
122–26, 151
Pocumtuck (tribal group), 19, 32,
55, 107, 155
Podunk (tribal group), 54, 56,
198n43
Pratt, William, 101
Praying Indian(s). *See* Natick
Praying Indian(s)
Prisoners and captives, 19–21, 23,
25–26, 28, 42, 53, 65, 69, 75,
81, 88–91, 131, 154. *See also*
Hostages

Providence, R.I., 68, 71, 121
Providence Plantations, 84, 193n78
Pulsipher, Jenny, 6, 10, 62, 184n14,
194n101
Puritanism: anti-Indian policies,
83–85, 91–92, 95; culture and
customs, 122–24; destruction
of Indian power, 41, 45, 79;
encroachment on Indian
beliefs, 33, 37–38; Great
Migration, 16, 37; racism and
genocide, 37, 103, 107, 185n25,
190n24, 206n58. *See also*
United Colonies
Pynchon, John, 79, 128, 151

Quabaug and Nashaway War,
184n10
Quabog (tribal group), 74
Quaiapen (Narragansett sachem).
See Sunk Squaw (Narragansett
sachem, aka Quaiapen)
Quannapohit, James, 188n12
Queen Anne's War, 220n22
"Queen's Fort, The" (Narragansett),
134, 136, 217n63, 218n74
Quinnipiac (tribal group), 37, 70–73,
154–55, 187n3, 189n16, 194n95

Racism/racial relations, 37, 107,
185n25, 190n24
Randolph, Edward, 5
Rations. *See* Equipment and rations
Reede, Thomas, 72
Rehoboth, Conn., 68
Reynolds, John, 201n98
Rhode Island Colony: about the
war effort and Indian policy,
9–12; Aquidneck Island, 85,
121, 205n43, 215n98; defense
costs and casualties, 4–5;
fortifications, 121; Indian
policies, 84–85; Puritanism
and religious beliefs, 85; role in
Great Narragansett War, 53–54;
role in Great Swamp Fight,
60–61

246 INDEX

Rhode Island War Council, 85, 121, 123
Rochambeau, Jean-Baptiste de, 146
Rockaway (tribal group), 86
Rockwell, Josiah, 201n98
Rogers, Robert, 162
Royal Colony of New York: Indian policies, 82, 85–87, 205n58; Indian population estimate, 19; land claims and boundaries, 186n27; role in Great Narragansett War, 9–10; support from Indians during war, 66–67
Royal Colony of New York War Council, 123–24

Sachem: authority and power, 8, 21, 33, 38–39, 194n101; cooperation with English authority, 95; inheritance politics, 21–22, 28, 30–31, 36; rise of "sunksquaws," 37–38, 64, 194n95
Sachem Sam (aka Sagamore Sam, Indian war leader), 67, 77
Salisbury, Neal, 18, 187n3, 188–89nn13–21
Sassacus (Pequot sachem), 21–22, 25–26, 190n31
Sassamon, John, murder of, 38–40
Saybrook Point (Conn.), 21, 100, 110–11, 213n68
Schaghticoke, N.Y., 65
Schroeder, Sissel, 17–18, 187n6, 188n10
Second Anglo-Dutch War (1665–67), 178
Seed, Patricia, 188n11
Seeley, Nathaniel, 152
Selesky, Harold, 7, 52, 143
Sepawcutt (Indian warrior), 72
Sequassen (Pequot sachem), 21
Sequatalke (tribal group), 86
Shantok (Mohegan fort), 28–29, 32
Shaumpishuh (Quinnipiac sachem), 194n95

Shultz, Eric, 6, 195n101
Simsbury, Conn.: defensive fortifications, 117; hostilities near, 55–56; loss/burning of, 5, 43, 46, 69, 88, 120, 132–33; Menowalett admission to burning, 74
Skulking Way of War (Malone), 140, 186n35
Slavery and indentured servitude: capture and sale of Indians, 3, 26, 42, 177, 206n68; Connecticut forbidding sale of Indians, 89; sentencing Philip's family to, 89–90; slaves as combatants, 130; Winthrop policy of leniency, 94
Springfield, Conn. (renamed Suffield), 16, 43, 47, 56, 74, 79, 83, 88, 91, 116, 128–30, 150–52, 181
Stamford, Conn., 57, 58, 206n58
Stamford River, 154
Stanley, John, 101
Stanton, John, 57, 67, 157–59
Stanton, Thomas, 32, 212n58
Stiles, Henry, 183n5
Stone, John, 189n22
Strachan, Hew, 5
Strategic consumption, 146, 220n20
Stratford, Conn., 60, 80, 113, 116–17, 206n58
Stratford River, 57, 154
Sudbury, Mass., 62, 68, 73, 140, 141, 191n46
Suffield, Conn. *See* Springfield, Conn.
Sunk Squaw (Narragansett sachem, aka Quaiapen), 64, 74, 90, 134, 143, 157, 159, 194n95
Sunksquaw (female sachem), 37–38, 194nn94–95. *See also* Women
Swansea, Mass., 35, 53, 79, 181
Symonds, Samuel, 30

Tactics and fighting ability: battlefield experience and,

101–102; battlefield maneuver, 164; colonial politics and management, 12, 127; countermarch, 164; European fortress strategy, 96–99; extirpative war, 140, 185n25; feints and demonstrations, 216n27; "hammer and anvil" operations, 159, 223n77; hand-to-hand combat, 197n26; Indian "cutting off way of war," 24–25, 53, 98, 136–37, 149, 159–62, 164–65, 169–70, 182; Indian "skulking way of war," 12–13, 24, 71, 112, 130–33, 140–43, 162, 173, 179, 209n4; Indian use of English tactics, 33; New Model Army influence, 102–104, 144–45; river-crossing operations, 55, 71, 162, 223n88; search-and-destroy operations, 72, 127, 143; "skirmishing," 33, 36, 61, 97, 102, 147, 159, 223n76; strategic consumption, 146, 220n20; use of dragoons and cavalry, 102, 127–29; use of horses, 52–53, 145, 148–50; use of Indian allies, 127–29, 141–44, 158–59, 178–79. *See also* Fort/fortresses; War; Weapons/weaponry

Talcott, John, 73–74, 90, 114, 126, 157, 166–71, 179, 180, 219n14
Tatobem (Pequot sachem), 190n27
Third Anglo-Dutch War (1672–74), 11, 147, 170
Thirty Years' War (1616–48), 21, 23, 103–104, 191n51
Tiawakesson (aka Watawaikeson, Narragansett), 88
Tomsquash (Indian ally), 130
Tougias, Thomas, 6, 195n101
Trainbands. *See* Militiamen (trainbands)
Treat, Robert: actions against hostiles, 129, 131, 167; at Battle of Bloody Brook, 140, 157, 161–64; battlefield experience, 151–52, 170–71; at Great Swamp Fight, 61; military leadership, 57, 126, 179–80; use of Indian allies, 82
Tunxis (tribe), 90, 175
Turner's Falls, Battle of, 52, 72–73, 140, 148, 197n26
Turramuggus (sachem), 207n79
Tuscarora (tribal group), 135–36, 160

Uncas (Mohegan sachem): advice on military operations, 171; alliance with the English, 7–8, 11, 15–16, 25–33, 36, 91–92, 175; authority as sachem, 44, 47; conflicting tribal loyalties, 75–77; distrust of Narragansetts, 54, 60, 63, 127, 129, 176; leadership style, 76; mistreatment of other tribal groups, 81–82; rejection of Christianity, 37; role in Mystic fort attack, 25–26; role in peace negotiations, 94–95; support of Connecticut Colony, 16, 21–22. *See also* Mohegan (tribal group)
Underhill, John, 191n37
United Colonies: conducting offensive operations, 60, 67; coordination among colonies, 151–53; directing the war effort, 123; exclusion of Rhode Island, 85; Indian policies, 30–31, 90–91, 93–95; military command and control, 41–42, 45, 123, 151–52; relationship with Narragansetts, 85, 194n90. *See also* New England; Puritanism
Unlimited warfare, 185n25

Vauban, Sebastien de, 97
Vaughan, Alden T., 10, 39, 185n25, 195n107
Vermont, 55, 72

248 INDEX

Wabbaquasett (Nipmuck subtribe), 47, 66, 91, 200n80
Wadsworth, John, 122
Wadsworth, Samuel, 73, 140–41
Wampum. *See* Fur and wampum trade
Wampanoag (tribal group): account of King Philip' death, 3–4; initiation of war, 44; King Philip as sachem, 5–6, 38–39, 62; murder of John Sassamon, 38; population estimate, 19, 62, 189n20; relationship with Pilgrim settlers, 8, 79, 194n90, 205n45; relationships to other tribal groups, 84–85, 203n4; as war combatants, 9, 16, 36, 53–54, 64, 76, 161–62; women in leadership roles, 37, 194n95
Wamsutta (aka Alexander), 36
Wappinger (Algonquian tribal group), 154, 156, 193n77
War: American fear of standing armies, 113; European fortress strategy, 96–97; Indian cultural objectives, 24–25; New Model Army influence, 101–103, 144, 148; theory of "American way of war," 140, 219n5; theory of strategic consumption, 146, 220n20; waging "limited war," 144, 146, 148, 185n25. *See also* Tactics and fighting ability
War and Society in Colonial Connecticut (Selesky), 7
War Council(s), formation and authority, 122–26, 180–81. *See also entries for individual colonies*
Ward, Robert, 104
Warfare and tactics. *See* Tactics and fighting ability
Warfare in Woods and Forests (Clayton), 142
Warner, Thomas, 200n84
Warwick, R.I., 121, 215n99, 218n74

Washington, George, 146
Waterhouse, Jacob, 101
Weapons/weaponry: artillery, 41, 97–98, 110, 114, 130, 145, 191n47; bows and arrows, 50, 80, 147; carbines ("fusils"), 52; confiscation of firearms, 32, 79–80, 86–87, 91, 95; flintlock muskets, 50, 52, 80, 147, 197n23; gunpowder revolution, 208n2; pikes, 147, 164; swords and bayonets, 51–52, 147–48, 197n24. *See also* Equipment and rations; Tactics and fighting ability
Webster, Noah, 114
Weetamoo (Wampanoag sachem), 194n95
Weigley, Russell, 219n5
Wells, Samuel, 122
Wequash (Pequot sachem), 26
West Kingston, R.I., 61, 133, 165
Western Niantic (tribal group): cooperation with the English, 40, 94, 128–29, 195n107; lineage and linguistics, 193n81; relationship with Pequots, 13–14, 20–21; tribal relations after Pequot collapse, 26, 32, 193n83
Westfield, Mass., 55, 151–52
Wethersfield, Conn., 21
Wheeler, Thomas, 54, 79
William of Orange (king of Holland), 41
Williams, Roger, 84–85, 193n78
Windsor, Conn., 43, 69, 88, 110, 113–17, 131, 180, 198n43
Winslow, Josiah (governor), 61, 94, 141, 164–65
Winthrop, Fitz-John: battlefield experience, 102, 106; Indian policies, 94; invasion of Canada, 220n22; military training and experience, 164, 174; role in English-Dutch War,

212n47; use of Indian allies, 153
Winthrop, John, Jr.: Indian policies, 10, 15, 29–33, 178, 207n90; leadership as governor, 92–94; library collection, 211n42; military experience, 103–105, 174; objection to Great Swamp operation, 60, 123, 178; postwar treatment of Indians, 94–95; trust of local Indians, 79–80; use of Indian allies, 156
Winthrop, John, Sr., 29–30, 212n47
Winthrop, Wait: Indian policies, 94; military experience, 174; role in Great Narragansett War, 54; use of Indian allies, 153, 163, 171

Wolfe, James, 146
Women: assuming political leadership, 37–38, 194n94; deaths during combat, 165–66, 183n5; as impediment during combat, 128; noncombatant deaths, 16, 166, 183n5; sale into slavery, 88–89; as tribal sachem, 194n95. *See also* American Indian(s); Sunksquaw (female sachem)
Woronoco (tribal group), 55, 74–75

Yunan (tribal group), 155

Zelner, Kyle, 149, 150

Made in the USA
Middletown, DE
10 September 2025